THE CAMBRIDGE COMPANION TO EDMUND BURKE

Edmund Burke prided himself on being a practical statesman, not an armchair philosopher. Yet his responses to specific problems – rebellion in America, the abuse of power in India and Ireland, or revolution in France – incorporated theoretical debates within jurisprudence, economics, religion, moral philosophy, and political science. Moreover, the extraordinary rhetorical force of Burke's speeches and writings quickly secured his reputation as a gifted orator and literary stylist. This Companion provides a comprehensive assessment of Burke's thought, examining the intellectual traditions that shaped it and the concrete issues to which it was addressed. The volume explores all his major writings from his early treatise on aesthetics to his famous polemic, *Reflections on the Revolution in France*. It also examines the vexed question of Burke's Irishness and seeks to determine how his cultural origins may have influenced his political views – from his attitudes on religious toleration to his complicated response to Empire. Finally, it aims both to explain and to challenge interpretations of Burke as a romantic, a utilitarian, a natural law thinker, and founding father of modern conservatism.

DAVID DWAN is a lecturer in English at Queen's University Belfast. He is author of *The Great Community: Culture and Nationalism in Ireland* (2008) and has written a range of articles on intellectual history and modern literature.

CHRISTOPHER J. INSOLE is senior lecturer in theology and ethics at the University of Durham, U.K. He is the author of *The Politics of Human Frailty: A Theological Defence of Political Liberalism* (2005) and has written articles on Burke, Kant, philosophy of religion, epistemology, and intellectual history.

A complete list of books in the series is at the back of this book.

T0371084

THE CAMBRIDGE
COMPANION TO
EDMUND BURKE

THE CAMBRIDGE
COMPANION TO
EDMUND BURKE

EDITED BY
DAVID DWAN
Queen's University Belfast

CHRISTOPHER J. INSOLE
University of Durham

CAMBRIDGE
UNIVERSITY PRESS

CAMBRIDGE
UNIVERSITY PRESS

32 Avenue of the Americas, New York NY 10013-2473, USA

Cambridge University Press is part of the University of Cambridge.

It furthers the University's mission by disseminating knowledge in the pursuit of education, learning and research at the highest international levels of excellence.

www.cambridge.org
Information on this title: www.cambridge.org/9780521183314

First published 2012

A catalogue record for this publication is available from the British Library

Library of Congress Cataloguing in Publication data
The Cambridge companion to Edmund Burke / edited by David Dwan, Christopher Insole.
p. cm. – (Cambridge companions to literature)
Includes bibliographical references and index.
ISBN 978-1-107-00559-4 (hardback) – ISBN 978-0-521-18331-4 (paperback)
1. Burke, Edmund, 1729–1797. 2. Political science – Great Britain – History – 18th century. 3. Speeches, addresses, etc., English – History and criticism. 4. Politics and literature – Great Britain – History – 18th century. I. Dwan, David. II. Insole, Christopher J.
PR3334.B4Z59 2012
824´.6–dc23 2012002708

ISBN 978-1-107-00559-4 Hardback
ISBN 978-0-521-18331-4 Paperback

CONTENTS

CONTRIBUTORS

RICHARD BOURKE is a reader in the history of political thought at Queen Mary, University of London. He is the author of *Peace in Ireland and the War of Ideas* and co-editor of *Political Judgement*. He is the author of several articles on Edmund Burke and is currently preparing *The Political Life of Edmund Burke: Empire to Revolution* for publication with Princeton University Press.

PADDY BULLARD is a lecturer in the School of English at the University of Kent, Canterbury, and also teaches romantic literature at St. Catherine's College, Oxford. He is the author of *Edmund Burke and the Art of Rhetoric* and is co-editing (with James McLaverty) *Swift, the Text and the Book*. He is co-editor of the online Jonathan Swift Archive.

DAVID CRAIG is a lecturer in history at the University of Durham. He is the author of *Robert Southey and Romantic Apostasy: Political Argument in Britain, c. 1780–1840*. He has published articles on nineteenth-century political and intellectual history and is co-editing a series of essays entitled *Languages of Politics in Nineteenth-Century Britain*.

SEAMUS DEANE is Keough Emeritus Professor of Irish Studies at the University of Notre Dame. He is the general editor of the *Field Day Anthology of Irish Writing* and the author of several books: *Celtic Revivals: Essays in Modern Irish Literature 1880–1980*, *Reading in the Dark* (novel), *A Short History of Irish Literature*, *The French Revolution and Enlightenment in England 1789–1832*, and *Strange Country: Modernity and the Nation*. His most recent work is *Foreign Affections: Essays on Edmund Burke*.

HARRY T. DICKINSON taught at the University of Edinburgh for forty years and is now an emeritus professor there as well as being a concurrent professor at Nanjing University in China. A former president of the Historical Association and twice vice president of the Royal Historical Society, he has authored and edited many volumes, including *Bolingbroke, Liberty and Property: Political Ideology in Eighteenth-Century Britain; The Politics of the People in Eighteenth-Century*

Britain; Britain and the American Revolution; and *British Pamphlets on the American Revolution.*

SEÁN PATRICK DONLAN lectures in law at the University of Limerick, Ireland. In addition to publishing numerous articles on Burke, he edited *Edmund Burke's Irish Identities* and a reprint of Francis Stoughton Sullivan's *Lectures on the Constitution and Laws of England* (2nd edn, 1776). His primary research is on comparative law and legal history. His most recent work is as co-editor, with Eleanor Cashin-Ritaine and Martin Sychold, of *Comparative Law and Hybrid Legal Traditions.*

DAVID DWAN is a lecturer in English at Queen's University Belfast. He has written several articles on modern literature and intellectual history. His book, T*he Great Community: Culture and Nationalism in Ireland,* was published by Field Day in 2008.

IAIN HAMPSHER-MONK is a professor of politics at the University of Exeter. He is the founder and joint editor of the journal *History of Political Thought,* the author of *A History of Modern Political Thought,* and the editor of *The Impact of the French Revolution: Texts from Britain in the 1790s.* He is currently writing a monograph on the political thought of Edmund Burke and is preparing the Cambridge Texts edition of Burke's *Reflections on the Revolution in France.*

IAN HARRIS is a lecturer in early modern history at the University of Leicester and specialises in the parliamentary history of eighteenth-century Britain. He is the author of *The Mind of John Locke: A Study of Political Theory in Its Intellectual Setting* and is the editor of the Cambridge Texts edition of Burke's pre-revolutionary works. He has recently published articles on Hobbes, Locke, Kant, and Burke.

CHRISTOPHER J. INSOLE is a senior lecturer in philosophical theology and ethics at the University of Durham. He is the author of *The Politics of Human Frailty: A Theological Defence of Political Liberalism* and *The Realist Hope: A Critique of Anti-Realist Approaches in Philosophical Theology.* His most recent work includes articles on Kant and Burke.

F. P. LOCK is professor of English at Queen's University in Kingston, Ontario, Canada. He is author of *Edmund Burke* (2 vols., 1998–2000). His earlier books include *Susanna Centlivre* (1979), *The Politics of 'Gulliver's Travels'* (1980), *Swift's Tory Politics* (1983), and *Burke's 'Reflections on the Revolution in France'* (1985). He has also edited three collections of 'Unpublished Burke Letters' (*English Historical Review,* 1997, 1999, and 2003).

IAN MCBRIDE is a senior lecturer in history at King's College London. He is the author of *Scripture Politics: Ulster Presbyterians and Irish Radicalism in the Late Eighteenth Century* and the editor of *History and Memory in Modern Ireland*. His general history of Ireland between 1688 and 1800, *Eighteenth-Century Ireland: The Isle of Slaves*, was published in 2009.

JENNIFER PITTS is a professor of political science at the University of Chicago. She is the author of *A Turn to Empire: The Rise of Imperial Liberalism in Britain and France* and the editor of Alexis de Tocqueville's *Writings on Empire and Slavery*.

CHRISTOPHER REID is a senior lecturer in English at Queen Mary, University of London. He is the author of *Edmund Burke and the Practice of Political Writing*. He has published articles on eighteenth-century oratory and co-edited a series of essays entitled *Oratory in Action*.

RICHARD WHATMORE is a professor in intellectual history at the University of Sussex. He is the author of *Republicanism and the French Revolution: An Intellectual History of Jean-Baptiste Say's Political Economy*. He is the co-editor of *Economy, Polity and Society: Essays in British Intellectual History, 1750–1950* and *History, Religion and Culture: Essays in British Intellectual History, 1750–1950*.

FREDERICK G. WHELAN is a professor of political science at the University of Pittsburgh. He is the author of several books on the history of political thought. He has written several essays on Burke and is the author of *Edmund Burke and India: Political Morality and Empire*.

ACKNOWLEDGEMENTS

We would like to thank Richard Bourke, David Craig, Paul Langford, Fred Lock, Justin Mihoc, Ray Ryan, and Maartje Scheltens for invaluable support and advice on various aspects of the project.

Citations to Burke's texts are generally given parenthetically, although some additional references are included in notes to the chapters. References to *The Annual Register* are given by year and page number, or to the manuscript reference in the case of the Fitzwilliam Burke Papers. Otherwise references are to volume and page number.

AR   *The Annual Register.*

C   *The Correspondence of Edmund Burke,* (ed.) Thomas Copeland and others, 10 vols. (Cambridge: Cambridge University Press, 1958–78).

CD   *Cavendish Debates,* (ed.) Sir Henry Cavendish, *Government of Canada: Debates of the House of Commons in the Year 1774 on the Bill for Making More Effectual Provision for the Government of the Province of Quebec* (London: Ridgway, 1839).

N   *A Notebook of Edmund Burke,* (ed.) H. V. F. Somerset (Cambridge: Cambridge University Press, 1957).

NRO   Fitzwilliam Burke Papers, Northampton Record Office, Northampton.

PH   *The Parliamentary History of England from the Earliest Period to the Year 1803,* 36 vols. (London: T. C. Hansard, 1806–20).

Works   *The Works of the Right Honourable Edmund Burke,* 8 vols., Bohn's British Classics (London: Bohn, 1854–89). Used for texts that are not yet available in WS.

WS   *Writings and Speeches*, (ed.) Paul Langford et al., 8 vols. to date (I–III, V–IX), (Oxford: Oxford University Press, 1981–).

For ease of reference to other editions, the full titles of all works, letter, and speeches referred to in this volume from C, WS, and Works, are provided below:

From WS:

WS, I: 65–128	*The Reformer* 1748
WS, I: 129–184	*A Vindication of Natural Society* 1756
WS, I: 185–320	*A Philosophical Enquiry into the Origin of Our Ideas of the Sublime and Beautiful* 1757
WS, I: 321–331	*Fragment: An Essay towards an History of the Laws of England* c. 1757
WS, I: 332–552	*An Essay towards an Abridgement of the English History* (1757–?)
WS, II: 45–50	Speech on Declaratory Resolution 3 February 1766
WS, II: 51–53	Speech on Enforcement of Stamp Act 7 February 1766
WS, II: 54–57	*Short Account of a Late Short Administration* 1766
WS, II: 61–64	Speech on Townshend Duties 15 May 1767
WS, II: 67–73	Speech on Address 24 November 1767
WS, II: 94–100	Speech on Address 8 November 1768
WS, II: 102–218	*Observations on a Late State of the Nation* 1769
WS, II: 228–230	Speech on Middlesex Election 15 April 1769
WS, II: 241–322	*Thoughts on the Present Discontents* 1770
WS, II: 343–349	Speech on Jury Bill 7 March 1771
WS, II: 406–461	*Speech on American Taxation* 19 April 1774
WS, II: 463–465	Speech on Massachusetts Bay Regulating Bill 2 May 1774

WS, II: 471–473	Speech on Quebec Bill 10 June 1774
WS, III: 63–70	Speech at the Conclusion of the Poll 3 November 1774
WS, III: 102–169	Speech on Conciliation with America 22 March 1775
WS, III: 183–219	Second Speech on Conciliation 1775
WS, III: 288–330	*Letter to the Sheriffs of Bristol* 3 April 1777
WS, III: 344–346	Speech on Fox's Motion 2 December 1777
WS, III: 373–374	Speech on Repeal of Declaratory Act 6 April 1778
WS, III: 431–435	Notes for Speech on Dissenters Bill April 1779
WS, III: 481–551	Speech on Economical Reformation 11 February 1780
WS, III: 588–601	Speech on Duration of Parliaments 8 May 1780
WS, III: 626–634	Speech at Bristol Previous to Election 6 September 1780
WS, V: 41–123	*Policy on Making Conquests for the Mahometans* 1779
WS, V: 140–142	Speech on Bengal Judicature Bill 27 June 1781
WS, V: 144–189	*First Report Select Committee*: 'Observations' 5 February 1782
WS, V: 194–333	*Ninth Report of Select Committee* 25 June 1783
WS, V: 334–378	Eleventh Report of Select Committee 18 November 1783
WS, V: 378–451	*Speech on Fox's India Bill* 1 December 1783
WS, V: 454–459	Speech on Pitt's Second India Bill 28 July 1784
WS, V: 478–552	*Speech on Nabob of Arcot's Debts* 28 February 1785
WS, V: 552–616	Appendices
WS, VI: 79–91	Rohilla War Charge

WS, IX: 434–482	Tracts Relating to Popery Laws 1765
WS, IX: 496–503	Speech on Foreign Troops in Ireland 15 February 1776
WS, IX: 506–517	*Two Letters on the Trade of Ireland* 23 April and 2 May 1778
WS, IX: 543–563	*Letter to Thomas Burgh* 1 January 1780
WS, IX: 564–579	*Letter to Lord Kenmare* 21 February 1782
WS, IX: 594–639	*Letter to Sir Hercules Langrishe* 1792
WS, IX: 640–658	Letter to Richard Burke post 19 February 1792

From Works:

Works, II: 251–276	Motion Relative to the Speech from the Throne 14 June 1784
Works, III: 1–115	An Appeal from the New to the Old Whigs
Works, III: 269–281	Substance of the Speech on the Army Estimates 1790
Works, IV: 113–126	Speech on the Petition of the Unitarians 11 May 1792
Works VI: 92–102	Speech on the Acts of Uniformity 1772
Works, VI: 144–153	Speech on a Motion Made in the House of Commons 7 May 1782
Works, VI: 154–165	Speech on Powers of Juries in Prosecutions for Libels

From C:

C, I: 34–36	Burke to Richard Shackleton 1 November 1744
C, I: 44–46	Burke to Richard Shackleton 5 March 1745
C, I: 47–48	Burke to Richard Shackleton 15 March 1745
C, I: 67–68	Burke to Richard Shackleton 12 July 1746
C, I: 88–90	Burke to Richard Shackleton 21 March 1747
C, I: 110–111	Letter to Richard Shackleton 31 August 1751
C, I: 129–130	To Adam Smith 10 September 1759

C, I: 147–149	Burke to Charles O'Hara ante 23 August 1762
C, I: 242–243	John Ridge to Edmund and William Burke ante 8 March 1766
C, II: 136	Burke to Richard Shackleton 6 May 1770
C, II: 512–514	Burke to Adrian Henrich von Borcke 17 January 1774
C, III: 189–196	Burke to the Marquis of Rockingham 23 August 1775
C, IV: 8–10	Burke to Edmund Sexton Pery 18 July 1778
C, IV: 83–84	Burke to Dr. John Erskine 12 June 1779
C, IV: 223–225	Burke to John Merlott Esq. 4 April 1780
C, V: 34–36	Burke to James Boswell, Jr, 1 September 1782
C, V: 154	Burke to William Baker 22 June 1784
C, V: 252–257	Burke to Miss Mary Palmer 19 January 1786
C, V: 436–445	Burke to William Windham circa 24 January 1789
C, VI: 31–32	Burke to Charles-Jean-François Depont 4 November 1789
C, VI: 34–37	Burke to Earl Fitzwilliam 12 November 1789
C, VI: 55–58	Burke to Philip Francis 17 December 1789
C, VI: 67–76	Thomas Paine to Edmund Burke 17 January 1790
C, VI: 140–141	Burke to Charles-Alexandre de Calonne 25 October 1790
C, VI: 188–192	Burke to Sir Philip Francis 20 February 1790
C, VI: 216–219	Burke to John Trevor January 1791
C, VI: 241–243	Burke to the Chevalier de La Bintinaye March 1791
C, VI: 304	Letter to William Cusac Smith 22 July 1791
C, VI: 311–312	Burke to Dr French Laurence 2 August 1791
C, VII: 50–63	Burke to William Weddell 31 January 1792

C, VII: 173–178	Burke to Lord Grenville 18 August 1792
C, VII: 552–553	Burke to Earl Fitzwilliam 21 June 1794
C, VIII: 62–64	Burke to French Laurence 28 July 1796
C, VIII: 254–257	Burke to Sir Hercules Langrishe 26 May 1795
C, VIII: 425–435	Burke to Lord Loughborough circa 17 March 1796
C, IX: 112–118	Burke to John Keogh 17 November 1796
C, IX: 161–172	Burke to the Rev. Thomas Hussey post 9 December 1796
C, IX: 277	Burke to Sir Lawrence Parsons 8 March 1797
C, IX: 307	Burke to French Laurence 11 April 1797

CHRONOLOGY

1730	Burke born in Dublin (1 January; 12 January, NS).
1735–40 (?)	Lives with mother's relatives in the Blackwater Valley, County Cork.
1741–44	Attends Abraham Shackleton's school at Ballitore, County Kildare.
1744	Enters Trinity College, Dublin (14 April).
1748	Graduates from Trinity College, Dublin (February).
1750	Moves to London to study law at the Middle Temple.
1753 (?)	Drafts *A Philosophical Enquiry into the Origin of Our Ideas of the Sublime and the Beautiful*
1755	Abandons his study of law to seek a literary career.
1756	Publishes *A Vindication of Natural Society* (18 May).
1757	Marries Jane Nugent (12 March). Publishes *A Philosophical Enquiry into the Origin of Our Ideas of the Sublime and Beautiful* (21 April).
1758	Richard Burke born (9 February). Burke signs contracts for an *Essay towards an Abridgment of the English History* (25 February; subsequently abandoned; a fragment was published in 1812) and an *Annual Register* (24 April).
1759 (?)	Accepts position as private secretary to William Gerard Hamilton.
1759	First volume of the *Annual Register* published (15 May).

1761–4	Returns to Ireland for two periods (August 1761–Spring 1762; September 1763–Spring 1764) as secretary to Hamilton, who had been appointed Chief Secretary to the Lord Lieutenant.
1762 (?)	Begins *Tracts Relative to the Laws Against Popery in Ireland* (later abandoned; the surviving portions published in 1812).
1765 (?)	Breaks with Hamilton (before February 1765).
1765	Becomes private secretary to the Marquis of Rockingham, First Lord of the Treasury (11 July). Through the influence of Lord Verney, elected to the House of Commons for the borough of Wendover, in Buckinghamshire (23 December).
1766	First speech in the Commons (17 January). Publishes *A Short Account of a Late Short Administration* (4 August). Goes into opposition with Rockingham.
1768	Buys a house and 300-acre estate at Beaconsfield, in Buckinghamshire (April).
1769	Publishes *Observations on a Late State of the Nation* (8 February).
1770	Publishes *Thoughts on the Cause of the Present Discontents* (23 April).
1770	Elected London agent for the New York Assembly (21 December; Burke accepts the position early in 1771).
1773	Visit to France (January to March).
1774	Delivers *Speech on American Taxation* (19 April; published 10 January 1775). Elected MP for Bristol (2 November).
1775	Delivers *Speech on Conciliation with America* (22 March; published 22 May).
1776	American Declaration of Independence.
1777	Publishes *Letter to the Sheriffs of Bristol* (5 May).
1778	Publishes *Two Letters on the Trade of Ireland* (12 May).
1780	Delivers *Speech on Economical Reformation* (11 February; published 17 February). Dissolution of Parliament

(1 September). Seeks reelection at Bristol, but is forced to withdraw. Through Rockingham's influence, elected for the borough of Malton, in Yorkshire (9 December).

1781   Cornwallis surrenders at Yorktown (19 October).

1782   Lord North resigns (20 March). Rockingham forms a new ministry; Burke appointed Paymaster-General of the Forces (27 March). On the death of Rockingham (1 July), the King appoints Lord Shelburne as First Lord; Burke therefore resigns (11 July).

1783   Shelburne's administration defeated in the Commons (18 February) by a conjunction between the supporters of Lord North and Charles James Fox. The Fox–North Coalition (nominally headed by the Duke of Portland) formed; Burke again becomes Paymaster-General (2 April). Delivers his *Speech on Fox's East India Bill* (1 December). The Fox–North coalition is defeated in the House of Lords (17 December). The Coalition is dismissed (19 December), and William Pitt becomes Prime Minister.

1784   Parliament dissolved (25 March). In the ensuing election, Pitt secures a majority. Burke re-elected for Malton (1 April).

1785   Delivers his *Speech on the Nabob of Arcot's Debts* (28 February; published 23 August).

1786   Composes 22 'articles of charge' against Warren Hastings, the East India Company's Governor-General of Bengal 1772–85 (April–May).

1788   Trial of Hastings opens (13 February). Burke leads with a four-day speech (15, 16, 18, 19 February). In October, the King is taken ill, initiating the 'Regency Crisis'. Burke speaks frequently in the debates in the Commons.

1789   The King unexpectedly recovers, ending the 'Regency Crisis' (February). The storming of the Bastille (14 July).

1790   Publishes *Reflections on the Revolution in France* (1 November).

1791   *A Letter to a Member of the National Assembly* published (April, in French; May, in English). Public breach with Fox on the floor of the House of Commons (6 May). Publishes

An Appeal from the New to the Old Whigs (3 August). Writes 'Thoughts on French Affairs' (posthumously published in 1797).

1793   France declares war on Great Britain (1 February). Burke writes *Observations on the Conduct of the Minority* (September; unauthorised publication, 13 February 1797) and 'Remarks on the Policy of the Allies' (October; posthumously published 1797).

1794   Delivers the concluding speech at the trial of Hastings (over nine days, May–June). Retires from Parliament (25 June). Death of Richard Burke, Jr. (2 August).

1795   Hastings acquitted on all charges (23 April). Burke awarded a pension (August). Writes on the food crisis (December; a garbled text published as *Thoughts and Details on Scarcity* in 1800).

1796   Publishes *A Letter to a Noble Lord* (24 February). Publishes *Two Letters ... on the Proposals for Peace with the Regicide Directory of France* (20 October; pirated text published 19 October as *Thoughts on the Prospect of a Regicide Peace*).

1797   Burke dies (9 July).

DAVID DWAN AND CHRISTOPHER J. INSOLE

Introduction: Philosophy in Action

Edmund Burke is one of the most important figures in the history of modern political thought, yet his thinking about politics is not easily reducible to a general or fully coherent philosophy. This is partly because of the practical character of much of his intellectual enterprise: elected to parliament in 1765, he remained – despite a brief hiatus in 1780 – a practicing politician for almost twenty-nine years. During this time, he never set out to produce a systematic work of political philosophy, and he repudiated attempts to read his various pronouncements on politics in this way. His account of his most famous work, *Reflections on the Revolution in France* (1790) – 'I was throwing out reflexions upon a political event, and not reading a lecture upon theorism and principles of Government' – arguably applies to the whole sweep of his political writings (C, VI: 304). His 'works' are largely a compilation of disconnected performances urging practical responses to specific problems from rebellion in America to revolution in France to political corruption in England to the abuse of power in Ireland and India. Whether or not one can abstract from these contexts a general doctrine or corpus of thought is debateable. And if such abstraction is possible, it is far from clear that his thought was consistent across contexts. He boasted later in life that if 'he could venture to value himself on anything, it is on the virtue of consistency that he would value himself the most', but his critics would continue to insist that this was a virtue in which he was most derelict (Works, III: 24).

Thus Burke's writings are not swiftly convertible into a theoretical system and much of what he said might be regarded as explicitly hostile to any such endeavour. He was, after all, famously critical of abstract theory and called for a more modest and contextual approach to moral and political problems. 'I cannot stand forward,' he insisted, 'and give praise or blame to any thing which relates to human actions, and human concerns, on a simple view of the object, as it stands stripped of every relation, in all the nakedness and solitude of metaphysical abstraction.' 'Circumstances', he added, 'give in reality to every political principle its distinguishing colour, and discriminating effect. The circumstances are what render every civil and political scheme beneficial or noxious to mankind' (WS, VIII: 58). The extent to which Burke's views on political method should be recast as exegetical principles for reading him is, of course, an arguable question. Nevertheless, his criticisms of abstraction emphasise the conceptual risks of detaching his remarks from their specific circumstances in the service of a more capacious account of his overall outlook or system; it also reveals the potentially dogmatic character of committed assumptions that he had any such system. Of course, not everyone has been dissuaded. Burke has been credited with a highly methodical and philosophically ambitious approach to jurisprudence and to ethics and – despite his disgust for 'political metaphysics' (WS, VIII: 109) – his politics, for some, is informed by a broader metaphysical doctrine.[1] He also has been given a distinctive political credo and has been repeatedly cast as the principal theorist of modern conservatism.[2]

Here and elsewhere, the element of paradox in Burke's theories about the limitations of theory has been fully exploited: thus his elevation of practical reason over theoretical reason has been identified with a number of highly elaborate theoretical positions – utilitarianism, positivism, as well as a theologically honed scepticism.[3] In other accounts, Burke's emphasis on the extreme contingency of political reason has been situated within a broader tradition of common law, where legal norms are derived from historical precedent and customary practice.[4] Yet, for others, he remains a stalwart champion of classical conceptions of natural law (a law universal in scope and binding across all contexts), which he defends from distortion by modern enthusiasts of natural right.[5] However, Burke has also been seen as one of the initiators of a historical school that was hostile to the universalism and metaphysical commitments of a natural law tradition.[6] Each of these rival views risks exaggerating the systematic nature of Burke's enterprise, while the rivalry between them merely serves to expose this common flaw. Of course, the contradictions may reveal tensions in Burke, but the problems may equally stem from the over-ambitious pursuit of consistency itself.

This last view has much to recommend it, but it can also be brought to a point where it begins to distort Burke's intellectual practice. In his own opinion, at any rate, he had a coherent outlook on political affairs. Moreover, in his defence of that consistency, he hoped that people would learn to appreciate the distinction between 'a difference in conduct under a variation of circumstances, and an inconsistency in principle' (Works, III: 27). This was an invitation to interpret his words and deeds in context but also to recover some background principles that determined his responses to specific environments. The Companion takes up this invitation and explores the practical settings that shaped Burke's reflections on politics as well as the general ideas or principles he brought to bear upon them.

The interaction between context and principle in Burke's political life is outlined by Fred Lock in the opening chapter of the volume. Lock sets Burke's key speeches and writings in the context of various events, alliances, and conflicts, mapping his pre-occupations with Ireland, America, India, and then France. Lock relates these various political and intellectual concerns in a sustained chronological narrative. He allows that Burke's writings transcend their various contexts, in terms of their themes and their importance to subsequent generations. But as Lock demonstrates, only by restoring the historical context, can we properly grasp Burke's meaning and nuance. Accordingly, the Companion attempts to address the perennial thematic interest of Burke's writings, by combining extensive treatments of his key intellectual influences and achievements, followed by a set of chapters on the various political theatres of Burke's career, and concluding with a consideration of Burke's legacy.

Seen within context, Burke's resistance to theory was far from total. 'Whenever I speak against theory,' he explained, 'I mean always a weak, erroneous, fallacious, unfounded, or imperfect theory; and one of the ways of discovering that is a false theory is by comparing it with practice.' Burke's criticisms of 'fallacious' theory begged the question, but the general drift of his comments was clear: practice was the 'true touchstone of all theories'; it set the limits for our theories and operated as the test of their merits (Works, VI: 148). Our everyday practices provided the conditions of intelligibility for moral and political claims. Since our theories derived from our practices, it was wrongheaded to attempt to ground our practices on a more foundational set of ideas:

> It seems to be a preposterous way of reasoning, and a perfect confusion of ideas to take the theories, which learned and speculative men have made from that Government and then supposing it made on those theories, which were made from it, to accuse the Government as not corresponding with them. (Works, VI: 148)

For Burke, there was often something hubristic about those who would seek to step outside their received social contexts in an effort to find an objective ground for their values. But there was usually something incoherent in this search for transcendence: it either presupposed the social norms that it put in question or it precluded the very practices that it sought to guarantee.

Such incoherence, he often suggested, was endemic in attempts to derive political entitlements from natural rights. He insisted in 1782 that political rights presupposed the existence of established institutions and social norms, whereas the domain of natural right usually implied the absence of all such norms – given this, it was not clear how the impoverished category of natural rights could or should ground richer normative practices and institutions (Works, VI: 145). In 1791 he claimed that it was contradictory to cast the rights of the people as a natural right: 'a people' was an artificial entity; it was the product of political society not its legitimising condition (Works, III: 95). Thus, theories that pretended to be foundational for everything else inevitably borrowed from the social order that they would seek to challenge or to found. In some of his earliest writings, he insisted that the search for rational foundations for all our practices was fundamentally misguided: 'what would become of the World', he asked, 'if the Practice of all moral Duties, and the Foundations of Society, rested upon having their Reasons made clear and demonstrative to every Individual?' (WS, I: 136). His objections to such exhaustive demonstrations were largely practical, but they could also have a more theoretical bent: some things had to be taken on trust for rational enquiry to be possible; it was thus irrational to demand reasons for everything. Burke has been presented as a 'philosopher of unreason' in an age of Enlightenment, but it is more plausible to suggest that his aim was to expose the irrationality of some of the demands we place on reason.[7]

For Burke, the limits of our reasoning were set by our practices, but it is a mistake to draw an excessively sharp contrast between theory and practice when it comes to understanding his own parliamentary career. After all, the practice of politics was organised around systematic argument and habits of theorising. 'I do not put abstract ideas wholly out of any question,' he duly declared, 'because I well know that under that name I should dismiss principles; and that without the guide and light of sound, well-understood principles, all reasonings in politics, as in everything else, would be only a confused jumble of particular facts and details, without the means of drawing out any sort of theoretical or practical conclusion' (Works, VI: 114). As David Craig shows, it would be difficult to make sense of Burke's political life without commenting on the background theories that shaped it: received wisdom about the nation's 'ancient constitution'; pre-existing views about the role of trust in politics; classical debates about the dangers of faction and the sources of public corruption. His genius for conspiracy theory and his obsession with Court intrigue were informed by a clear-sighted understanding of parliament's role within a mixed constitution. He re-stated with unusual skill and acumen the importance of trust between king, parliament, and people and supplied with this a famous account of political representation as a type of trusteeship. Thus, representatives were entrusted to act in the interests of their constituents, but it was a condition of that trust that they maintained their independence from the people they would serve. However, his respect for the independence of representatives did not lead him to proscribe alliances between them. Here he provided a powerful defence of party – 'a body of men united, for promoting by their joint endeavours the national interest, upon some particular principle in which they are all agreed' – while retaining a conventional hatred of self-interested factions (WS, II: 317).

In these arguments, Burke lived up to his own definition of a politician as a 'philosopher in action', and in a series of responses to practical issues he made a lasting contribution to political thought (WS, II: 317). Understandably, Burke is often cast more as a rhetorician than as a political philosopher, but this distinction can be overdrawn and can credit one practice with too much interest in reason and truth, while allowing another all too little.[8] His rhetoric might easily be seen as opportunistic and emotionally manipulative; in Jeremy Bentham's eyes, Burke was a master of 'the art of misrepresentation – the art of misdirecting the judgment by agitating and inflaming the passions'.[9] However, his speeches were also exercises in reasoning and judgement; if their object was to persuade, Burke seemed to assume that systematic argument and theoretical speculation were valid means of persuasion.

Christopher Reid provides a study of Burke's famous oratory and shows how its venomous qualities were often jarringly at odds with contemporary ideals of eloquence. Burke's defence, drawing on Cicero, would be his sense of occasion: whether vehemence and passion is proper will depend upon the speaker, the subject, and the audience. Here, once again, Burke considers that circumstances can render an action that is right in one situation, wrong in another. When the correctness of an action is so vulnerable to context, high demands are placed upon the agent to perceive the salient circumstances. This is not to say that Burke's assessment of the circumstances was always correct. As Reid shows, his venomous rhetoric was deemed to lack propriety precisely with reference to the circumstances. Few believed, for instance, that he covered himself in glory during the Regency Crisis. His use of rhetoric in evoking the madness of the king was itself considered to put under question the sanity of the speaker, and to misjudge both the subject and the audience.

The study of Burke's rhetoric also reveals how his opinions were sifted from other thinkers, or were partly given to him in the form of readily available idioms. According to one of his best interpreters, he was not a creator of a school of thought, but 'a catalyst of pre-existing traditions of discourse'.[10] This volume examines Burke's use of these discourses and tries to situate his rhetoric within a broad set of intellectual traditions. Paddy Bullard shows

how Burke based his aesthetic theories on Lockean psychological principles, while his discussion of the sublime might owe as much to classical
sources – clearly Longinus, but also Lucretius. The polemical energy of his
Philosophical Enquiry (1757) is best recovered, according to Bullard, when
the Earl of Shaftesbury is identified as its main target. Thus, Burke objects
to Shaftesbury's excessively ethereal account of aesthetic phenomena and
attempts to reassert their material causes and bodily nature. He worries most
of all about Shaftesbury tendency to conflate aesthetic and moral orders of
experience – a point also brought into sharp relief by Richard Bourke.

Burke's frequent recourse to legal arguments and principles gleaned from
traditions of common law and natural law jurisprudence also need to be
interpreted within a broader historical and intellectual context. As Seán
Donlan argues, Burke could sing the praises of England's 'ancient constitution' as well as any other Whig, but he could also challenge parochial
views of English legal history and was especially critical of the insularity of
popular common law histories associated with William Blackstone. Instead,
he chose to emphasise the degree to which English law was the result of
frequent and constructive communication with the continent. Throughout
his life he expressed impatience at narrow or excessively positivist construc-
tions of law and insisted that all legal schemes must accommodate the particular manners and morals of nations as well as ethical constraints imposed
by human nature. Of course, critics have disputed the meaning and importance of these ethical constraints, and it is an issue that Christopher Insole
addresses in his chapter on Burke's use of natural law.

Insole finds Burke to be sketchy on some fundamental controversies about
the precise grounding and implications of 'the immutable, pre-existent law'
(WS VI: 350). Nonetheless, Insole argues that there is a loose pattern in
Burke's use of the language of natural law: he unambiguously gravitates
towards conceptions of natural law that focus on God as the source of
laws of nature, where the human being is conceived of as having a divinely
ordained purpose, manifested through the exercise of virtues such as prudence. Burke follows Aristotle and Cicero in maintaining that the task of
prudence is to discern the right action – oriented to a substantive conception
of the 'good' – by attending carefully to the whole range of contingent circumstances that frustrate, limit, or promote this endeavour. This conception
of the role of prudence leads directly to Burke's critique of those who are
'metaphysically mad' enough to seek geometrical patterns of reasoning in
politics (Works, VI: 101). On this issue, Burke clearly distances himself from
some of the more systematic early modern reconstructors of natural law
language, who were fascinated by and covetous of the certainty delivered by
geometrical methods.

Burke has been cast as a natural law thinker on the one hand or as a utilitarian on the other, but as David Dwan argues, this dichotomy is over-drawn and imposes a false set of alternatives on Burke's intellectual practice. Dwan also cautions against viewing Burke as a 'utilitarian' – at least in the way that term was defined by Jeremy Bentham and by the Mills. 'Utility', for Burke, is a broad concept that describes the fitness of means to an end. Everything depends upon what the end is judged to be, and what the means are that are considered appropriate. On neither front does Burke look like a 'utilitarian' in any meaningful sense: the end is the 'good', constituted by a range of different and irreducible moral values, including, it is true, hap-piness, but not in the crude sense of pleasure, or even the slightly enlarged sense of satisfied desire. Oriented to a broad and objective sense of the human good, utility need not be incompatible with an attachment to justice or natural law, both of which for Burke have a reference to objective human purposes, and so to utility. A narrow conception of utility, on the other hand, is self-undermining – a fact that was lost, he suggested, on the 'oeco-nomical politicians' who increasingly hold sway in France and in England (WS, VIII: 130).

Burke had a strong interest in the developing science of political economy throughout his career. This was the archetypal science of political reform, according to Richard Whatmore; moreover, it twinned proposals for domes-tic improvements with a wide-ranging assessment of international relations. Even the most level-headed of Burke's contemporaries feared that Europe was on the verge of another decline and fall: the monarchies of France and Britain faced the prospect of bankruptcy and exhaustion through war. Consequent threats of domestic revolution loomed, while some anticipated the reawakening of religious conflict across Europe. To add to this dark picture, oriental despotism was anticipated by some to become a dominant state form, or at the very least, Europe's borders appeared to be vulner-able to renewed barbarian invasions from the East. Thus, reform of the European system of states was vital to prevent catastrophe – a process that entailed discussion about the security and merits of small and large states, the political prospects for rich and poor countries and the general relation-ship between commerce and government. This triggered questions as to whether trade could be moralised, whether it might be made immune to luxury and conducive to equality, whether it was compatible with particular forms of government and could be fully harmonised with empire. Burke's interest in contribution to these debates is evident across the whole sweep of his writings from An *Account of the European Settlements in America* – a work co-authored with William Burke and published in 1757 – to his late 'Thoughts and Details on Scarcity' (1795).

Here Burke emerges as very much a figure of enlightenment, committed to the ameliorating influence of modern social science. He is best remembered, of course, for his assault on the follies of 'this enlightened age' during the furious debates surrounding the French Revolution (Works, III: 17). Advocates of a naïve and self-undermining rationalism, he believed, had claimed for themselves a monopoly on enlightenment, and in this context he was happy to relinquish the prize to his adversaries. Against the emissaries of 'new light', he seemed to prefer 'the sober shade of the old obscurity' (Works, III: 67). But, as Richard Bourke argues, Burke was a self-conscious defender of enlightened principles for much of his career. From his early days at Trinity College, he defended the rational methods of 'enlightened times' and contrasted this with scholastic logic – a relic from the 'days of ignorance' (C, I: 89). If, as Ernst Cassirer once suggested, 'the Enlightenment begins by breaking down the older form of philosophical knowledge, the metaphysical systems', then Burke is located squarely within it.[11] In his *Account of European Settlements in America* and in his unfinished histories of England, he placed the growth of enlightenment within a broader and conventional narrative: the growth of modern science and humanist scholarship had led to a general improvement of minds and manners; this had vouchsafed the growth of commerce which in turn fostered civility; all was guaranteed by the rule of law and the consolidation of modern monarchies throughout Europe.

Religion, for Burke, was an essential constituent of this improvement: it softened manners and fostered learning. Burke is clearly a staunch critic of enlightenment if this is to be identified with anti-clericalism and religious scepticism, but there is no good reason why matters should be cast in this way.[12] For Burke, religion was perfectly compatible with 'ingenuous science' (WS, I: 322). This was partly due to the rational limits of both practices. Like many successors of Locke, he combined a confident empiricism with an intense awareness of the limitations of knowledge. It was precisely because knowledge derived from the senses that our grasp of metaphysical issues was always limited. He was convinced that the 'great chain of causes, which linking one to another even to the throne of God himself, can never be unravelled by any industry of ours.' 'When we go but one step beyond the immediately sensible qualities of things,' he added, 'we go out of our depth' (WS, I: 283). Religious truths could not be fully verified, but this exposed the limits of justification, not the errors of our belief.

However, the utility of religion could be known, and, as Ian Harris shows, he repeatedly emphasised the social benefits of religious practice. He insisted that it was both mistaken and impious to regard religion as 'nothing but policy' (WS, VIII: 486), but he also believed that 'its excellent policy instead of being an objection to it, was one of the greatest proofs of its divinity.'[13] It was on the basis of their perceived utility that he discussed with approval the rise of monasteries in England and controversially defended their main-tenance in France. For similar reasons, he endorsed the religious institutions of India, both 'Hindoo' and 'Mahometan' (WS, V: 422). Burke was a strong advocate of religious toleration and seemed to associate himself with those who would 'protect all religions, because they love and venerate the great principle upon which they all agree, and the great object to which they are all directed' (WS, VIII: 199). However, he had little tolerance for atheism – 'a foul, unnatural vice, foe to all the dignity and consolation of mankind' (Works, III: 273) – and his assaults on 'atheistical fanaticism' in *Reflections on the Revolution in France* (1790) are not without their own kind of zeal (WS, VIII: 202).

Having covered extensively the range of Burke's theoretical commitments and allegiances, the Companion moves into a detailed consideration of each of Burke's political theatres of action. Although each of these contexts has its own distinctive properties, his interventions on Ireland, America, and India all revolve in different ways around issues of empire and colonial power. Prior to chapter length treatments of each of these areas, Jennifer Pitts con-siders the extent to which Burke's outlook was more broadly guided by a theory or theories of empire. Pitts suggests that Burke's interest in the par-ticularity of each situation did not prevent his theorising empire as a political form with more depth than any of his contemporaries. To govern an empire was a high calling, which required the exercise of power with restraint and for the benefit of those governed. Unlike his contemporaries, who tended to focus on issues of how to control and stabilise the governed, Burke saw the main threat to empire being a failure of moral and political imagination in the governors. The British state and public Burke considered to be mor-ally and institutionally ill-prepared to run an empire, showing themselves neglectful of the deep structural liabilities of imperial rule, with its intrinsic momentum towards violence, instability, and oppression. In each political theatre that Burke attended to, he paid close attention to the source of the corruption and the abuse of power, setting out his diagnosis as part of the case for reform.

The colonial momentum towards oppression had gained an unusual lon-gevity in the context of Ireland. Ian McBride explains that although 'colon-isation' did not, for Burke, carry the immediate connotations of illegitimacy that it has since accrued, he considered the particular nature and history of the colonial rule in Ireland to be lamentable. Conquerors in other contexts, such as the Normans in England, had blended imperceptibly with the con-quered population, but not so in Ireland. McBride shows how Burke lays the heavy responsibility for this at the door of the Protestant Ascendancy, a 'plebeian oligarchy', whose garrison mentality had oppressed the majority of the people, stripping Catholics of their property and their traditional religion, two of Burke's pillars of civilisation (WS, IX: 600). Even the Whig shibboleth of the Glorious Revolution of 1688 is capable of becoming a political evil, in the wrong circumstances: Burke considered that the impact of the Revolution had the opposite effect in England, as it had in Ireland, where it consolidated the arbitrary power of a privileged minority, rather than the liberties of the nation as a whole.

Harry Dickinson explores Burke's response to American affairs, defending the cogency and nuance of Burke's contribution during the American crisis. Burke supported the Declaratory Act of 1766, which upheld the superintending power of the British parliament over the American colonies. At the same time Burke was heavily critical of much of the legislation imposed upon America by Britain. Both at the time and subsequently, Burke has come under criticism for his inconsistency, and for backing half-measures that failed to grasp that the real problem was the Declaratory Act itself. Dickinson puts the case that Burke was exploring a more subtle and pragmatic arrangement. Whilst avoiding split sovereignty, Burke considered that the colonists should be granted considerable self-government, with the British parliament imposing real restrictions on the exercise of its own sovereign authority. To repeal the theoretical superintendence of parliament would not address the practical issues, and could lead to unforeseen and extreme consequences. Here we see demonstrated in context Burke's consistent preference for practical measures with predictable consequences and benefits, rather than clean theoretical solutions, with undesired and precarious consequences.

As with America and Ireland, Burke's consistent preoccupation in India is with the abuse of power. Frederick Whelan sets out Burke's diagnosis of the particular source of these abuses: in India, the abuse of power is inevitable when young men are removed from the constraints and formation of their background and given authority, without accountability, in an alien environment. Burke's disgust with British actions in India is consistent with principles that he applies across a range of contexts: the British violate and uproot an ancient and refined civilisation in India that can boast – in a way that parallels Europe – institutions of law, religion, property, and orders of nobility. So dramatic is this destructive process in Bengal that the British must be conceived of as promulgating a 'revolution', and not a glorious one. In carrying out this revolution, the British violate natural law and fail to exercise the trust of authority.

The cumulative message of these chapters is that even when attending to Burke at his most contextual – when he is responding to crises and at times fast-moving events in Ireland, America, and India – we find a cluster of common concerns and patterns of analysis. It does Burke's thought a disservice to remove it from the sphere of political action in which he lived and moved, but his actions are also misunderstood when deprived of all philosophy and identified with a free-floating pragmatism devoid of theoretical commitments.[14] The philosophical ambition manifested in Burke's reaction to events reaches a new intensity in the context of France, and Burke is best remembered of course for his *Reflections on the Revolution in France*. A chapter of the Companion is devoted to exploring the main lines of argument of this extraordinary work.

Burke's *Reflections* was drafted as a letter and contain all the artful spontaneity, colour, and lack of system that one might anticipate from this style of address. It also contains a dizzying number of preoccupations – it is a history lesson on the meaning of the Glorious Revolution; a survey of the rise of civility across Europe and an account of its demise; a tract on the intimate relationship between manners, law, and commerce; a lecture on political economy; an analysis of the ideological origins of revolution and a psychopathology of its participants; an *ubi sunt* to a lost age that is at once lachrymose, furious, and strangely clear-sighted. As Iain Hampsher-Monk demonstrates, *Reflections* is above all a sustained discussion of the conditions and limits of reason in political life. In their pursuit of metaphysical certainties, the French turn their back on the things that give us orientation in moral space: customary practice, established institutions, and historical entitlements. These are sources of a rational confidence – if not certainty – in politics, and abstract speculation destroys confidence in the political word just as much as it does in economic life. Hampsher-Monk also shows how Burke continued his attacks on the French Revolution in a series of later writings. Here his commitment to war with France never wavered, although his justification for military intervention underwent a series of intriguing shifts.

Burke's polemic against the French Revolution secured his lasting reputation. Such fame has inevitably led to some de-contextualisation of his arguments and to an anachronistic understanding of his principles. Admittedly, the problem of anachronism was internal to Burke's own situation: he stood before a 'total revolution' that recast the terms of political debate in Europe so that things would appear different on either side of the chasm (WS, VIII: 338). Of course, interpreters from Guizot to Tocqueville would question Burke's account of the Revolution as a cataclysmic 'schism with the whole universe' and would present it as a culminating moment in a general narrative of incremental change, or as an after-effect of an earlier rupture caused by absolute monarchy (WS, IX: 249). The true nature of the Revolution continues to be debated, but it is clear that it helped to produce a new political language, while established vocabularies now meant something else. By his own rhetorical lights, Burke hoped to preserve the proper meaning of political concepts as these were bequeathed to him within a Whig constitutional tradition ('rights', 'liberty', 'trust', or the political significance of terms such as 'the people'), but, partly because of the appearance of new alternatives, the prior meanings of these terms were no longer fully available to him – not to mention his later interpreters. Here his defence of British constitutional principles may have looked less 'liberal' than it once did.

Yet theories of Burke's 'conservatism' often misrepresent the Whig values he was trying to conserve or tend to overlook his own sense of nature's paradoxical law: change is a necessary means of conservation (WS, IX: 634). He was a political reformer for much of his career and for all his esteem for forefathers and legacies, he had little time for those who would defend the 'inheritance of absurdity, derived to them from their ancestors' (WS, III: 491). Here and elsewhere he was often prepared to argue against the authority of prescription in the interest of enlightened reform.[15] On a whole raft of issues – colonial administration in Canada and India, reform of criminal law, trade and public finance, slavery, or religious toleration – he was far from being a defender of the status quo – and even when he attempted to defend the existing constitutional balance, usually from its perceived infringement from the crown, he frequently struck the pose of a dissident. The fury of his attacks on Lord North and George III shocked many for their disrespect, while the limits of his deference are obvious in his famous *Letter to a Noble Lord* (1796). He championed an aristocratic interest as checks to pure democracy and absolute monarchy, but he declared himself 'no friend to aristocracy' (WS, II: 268). Indeed, pure aristocracy, he claimed, was 'the worst imaginable government' (WS, I: 547).

These details are easily suppressed by accounts of Burke's 'conservatism', 'traditionalism', or reactionary politics. Nor has his thought been best served by modern conservatives in search of an intellectual pedigree and coherent apologist for their political beliefs. In Britain, Burke has been anachronistically cast as a proleptic critic of the European Union and – even more churlishly – as an antagonist of political correctness.[16] As Seamus Deane argues in the final essay of this volume, the problem of anachronism has also been a pronounced feature of American discussions of Burke. In the 1950s in the United States, those in search of the intellectual origins of the conservative mind circled around Burke and found that his critique of Jacobinism could be infinitely re-adapted to suit Cold War conditions.[17] Here and elsewhere the 'natural law' elements of Burke's political thought were emphasised at some expense to his sense of history and context. More subtle interpretations of Burke subsequently appeared, particularly within larger debates between liberals and communitarians, while recently a more 'liberal' Burke has arisen as a challenge to conservative cartoons. But, according to Deane, the Disneyland version of Burke still persists. Part of the problem may lie in Burke's infinite quotability: each time bad men combine, tannoys call on the good to associate, while little platoons spring up in defence of every kind of purpose from the family to the local firm. Burke's tendency to express matters in Manichean terms – albeit in reaction to specific evils – has not always served him or others well. The best remedy, perhaps, is not just to quote Burke but to read him – and with reference to the contexts in which he lived.

NOTES

1 See Joseph L. Pappin III, *The Metaphysics of Edmund Burke* (New York: Fordham University Press, 1993).

2 For an ambivalent account of this construction of Burke, see Robert Eccleshall, *English Conservatism since the Restoration: An Introduction and Anthology* (London: Allen & Unwin, 1990), pp. 71–4. For more committed views, see Roger Scruton, 'Man's Second Disobedience: A Vindication of Burke' in Ceri Corssley and Ian Small (eds.), *The French Revolution and British Culture* (Oxford University Press: 1989), pp. 187–222; Michael Gove, 'Edmund Burke and the Politicians' and John Redwood, 'Edmund Burke and Modern Conservatism' in Ian Crowe (ed.), *Edmund Burke: His Life and Legacy*, (Dublin: Four Courts Press, 1997), pp. 152–8; pp. 189–97.

3 The interpretation of Burke as a utilitarian and a positivist owed most to John Morley's two books: *Edmund Burke: An Historical Study* (London, 1888) and *Burke* (London, 1867). For an interesting account of the religious sources of Burke's 'fideistic politics', see Iain Hampsher-Monk, 'Burke and the Religious Sources of Skeptical Conservatism' in J. van der Zande and R. H. Popkin (eds.), *The Skeptical Tradition around 1800*, (Dordrecht: Kluwer, 1998), pp. 235–59.

4 See J. G. A. Pocock, *The Ancient Constitution and the Feudal Law: A Study of English Historical Thought in the Seventeenth Century*, 2nd ed. (Cambridge: Cambridge University Press, 1987), and 'Burke and the Ancient Constitution: A Problem in the History of Ideas', *Historical Journal*, 3.2 (1960): 125–43.

5 See, in particular, Peter J. Stanlis, *Edmund Burke and the Natural Law* (Ann Arbor, Michigan: University of Michigan Press, 1958); Francis S. J. Canavan, *The Political Reason of Edmund Burke* (Durham, NC: Duke University Press, 1960).

6 Friedrich Meinecke, *Historicism: The Rise of a New Historical Outlook*, trans. J. E. Anderson (London: Routledge & Kegan Paul 1972), p. 223. For an account of this historical turn as less programmatic and more inadvertent, see Leo Strauss, *Natural Right and History* (Chicago: The University of Chicago Press, 1953), pp. 314–23.

7 Alfred Cobban in *Edmund Burke and the Revolt Against the Eighteenth Century: A Study of the Political and Social Thinking of Burke, Wordsworth, Coleridge, and Southey.* (London: Allen & Unwin, 1960), p. 75.

8 The view that Burke was a 'splendid rhetorician and advocate' but 'not a philosopher' or 'seeker after truth' was put forward most starkly by Robert M. Hutchins, 'The Theory of the State: Edmund Burke', *Review of Politics*, 5 (1943): 139–55. But the view has been repeated on a more subtle basis ever since.

9 Jeremy Bentham, *Works* (Edinburgh, 1848), vol. X, p.510. Cited in James T. Boulton, *The Language of Politics in the Age of Wilkes and Burke* (London: Routledge, 1963),p. 123.

10 J. C. D. Clark 'Introduction' in Edmund Burke, *Reflections on the Revolution in France* (Stanford, 2001), pp. 23–111, 98.

11 Ernst Cassirer, *The Philosophy of the Enlightenment* trans. Fritz C. A. Koelln and James P. Pettegrove (Princeton University Press, 1951), p. vii.

12 On this point see J. C. D. Clark, 'The Enlightenment, Religion and Edmund Burke', *Studies in Burke and His time*, 21 (2007): 9–38.

13 Edmund Burke, 'An Extempore Commonplace on the Sermon of our Saviour on the Mount' in Ian Harris (ed.), *Pre-Revolutionary Writings* (Cambridge University Press, 1993), p. 3.

14 Frank O'Gorman cast Burke as a pragmatist with no broader theoretical agenda in *Edmund Burke: His Political Philosophy* (London: Unwin, 1973).

15 On this point see Richard Bourke, 'Edmund Burke and the Politics of Conquest', *Modern Intellectual History*, 4.3 (2007): 403–32.

16 Jim McCue, 'Edmund Burke and the British Constitution' and Redwood, 'Edmund Burke and Modern Conservatism' in Crowe (ed.), *Edmund Burke: His Life and Legacy*, pp. 170–8; 170, 190.

17 See, in particular, Russell Kirk, *The Conservative Mind: from Burke to Santayana* (Chicago: Regnery, 1953).

I

F. P. LOCK

Burke's Life

More than with most figures in the Western intellectual tradition, understanding Burke's contributions requires some knowledge of his biography.
This is especially important for his political ideas, for he wrote no sustained
and systematic work of political theory. His views have to be derived from a
long and varied series of writings and speeches, all of which were responses
to particular occasions and problems. Without knowing these contexts, readers are liable to misconstrue his arguments. A succinct narrative of Burke's
career thus provides an essential background for detailed thematic studies,
for his life both generated and constrained the production of the writings
and speeches that are his legacy to the world.[1]

Early years: 1730–1765

Born in Dublin in 1730, Burke lived in Ireland until 1750, when he left to
study law in London. The importance of his Irishness is universally acknowledged, though scholars disagree about the precise nature of its influence.[2]
His father was a Protestant and an attorney, possibly, but probably not a
convert from Roman Catholicism. Nothing is known of his father's background. His mother came from a well-documented family of Catholic gentry, who had lost much, though not all, of their property. Burke was one of
four children who survived infancy. As a child, he suffered poor health, and
was sent to stay with relatives in the Blackwater valley in County Cork,
perhaps for as long as five years (1735–40). In 1741, he was sent to a board-
ing school at Ballitore, County Kildare, kept by Abraham Shackleton, a
Quaker who had emigrated from Yorkshire. Burke retained fond memories
of Ballitore and his master. In 1744, he entered Trinity College, Dublin, then
a bastion of the Protestant establishment, and still primarily a training college for the Church of Ireland. There he followed the regular four-year arts
course, graduating in February 1748. His academic record was undistin-
guished. Shortly after graduating, he helped to write and edit the *Reformer*,

a short-lived periodical on the plan of the *Spectator*. The remainder of his time in Dublin is a blank. From this bare outline, one conclusion can confidently be drawn: Burke's Irishness was a complex inheritance.

In 1750, Burke arrived in London to study law at the Middle Temple. He was supported by his father, who intended him to practice at the Irish bar, for which keeping terms at one of the London Inns of Court was required. For about five years, Burke maintained a pretence at least of studying the law. These proved five unhappy years: Burke suffered some kind of breakdown, from which he was rescued by a kindly doctor, Christopher Nugent, whose daughter Burke subsequently married. Burke began to write, soon abandoning poetry (which he had cultivated as an undergraduate) for prose. By 1753, he had at least drafted his early masterpiece, *A Philosophical Enquiry into the Origin of our Ideas of the Sublime and Beautiful*.

Symptomatic of the uncertainty and drift of these years is that he made no attempt to publish his *Enquiry*. Gradually, however, Burke began to emerge from this slough of despond. In 1754, he applied for a colonial job, obviously in an attempt to achieve financial independence, though in 1755 he still professed willingness to follow his father's path. Between 1756 and 1759, he finally achieved emancipation. In 1756, he published his first book, *A Vindication of Natural Society*, a parody of the subversive 'philosophy' of Henry St John, Viscount Bolingbroke. In addition, he helped William Burke (a distant relation whom he met soon after his arrival in London and who became a close and lifelong friend) with the writing of *An Account of the European Settlements in America* (published in 1757), a book intended to capitalise on the interest in the American colonies stimulated by the outbreak of the Seven Years War in 1756. In 1757, he finally published his *Philosophical Enquiry* and married Jane Nugent. Two children followed, both born in 1758. In the longer term, the marriage proved enduringly happy and provided Burke with a welcome haven of comfort from the vexations and frustrations of his political career. Also in 1758, he signed a contract for a short history of England. With great rapidity, he wrote the narrative as far as 1215, and this was actually set in type for imminent publication. Still in 1758, he signed another contract to produce an *Annual Register*, a digest of contemporary history combined with a wide range of miscellaneous reprinted articles. But such journalism could not support a family, so in 1759 Burke accepted a vaguely defined position as private secretary or companion to William Gerard Hamilton, an independently wealthy MP.

Unfortunately, the connection proved stifling. For six years, Hamilton absorbed all Burke's time and energies. Following Hamilton (who had been appointed chief secretary), and serving as his 'jackal', Burke spent two winters (1761–2 and 1763–4) in Dublin. He continued to edit the *Annual Register*, which he established as a standard resource (indeed, a descendant is still published), and in 1763, he achieved financial security with the award of an Irish pension obtained by Hamilton. To these years also belongs his unfinished 'Tract on the Popery Laws', a powerfully written indictment of the tyranny of what would later be called the 'Protestant Ascendancy'. Burke also extended his acquaintance, meeting many eminent figures in the worlds of literature, politics, and culture, such as Samuel Johnson and Joshua Reynolds. By 1765, however, he had reached a breaking point. The final provocation was an ill-judged attempt on Hamilton's part to bind Burke by some kind of formal contract. Burke's patience snapped. He severed relations with Hamilton, resisted overtures for a reconciliation, and even resigned his pension. These were less quixotic gestures than they may appear. Burke had by now realised that his talents could find other markets. While he still needed patrons, he had some in view whose service would be less inhibiting and who would allow him to emerge out of the shadows.

Politics and party: 1765–1784

Burke entered politics as the result of a series of chances. The determination of George III, on his accession in 1760, to take a more active role in the choice of ministers led to a period of political instability and a succession of short-lived governments. In no other circumstances would the inexperienced Marquis of Rockingham have been offered the position of first lord of the treasury, and few other potential ministers would have lacked a competent man of business to act as private secretary. Burke was personally unknown to Rockingham. He owed his position proximately to the recommendation of Lord Cavendish; who recommended him to Lord John is unknown. Nor was even this appointment, fortunate as it seemed, enough on its own to propel Burke into prominence. He owed his seat in the Commons to another source, Earl Verney, who controlled the pocket borough of Wendover in Buckinghamshire. William Burke had somehow achieved a remarkable influence over Verney, and when Verney offered to bring him into the Commons, William generously allowed Edmund to take the first vacancy (he was himself subsequently elected on Verney's interest at Carmarthen).

Even this second stroke of good fortune would not have been enough had not Burke served an unconscious apprenticeship, having acquired (in part through his work on the *Annual Register*) an extensive knowledge of political and economic topics. Finally, he owed his fame to a quite unsuspected talent. Within a few days of entering the Commons, he discovered his readiness in debate. This was the decisive factor in opening the road to fame. Of the 558 MPs in the Commons, no more than about forty were regular speakers, and many of these were weak at impromptu debating. Burke could dissect an opponent's case and mount an immediate riposte. This ability made him invaluable to Rockingham and the group of mainly aristocratic Whigs who acknowledged his leadership. The party was short of good speakers, and Burke soon achieved a prominence he could not otherwise have achieved in such a party.

During Burke's first nine sessions in Parliament (from 1765–6 to 1772–3), no great issue was agitated that greatly interests posterity. Nevertheless, some attention to these years is justified, if only for the part they played in shaping his later opinions and attitudes. The most important issue that faced Rockingham's government in 1766 was how to respond to the American defiance of George Grenville's Stamp Act. Its solution was to repeal the Stamp Act, and to pass instead a Declaratory Act, which firmly asserted (in theory) parliamentary sovereignty over the colonies. Loyalty to this compromise determined the American policy of the Rockingham party for many years. Only with great reluctance was it constrained eventually to accept the fact of American independence.

Rockingham's ministry lasted only a year. In July 1766, the king turned to the elder William Pitt (ennobled as Earl of Chatham) to form a new ministry. Burke had no official position to resign, and was not at this stage so committed to Rockingham that he could not have taken office under Pitt. Indeed, with little visible means of support (only a small Irish estate that he inherited from his elder brother, who had died in 1765), he had every incentive to do so, and was actually approached by William Conway, one of Chatham's subordinates. Burke, however, set impossible conditions. Not for the last time, he preferred a pose of high-minded integrity to the messy scramble for jobs. It proved a momentous decision. For the next sixteen years, he followed Rockingham in opposition, where he proved an able and versatile debater. Indeed, he was perhaps by temperament best suited to this role of constant critic. In any case, so long an experience of opposition left its mark, making Burke increasingly self-righteous, inflexible, and convinced of the folly or knavery of those who disagreed with him.

Apart from his service in the Commons, Burke also wrote what came to be regarded as the Rockingham party's creed, *Thoughts on the Cause of the Present Discontents* (1770). Rarely has a partisan polemic been so happily elevated and generalised into a statement of general principles: so much so that the pamphlet is regularly accorded a place in histories of the 'rise' of parties in British politics. As with all of Burke's political writings, it does indeed embody reflections of permanent interest and value. But it grew out of the discontents of the Rockingham party as they faced the prospect of perpetual opposition.

One non-political episode of these years merits attention: Burke's purchase in 1768 of a 300-acre country house and estate at Beaconsfield, about twenty-four miles northwest of London. He acquired this handsome property on the strength of profits that William Burke, in conjunction with Lord Verney, expected to make from speculating in the stock of the East India Company. Burke paid £20,000, all of it borrowed. Thereafter, Burke's year was divided between parliamentary sessions in London and summers (and shorter breaks during the session) at Beaconsfield. For the first time, Burke possessed a real home, and as a landed gentleman could mix on more equal terms with his political associates. He became an enthusiastic amateur farmer, and took great pleasure in the estate. Yet he paid a high price in terms of lifelong financial insecurity. In 1769, East India stock crashed, and William's paper fortune proved a mirage. Meanwhile, interest on the mortgages exceeded the income from the estate, so that Burke fell increasingly into debt, kept afloat by periodic loans from Rockingham. Financial exigency was undoubtedly his main reason for accepting, in 1771, the position of London agent for the New York Assembly, a role that awkwardly compromised his political independence, but that paid £500 a year.

News of the Boston Tea Party reached England in January 1774, and for most of the next decade the American crisis was the leading political issue. Burke, and the Rockingham party, blamed the British government for the conflict. Relations with the Americans would have remained cordial, they argued, if the wise compromise effected by the first Rockingham administration in 1766 had been allowed to stand. In defence of this argument, Burke gave the first of his great speeches, on 19 April 1774. Subsequently prepared for publication, and now generally known as his *Speech on American Taxation*, it was by far his most elaborate parliamentary effort to date. Like most of its successors, it was admired, but failed to convince. Only when the policies it opposed were seen as having manifestly failed did it acquire a retrospective aura of prophetic wisdom. Still, even at the time it raised Burke's reputation, not least among those who disagreed with him.

The speech probably also contributed to Burke's one triumph in popular politics, his election on 2 November 1774 as MP for Bristol, then one of the country's leading commercial centres. As with other events in Burke's life, this was the result of a series of accidents. Lord Verney, financially embarrassed as a result of his East India speculations, could no longer provide Burke with a free seat at Wendover, nor was Burke in a position to buy one elsewhere. Westminster and Bristol, popular constituencies, seemed at first possible, but these hopes were dashed. Rockingham came to the rescue, ensuring Burke's election at his pocket borough of Malton in Yorkshire. Then events in Bristol took a new turn. One of the sitting members decided not to contest the forthcoming election, opening the way for Burke's late entry into the race. After a long and grueling campaign (which he hated), he was elected, coming second at the poll. To represent Bristol was a signal honour, and for the first time Burke had something like an independent base. There were, however, drawbacks. Bristol had a numerous and exigent electorate, that expected a good deal from its MPs. Burke worked reasonably hard at helping his constituents in their dealings with government, though as a leading oppositionist he was not ideally placed to do so. Yet he was unwilling to visit Bristol and maintain a running canvas, which would have done more to preserve his interest among the voters at large. In fact, he visited Bristol only twice (once in 1775 and once in 1776) before the 1780 election. He probably realised that the unusual circumstances of 1774 were unlikely to be repeated, and that he had no realistic chance of re-election.

In the following session, on 22 March 1775, Burke gave the second of his great American speeches, subsequently published and now known as his *Speech on Conciliation with America*. Even more powerfully argued and eloquent than the *Speech on American Taxation*, it met with a similar fate. It failed to convince its auditors, but in retrospect came to be admired as a manual of wise statesmanship. Popular opinion ran too strongly against the Americans for Burke to make any headway against the policy of coercion. Burke was reluctant to accept this policy. Increasingly, he came to believe that Lord North's parliamentary majority was corruptly bought, not genuinely convinced by the government's case. In 1777, as a protest, the Rockingham party staged a temporary secession from parliament. When it failed to have any effect, Burke wrote a justification, his *Letter to the Sheriffs of Bristol* (1777).

Parliament might be solidly in support of Lord North and against the Americans, but a protest movement was emerging in the country at large. Burke distrusted such movements, and was always unwilling to enter into alliance with them. In 1779–80, however, the Rockingham party did join the Petitioning Movement, partly in the hope of moderating its aims and defusing demands for reform of parliament (which was always anathema to Burke). Instead, the Rockingham party, and Burke in particular, championed what they called 'Economical Reformation'. The aim of this species of reform was to reduce the number of sinecures and other rewards available to influence MPs and thus to make the House of Commons more independent of the executive. Burke drew up a specific measure, which he presented in his *Speech on Economical Reformation*, delivered on 11 February 1780 and subsequently published to great acclaim. It remains the wittiest and most enjoyable of all his long speeches, despite its subject being so local and temporary. After a long and often exciting struggle, during which one clause was successfully passed after a dramatic debate, the bill was lost.

Later in 1780, partly to take advantage of the burgeoning turn towards the government in the aftermath of the Gordon Riots, Lord North called an early election (not due until 1781). Burke's prospects in Bristol were dim. Warned by his friends that he stood little chance and that money for a campaign would not readily be forthcoming, Burke decided not to seek re-election. When he reached Bristol, however, intending to announce his formal withdrawal, a sudden change of feeling among his friends determined them to nominate him after all. In a dramatic reversal, they marched to the Guildhall, where Burke made a fighting speech, often quoted as a masterly exposition of the principle of parliamentary representation as he understood it. Even this great speech, however, could not compensate for the lack of money and of an effective grassroots organisation. Burke was soon compelled to withdraw. For a time, his exclusion from parliament seemed probable, but eventually Rockingham came again to the rescue. One of his members for Malton obligingly resigned, and Burke was duly elected in his place.

Meanwhile, military failures and ever-increasing costs were making the American war unpopular. Eventually, even Lord North was constrained to concede that coercion had failed. In March 1782, he resigned, and the king (still convinced that the war was winnable) was forced to ask Rockingham to form a new ministry. This should have been a moment of triumph for Burke. But the new ministry was not the pure party government that Burke had envisaged in his *Thoughts on the Cause of the Present Discontents*. Instead, it was an uneasy coalition between Rockingham and the Earl of Shelburne, the leader of another opposition faction. Consequently, Rockingham had few cabinet places at his disposal. Burke received only the lucrative consolation prize of the position of Paymaster-General of the Forces, one of the offices that his plan of Economical Reformation would have reformed. A truncated form of his bill was to be enacted, but Burke would still receive a salary of £4,000 a year, enough to have retrieved his finances had he held it for long enough. But Rockingham, who had never enjoyed robust health, died on 1 July. Burke's career was blighted just as he appeared on the threshold of reaping the reward for sixteen years of dispiriting opposition.

Rockingham's death split the fragile coalition. The king appointed Shelburne as his successor, and most of Rockingham's followers (including Burke) preferred to resign. Thus after just three months, Burke was again in opposition. Shelburne, however, was unpopular and widely distrusted, so that almost at once intrigues began to oust him. When parliament resumed in December 1782, the Rockingham party (now led nominally by the Duke of Portland, in effect by the more charismatic Charles James Fox) joined with Lord North and his supporters, and in February 1783 they defeated the treaty of peace that Shelburne had negotiated with the Americans and French. The king resisted this new coalition as long as possible, but in April was forced to accept it. Burke returned to office as Paymaster-General. His main contribution to the Fox-North coalition was to the drafting of two bills reforming the East India Company. His attitude towards the company had changed since 1767–73, when he had vehemently opposed government intervention in its affairs. Tales of corruption and oppression in India had convinced him, along with many others, that reform was needed. On 1 December 1783, he delivered a long speech on the subject, subsequently published and known as his *Speech on Fox's India Bill*. The most accessible of his Indian speeches, it shows a remarkable grasp of the problems and issues. But the question was not to be decided on its merits. One of Fox's bills could plausibly be represented as an invasion of chartered property rights, and the popularity of this specious topic emboldened the king to encourage his friends in the House of Lords to vote against it. When they defeated it (on 19 December), he dismissed the coalition and appointed the young William Pitt to the treasury, confident that, if an election were forced, Pitt would secure a majority. After several weeks of wrangling, parliament was dissolved, and the ensuing election gave Pitt a comfortable majority. Burke, of course, was re-elected at Malton, but many of Fox's supporters lost their seats. Burke became increasingly isolated, even within his own party. In the short post-election session, he moved a gargantuan resolution condemning the king's actions but found only a single loyal supporter to second it. This humiliation marked one of the two low points of his political career.

India and the French Revolution: 1784–1795

After such a *débâcle*, another politician, sensing that a younger generation had taken control, might have begun to take a less active part. Burke was irrepressible and indomitable and determined to maintain, indeed to intensify the struggle, on his own if necessary. Realising that he would have little influence with Fox and his cronies on current policies and strategies, he decided to revisit the past, determined above all to vindicate Fox's India Bill, of which he was widely considered the chief architect. Because he attributed much of the blame for misgovernment in India to corrupt officials who ignored or subverted their instructions from London, chief among them Warren Hastings (governor-general of Bengal, 1772–85), he determined on a judicial action, an impeachment. In this process, the Commons present a case to the Lords, before whom the accused is tried. This was an ancient constitutional practice, originating in the fourteenth century and revived in the seventeenth, but little used in the eighteenth. No colonial governor had ever been impeached. Initially, Burke expected his attempt to fail even to reach the Lords. Instead, he hoped to convict Hastings before the bar of public opinion. He therefore paid no attention to the legal niceties that might have secured a conviction, preferring to allege a mass of miscellaneous charges that could never have been 'proved' in a legal sense. This decision would cost Burke dearly at the later stages of the impeachment, though of course he never admitted as much.

With the help of some personal associates, and especially of Philip Francis, a former colleague of Hastings in India and since his most implacable enemy, Burke drew up a formidable indictment in the form of twenty-two 'articles of charge'. These were presented to the Commons in April and May 1786. After Hastings was heard in his own defence, the Commons began to debate the charges. The first, thought to be the strongest, was rejected; but the second, thanks to the unexpected support of Pitt, was approved. Further progress was then postponed to the session of 1787, during which a further string of charges was approved. Against all expectation, Hastings would be tried before the Lords. A committee was appointed to conduct the case, consisting of Burke and his associates. To that extent, Burke had triumphed. Without his energy and tenacity, there would have been no impeachment.

The trial itself began on 13 February 1788, in Westminster Hall, before a large crowd. Special stands were erected to accommodate participants and spectators, and for a time the impeachment became one of the curiosities of London. The first two days were occupied by a tedious reading of the charges and replies. Then, on 15 February, Burke began a four-day speech that outlined the prosecution's general case. But he had little regard or patience for legal, as opposed to moral or rhetorical, proofs. The moment he sat down on 19 February, at the end of his long speech, was probably, from his point of view, the acme of the impeachment. Almost at once, the trial degenerated into a series of interminable wrangles about procedure and evidence, punctuated by occasional speeches. Burke took more than his fair share in the disputes. But they were wearisome, tedious, and often brought out the worst in his character. By the end of the session, thirty-five days had been consumed, and only two of the charges presented.

Worse was soon to come. In October 1788, the king was taken ill. Unable to conduct business, he was soon suspected of insanity. The fortunes of politics depended on his chances of rapid recovery. If his incapacity proved permanent, a regent would have to be appointed. This could only be the Prince of Wales. Since he was at odds with his father, and a crony of Fox, his regency was expected to lead to a change of government, with Fox replacing Pitt. Burke stood to return to office, if only, again, in some subordinate but lucrative position. The ensuing parliamentary debates were awkward, and called for tact and restraint. Burke exhibited neither. Indeed, so intemperate and embarrassing were his contributions that he was accused of being as mad as the king, and he was cruelly caricatured as a lunatic. Then, the king unexpectedly recovered, and all prospect of a regency disappeared. If this were not enough, the short 1789 session of the impeachment made virtually no progress, being consumed with arguments about evidence which the prosecution generally lost. By the end of the parliamentary session, Burke's reputation had sunk as low as possible, lower even than its nadir in 1784. He seemed a spent force, a garrulous and obsessive old man. For a second time, however, Burke rose from the depths of derision and contempt. Within little more than a year, he would again be hailed as a master of political wisdom.

Burke was saved from ignominy and oblivion by the outbreak of the French Revolution. During its early stages, in 1789–91, many observers in Britain hailed it as a great event, the dawn of a spreading liberty. Burke, more impressed with its destructive nature, correctly predicted that it would end in despotism, and was retrospectively recognised as a prophet. His *Reflections on the Revolution in France* (published on 1 November 1790) has proved the most enduring book on the Revolution, perhaps the most momentous event in modern history, and one that remains contested and contentious. Remarkably, what Burke has to say about it still commands respect. Yet the book is no dispassionate, formal analysis. It was written in response to a young Frenchman, who had met Burke on a visit to England, and who asked for his opinions. Of course, the *Reflections* soon outgrew the bounds of a letter. But, characteristically, Burke preferred to retain the original epistolary form, and much about the book still reflects its origin in a personal correspondence.

The publication of the *Reflections* completed Burke's alienation from his former friends in the Whig party, most of whom at first welcomed the Revolution. Relations had, indeed, been cooling since 1784, and especially since the Regency Crisis, when Burke felt himself slighted and marginalised. In stages, the break became increasingly public and acrimonious. In May 1791, Burke denounced Fox on the floor of the House of Commons. In August, he published a personal manifesto, *An Appeal from the New to the Old Whigs*, in which he staked his claim to represent the true, genuine principles of the Whigs, which he accused Fox and his cronies of subverting. Yet he still maintained a certain distance from Pitt and the government, supporting them from a position of independence.

Meanwhile, the impeachment continued, and required a minimum of co-operation between Burke and his old friends. Most of the latter, indeed, had now lost all interest in the outcome, which seemed increasingly irrelevant in the new world created by the French Revolution. Burke maintained his dedication to the cause to the end. When the defence began to present its case, he was the most active manager in cross-examining witnesses and evidence. Finally, in 1794 he concluded the prosecution with a formal replication that took nine sittings to deliver. Because Burke took so long, judgement was deferred until the session of 1795, when Hastings was, as expected, acquitted on all charges.

Last Years 1794–1797

Burke retired from the Commons at the end of the session of 1794. To his great delight, Earl Fitzwilliam, who had inherited Rockingham's interest at Malton, offered his seat to his son, Richard Burke, Jr. Tragically, Richard, who had been ill for some time, died a few days after his election. Burke was much embittered by this blow, for since the purchase of his estate at Beaconsfield in 1768, he had dreamed of founding a family. As in the case of earlier blows and defeats, however, even the death of his son did not cause Burke to retreat from public life.

The French republic had declared war on Britain in February 1793. Burke strongly advocated a vigorous and aggressive strategy that would destroy the republic and restore the *ancien régime*. Pitt was content with more defensive aims, and conducted the war rather half-heartedly. These differences prevented any cordial coalition between Burke and Pitt, so that Burke remained independent and isolated. Indeed, when Pitt seemed willing to negotiate with the republic, Burke wrote a series of pamphlets attacking any compromise with the 'regicide' republic. *Two Letters on the Prospect of a Regicide Peace* was published in 1796. (Two other letters, one written earlier and one later, were published posthumously.)

Awkward as relations were between them, Pitt was prepared to acknowledge Burke's contribution to splitting the opposition by the award of a much-needed pension. By then selling the pension for a capital sum, Burke was able to discharge most of his debts. By the standards of the day, his reward was late in coming, and not especially generous. Many politicians received more for doing less. But his opponents naturally pilloried Burke's acceptance of it as inconsistent with the principles of public economy that he had advocated in 1780. This was hardly a valid criticism. Burke had never opposed pensions as a reward for service, only secret pensions that bought present support. He was particularly stung by his chief antagonist being the

Duke of Bedford, whose family fortunes were founded on grants from the Crown (unmerited in Burke's opinion) to the first Lord Russell in the reign of Henry VIII. For Burke, Bedford exemplified the 'democratic' aristocrats, those traitors to their order and their country, who had done so much to forward the French Revolution. In revenge, he wrote one of his best pamphlets, *A Letter to a Noble Lord* (1796), in which he both vindicates himself and excoriates the duke. In this last great work, Burke is at the height of his literary and rhetorical powers. Taken with his first book, the *Vindication of Natural Society*, it shows what a powerful satirist was lost to English literature when Burke turned his mind to politics.

In the summer of 1796, Burke's health began to deteriorate. After a long illness, which the medicine of the day was able neither to diagnose nor to alleviate, much less to cure, he died early in the morning of 9 July 1797. Though he failed to found a family, he left a legacy that has enriched the minds of every subsequent generation, and that is still studied, even by those who do not share his values, not as an inert body of historical texts, but as a living contribution to debates of continuing relevance and urgency. His writings transcend his life, but they grew out of it, and those who would understand his ideas must study his biography.

NOTES

1 For a full account of Burke's life, and for documentation, I refer readers to my *Edmund Burke*, 2 vols. (Oxford: Clarendon Press, 1998–2006).
2 William O'Brien, *Edmund Burke as an Irishman* (Dublin: Gill, 1924); Thomas H. D. Mahoney, *Edmund Burke and Ireland* (Cambridge, MA: Harvard University Press, 1960); Conor Cruise O'Brien, *The Great Melody: A Thematic Biography and a Commented Anthology of Edmund Burke* (Chicago: University of Chicago Press, 1992); Luke Gibbons, *Edmund Burke and Ireland: Aesthetics, Politics, and the Colonial Sublime* (Cambridge: Cambridge University Press, 2003); Seán Patrick Donlan (ed.), *Edmund Burke's Irish Identities* (Dublin: Irish Academic Press, 2006).

2

RICHARD BOURKE

Burke, Enlightenment and Romanticism

In a letter sent to his Quaker school-friend, Richard Shackleton, at the start of his third year as an undergraduate at Trinity College, Dublin, Burke identified a mania for syllogistic reasoning with the dark days of Scholastic philosophy, contrasting its procedures with those of 'these enlightened times'. He had encountered neo-Aristotelian logic through the textbooks of Franciscus Burgersdicius and Martinus Smiglecius during his first year at university; at the same time, he was exposed to the *Logica* of Jean Le Clerc. By the mid-1740s he was associating the former with the kind of pre-enlightened 'ignorance' that modern philosophy had helped to overcome (C, I: 89). A decade later, in the *Account of the European Settlements in America,* which Burke composed with his close friend, William Burke, the passage from ignorance to enlightenment is set within a conventional, Protestant historiographical framework. Technological and scientific progress, along with humanism and the Reformation, are presented as having created the conditions for material and intellectual improvement. These developments, moreover, are shown to have occurred in tandem with the consolidation of modern monarchies, the revival of politeness, and the establishment of a 'rational' – meaning prudently oriented – politics. Altogether, learning prospered, manners improved, and policy became enlightened[1]. In a fragmentary 'Essay towards an History of the Laws of England', which Burke undertook around the same time, the slow, faltering march towards a government of laws is taken to have been 'softened and mellowed by peace and Religion; improved and exalted by commerce, by social intercourse, and that great opener of the mind, ingenuous science' (WS, I: 322). What these diverse observations illustrate is that enlightenment for Burke encompassed the progress of society through the expansion of commerce under the protection of law, the improvement of morals under the government of Providence, and the liberalisation of religion under the influence of science.[2]

However, although Burke saw religion as having benignly influenced progress towards an enlightened society and politics, he also knew that sectarianism had threatened it with destruction. Along with his contempt for Scholastic philosophy, Burke's alarm about sectarianism can be traced to his teenage years. As a first year university student, he confided his belief to Shackleton that modern 'Sectaries' often dissented from established doctrine out of frivolous self-regard rather than on the basis of conscientious commitment. However, despite the excessively orthodox stance implied by his worry about the 'great Crime [of] Schism', his very relationship with Shackleton is clear evidence of an early devotion to the principle of toleration (C, I: 35). At the same time, it seems that this commitment was matched by optimism about the prospect of bridging differences in religious opinions. As Burke viewed things at this early stage in his development, while prejudice continually compromised the achievement of enlightenment, rational debate and candid criticism promised to correct the errors of 'Common' sense (C, I: 45). Pride confirmed prejudice and hoodwinked reason, and the ensuing bigotry inflamed sectarian animosity. By the same token, the dispassionate love of truth under a regime of toleration kept superstition and barbarism at bay (C, I: 48).

In the course of the 1750s, Burke abandoned his early faith in the ability of rational enquiry alone to foster enlightenment and dispel bigotry. This set him against the agenda of Bolingbroke and Voltaire, encouraging a more sceptical estimation of human reason together with its capacity to overcome sectarian hostility. For Burke, the 'deistical Enlightenment' threatened to extinguish toleration in pursuit of a dogmatic assault on religion. In the process, it risked undermining the foundations of civil society and the terms of international cooperation. Liberal, conservative, and Marxist historiographies have all mistaken Burke's enlightened opposition to doctrinaire attacks on organised religion for a wholesale counter-enlightenment crusade.[3] This confusion has been encouraged by a secular teleology anxious to reduce enlightenment to the criticism of religion.[4] As a result, Burke's espousal of sceptical Whiggism and Protestant toleration is curiously reinterpreted as hostile to the very principles of enlightenment he was in fact defending. In this vein, one of the earliest attempts to re-brand Burke as an antagonist of enlightenment was obliged to cast him as engaging in a 'revolt' against his own century, thus laying the foundations for the emergence of a 'Romantic' era.[5] There can be no doubt that Burke's writings in the 1790s resonated with many of the tenets espoused by Romantic writers in Britain and Germany. But this should not seduce us into equating his ideas with the principles generally associated with Romanticism.

Reason and Imagination

Alfred Cobban's account of the emergence of Romanticism in terms of a repudiation of the dominant Lockianism of the eighteenth century was indebted to C. E. Vaughan's *The Romantic Revolt*. In 1907, Vaughan presented Burke as a figure who broke free of the 'individualist' premises of seventeenth-century political thought, in the process laying the groundwork for a new conception of political community.[6] As Vaughan was later to elucidate the character of this new conception, it hinged on a rejection of social contract theory.[7] In reproducing Vaughan's thesis, Cobban added a particular inflection of his own. As Cobban saw it, Burke's originality lay in his innovative conception of the state. While Burke was alleged to have accepted the rule of expediency as an appropriate criterion by which to judge political action, at the same time he was taken to have abandoned the utilitarian moral psychology that Cobban identified as underpinning political thought from Locke to the *philosophes*. On this basis, Cobban proceeded to depict Burke as 'a philosopher of unreason in the great age of Reason'.[8] Reason here was understood as a means of correcting prejudice, with Voltaire, building on the legacy of Locke, represented as its champion. However, Cobban's scheme of analysis failed to recognise, that excessive trust in reason came to seem unreasonable to Burke. We need to interpret Burke's preparedness to credit educated prejudice as an antidote to its bigoted forms in terms of this commitment.

Burke moved towards a more positive valuation of the prejudicial attachment to habits and customs characteristic of human behaviour at some point in the early 1750s, after completing his undergraduate studies and taking up residence in London. This did not entail a renunciation of reason, but a suspicion of its inordinate pretensions. Burke adopted as his own the Horatian motto, 'Sapere aude', in a fragmentary essay that he composed between 1752 and 1756 on the subject of 'Philosophy and Learning'. He then commented: 'it requires some boldness to make use of one's reason' (N, 95). But such temerity had to be tempered with due caution: 'Great subtleties and refinements of reasoning are like spirits which disorder the brain' (N, 90). Where the reasoning faculty is set to work with the sole purpose of subjecting customary assumptions and arrangements to forms of criticism designed to undermine their operation, philosophy is put at odds with human nature, thereby corrupting rational inquiry, perverting natural sentiment, and reversing the process of enlightenment. Among the more conspicuous exponents of critical reasoning at this time was Henry St. John Bolingbroke, whose *Letters on the Study and Use of History* appeared posthumously in 1752. In a letter to Lord Bathurst included in the second volume of that work, Bolingbroke recommended the interrogation of first principles on the basis of the authority of reason alone as the only satisfactory method of defeating the delusive promptings of prejudice.[9] Two years later, the fruits of this approach appeared in a collected edition of his

Philosophical Works, exposing revealed religion to derision and contempt. Burke in due course embarked upon a satirical response.

Burke's satire on Bolingbroke appeared anonymously in 1756 as *A Vindication of Natural Society*. In the Preface, added to the second edition of 1757, Bolingbroke's conclusions are described as inhabiting a 'Fairy Land of Philosophy' (WS, I: 135). Voltaire had defended Bolingbroke's *Letters* in 1753 as a sober attempt to submit matters of faith before the 'tribunal of pure reason'; by contrast, Burke was describing his *Philosophical Works* as an exercise in fiction.[10] For Burke, Bolingbroke's posthumous writings were a kind of a bogus philosophy – a series of paradoxical reflections aiming to challenge the achievements of 'Science' but leaving its great landmarks undisturbed (WS, I: 133). The science in question comprised the monuments of theology, ethics, and jurisprudence, which Bolingbroke promised to deliver from superstitious prejudice. However, as Burke saw it, Bolingbroke's approach involved pursuing this deliverance at a cost of annihilating the legitimating principles of religion and society altogether. The spirit of paradox led to a habit of self-contradiction: reason was exalted, while it was compromised in practice; virtue was invoked, while its enabling conditions were undermined; piety was appealed to, while its foundations were destroyed. In short, irrationalism was championed under the enchanting 'Name of Philosophy' deployed as a cover for empty sophistry (WS, I: 134).

Underlying Burke's assault on Bolingbroke is a general dismay about the pretentions of socinian and deist rationalism.[11] John Toland, a pivotal deist precursor of Bolingbroke, had proclaimed in his *Christianity not Mysterious* that '*Reason* is the Foundation of all Certitude'.[12] Burke believed that pronouncements of this kind generated contradictory expectations and conclusions. On the one hand, in subjecting metaphysical ideas to empirical scrutiny, critics of the tenets of religious faith tended to reduce understanding to rudimentary sense perceptions, returning the mind in the process to its original 'savage' condition. On the other hand, Burke reckoned that the thrill of appearing to explain the mysteries of nature disposed the philosopher to exalt reason beyond its proper limits, inadvertently substituting imagination in the place of understanding. But imagination was vulnerable to enthusiasm or inspiration, laying the mind open to the extremes of passion and self-regard. The *Vindication* was intended to correct this corrosive 'Abuse of Reason' whereby zeal combined with imagination to undermine the assumptions of educated common sense (WS, I: 136). The human intellect was not equipped to reason demonstratively about moral and religious truths. As Burke had learned from his common law studies in the early 1750s, we reason probabilistically in the face of uncertain evidence.[13] The problem was that imagination could make absurdities look probable. Burke cited Coke to underline the point: 'Interdum fucata falsitas in multis est probabilior, et saepe rationibus vincit nudam veritatem' ('In many instances a painted untruth appears more likely, and often defeats the naked truth by reasoning') (WS, I: 136). Reason, when it lacks restraint, loses the quality of reasonableness; it is derailed by a native enthusiasm for invention.

In shunning rational argument, excessive enthusiasm, like primitive empiricism, was detrimental to enlightenment. As John Leland observed in commenting on Henry Dodwell's *Christianity not Founded on Argument*, resorting to inspiration as a touchstone of faith involved squandering the advantages that attended living in 'an enlightened or civilized age'.[14] Burke admired Leland's *View of the Principal Deistical Writers*, but he was also keen to resuscitate enthusiasm so long as it could be limited to its appropriate function. Having evicted imagination from the faculty of understanding, Burke reintroduced it as an aid to religious conviction and social life, reclaiming inspiration from a long history of denigration stretching back at least as far as Plato's *Ion*. Robert Lowth had drawn on pseudo-Longinus to equate the experience of sublimity with enthusiastic imagination in his *De Sacra Poesi Hebraeorum* of 1753.[15] Burke accepted the implication that imagination was integral to the religious nature of man. Whereas enthusiasm in this sense could not be extinguished, it could be disciplined by feeding it with worthy objects of admiration instead of permitting its decline into self-conceit. In an early draft essay on the public utility of religion, Burke recognised that enthusiasm was an ineliminable part of 'our Nature' that could nonetheless be checked by the faculty of reason (N, 68–9). Confined in this way within its proper bounds, imagination could be aroused in support of legitimate authority while acting as a stimulus to reasonable belief. To this extent, there was in Burke's mind a powerful 'aesthetic' dimension to politics and religion. Nonetheless, he was also concerned lest our imaginative responses become unmoored from consequential and moral reasoning, thereby reducing human preferences to mere matters of taste. In that case, imagination would be threatened with corruption and derangement, and the business of enlightenment would be undone.

Enlightenment and Revolution

Enlightenment in Burke's eyes was indeed precarious. At the beginning of his mammoth speech opening, the second day of proceedings in the impeachment of Warren Hastings, he reminded his packed audience in Westminster Hall of Britain's failure to enlighten her empire in the east. He recalled that the history of British power on the sub-continent had begun in earnest in

1756, with the entrenchment and expansion of the Empire under Robert Clive. This counted, Burke noted, as a 'memorable aera in the history of the world' since it introduced a new political order – 'with new manners, new customs, new opinions, new laws' – into the 'Bosom of the East' (WS, VI: 314). Given this opportunity for social and political improvement created by the subordination of an ancient civilisation to an enlightened European monarchy, the expectation that Indian society might advance under the protection of justice appeared well grounded. As Europe had emerged from its own dark period of barbarism into light, so India might have been liberated from the ongoing confusion sustained by the selfish ambition of its own 'grandees' (WS, VI: 315). This promise was held out by the prospect of introducing the spirit of liberty associated with the British system of government into a rank ordered society that operated under law but in the absence of constitutional freedom. The hope was that some progressive fusion might occur, that the spirit of liberty might encourage the development of a more enlightened form of government.

This hope was founded on the cultural heritage of the English polity, a heritage rooted in the history of its progressive civilisation. As Burke saw it, at the start of the Seven Years' War, the East India Company went forth from 'a learned and enlightened part of Europe' – indeed, from its 'most enlightened' portion in the 'most enlightened period of its time' – on the basis of its liberal politics and 'improved', Protestant religion (WS, VI: 315). But the hope of enlightenment was soon disappointed as practical exigency put the procedures of civilisation under stress, and corrupt morals replaced Indian law with the domineering whims of Company power. A disregard for norms of justice cultivated with due deference to a superintending intelligence was a principal agent of corruption in Burke's view, with Hastings acting as the consummate embodiment of secular rapacity born of irreligious scorn. The destruction of piety, on this conception, represented a terminal threat to enlightenment. But within two years of the launching of the impeachment, the enemies of enlightenment in Burke's vision were assaulting one of the strongholds of civilisation in its name.

The stronghold referred to here was of course the monarchy of France – a member, as presented by Burke in 1788, of the more enlightened part of Europe, albeit less enlightened than its northern commercial rival. Enlightenment in this context denoted a relative scale of achievement, and the comparative barbarism of France, when set alongside Britain, was underscored by Burke in February 1790. In his speech on the army estimates delivered in that month, he recognised how, in the previous century, Louis XIV had developed an unaccountable system of government presiding over an intolerant ecclesiastical regime.[16] And yet, as Burke went on to insist nine months later in the *Reflections*, this despotism flourished under the influence of gallantry and manners, conferring on it a relatively enlightened condition. As shown, in comparative terms, the French state appeared as a progressive bastion of civilisation. In fact, one of the main thrusts of the *Reflections* was to argue that the summoning of the Estates General for May 1789 had created the opportunity for reforming this polite and civilised monarchy into a more dependably enlightened regime. Instead, the initiative was seized by enthusiastic atheists and deists, abetted by conspiring socinians in Britain, to overturn the foundations of the French polity, and with it any chance of progressive reform (WS, VIII: 175–6).

Burke noted sarcastically how England's dissenting champions of the Revolution in France presumed to defend their cause under the banner of enlightenment. Richard Price is singled out for his perverse application of the enlightened ideal of overcoming superstition and error: in Price's hands, enlightenment was no better than popular oppression akin to the persecuting tyranny of levelling enthusiasts in the dying days of the regime of Charles I (WS, VIII: 115). If this is what agitators of Price's persuasion understood by enlightenment, Burke later commented, then they were welcome to appropriate that contaminated term (WS, VIII: 138).[17] This rhetorical strategy on Burke's part contributed to the systematic misinterpretation of his position as amounting to a polemic against the principles of enlightenment. Together with his celebration of 'high and romantic sentiments' in opposition to the morals of utilitarian 'calculators', this facet of his writing has often led to his being represented as one of the progenitors of a distinct 'Romantic' ideology (WS, VIII: 86, 127).[18] Criticism of the principle of utility as a basis for moral motivation looks back to the disinterested aestheticism of the Third Earl of Shaftesbury and Francis Hutcheson. The restiveness that Burke exhibits in the *Reflections* about the reduction of moral life to utilitarian sociability absorbs elements of Shaftesbury's equation between ethical sentiment and the judgement of taste. Yet whereas moral norms were conflated with aesthetic preferences in the *Characteristicks*, taste for Burke was a supplement to rather than a substitute for duty.[19]

In his dialogue, *The Moralists*, Shaftesbury proposed a method for extinguishing the irrational extremes of religious enthusiasm by reclaiming the experience of transport for the aesthetic contemplation of nature. 'Nature' here meant Stoic nature, a divinely orchestrated harmonious whole, in which human society was sustained by benevolent affection, and religious sensibility by an appreciation of divine craftsmanship. Lurking within this apparently pious construction was an unorthodox agenda readily associated with deism. Benevolent transport was identified by Shaftesbury with a sort of divine eros in which human goodwill was a function of the love of intelligent design. However, as readers of the *Characteristicks* promptly noted, Shaftesbury's professedly 'romantick' worshipper of sublime nature was freed from the fear of divine retribution: in promoting admiration for the almighty intelligence of the creator, Shaftesbury separated moral motivation from the expectation of rewards and punishments.[20] As a result, ethical norms were collapsed into sensibility and taste instead of answering to the tribunal of duty. Throughout his career, Burke appreciated the social significance of a 'moral imagination' as espoused in the work of Shaftesbury and Hutcheson, but he felt that it had to be underpinned by ethically sanctioned obligations. Otherwise, norms would become a matter of pure imaginative preference, driven by the changing worlds of opinion, fashion, and taste. So, while Burke was drawn to the aesthetic ideal of disinterested sentiment, he insisted that the beauty of manners had to be grounded on a substructure of morality. Romantic sentiment was potentially ennobling for Burke, but it had to be accountable to virtue.

Rousseau and Romanticism

Romantic sentiment as understood by Burke found its most compelling literary embodiment in the genre of medieval romance which captured at once the spirit of fidelity and chivalry – of deferential loyalty to rank on the one hand, and selfless devotion to the female sex on the other. In both cases, romantic sociability could be contrasted with self-regarding appetite. It was sympathetic and humane, and thus transcended relations of utility. But it was also based on immediate, personal attachment rather than arising out of cosmic, Shaftesburean disinterestedness. Moreover, it flourished in the context of Christian ethics, the primary vocation of which lay in the subjugation of pride: 'True humility, the basis of the Christian system, is the low, but deep and firm foundation of all real virtue', as Burke argued in his *Letter to a Member of the National Assembly* in 1791 (WS, VIII: 313). The great antagonist of this principle in contemporary Europe was the modern '*philosophy of vanity*' perfected by Rousseau. Burke had followed Rousseau's writings in the 1750s and 1760s, reviewing the *Letter to d'Alembert* and *Emile* for the *Annual Register* (AR, 1759: 479–84; AR, 1762: 227–39). His earlier ambivalent admiration mixed with fundamental suspicion now gave way to an unambiguous abhorrence.[21] It appeared to Burke that Rousseau's works had been adopted as the guiding canon of revolutionary fanaticism. This canon supplied a doctrine for a world turned upside down, while the doctrine itself encompassed a moral code propagated with the aid of irony. What this irony facilitated was an expression of universal benevolence masking the reality of utter self-absorption.

Irony is the weapon of a moralist like Socrates, at odds with public norms and resorting to paradox as a means of subversion. Although Burke dubbed Rousseau the 'insane *Socrates* of the National Assembly' (WS, VIII: 314), he further recognised that his method was doubly dissembling. As a consequence, Rousseauian irony unmasked is revealed to be nothing but hypocrisy: in saying one thing, Rousseau means another, but his real meaning is less a revelation than a sham. Burke alleges that he succeeded in the *Confessions* in perfecting this duplicity: sincerity is employed as a ruse for self-justification, self-justification as an instrument of self-promotion. So, notoriously, by proclaiming his guilt in the episode concerning the theft of a ribbon at the end of Book Two of the *Confessions*, Rousseau deftly succeeds in advertising his honesty: he reveals that he is a thief, but ironically the revelation is a statement of integrity, except the integrity is proclaimed in the service of self-exculpation, the parade of which is construed by Burke as an index of boundless vanity.[22] In this way, Burke exposes *amour-propre* as the motive for sincerity. At the same time, vanity is presented as an amoral force underlying a pretend commitment to morality. In this vein, Rousseau's outward devotion to universal benevolence is alleged to veil an inner heartlessness and indifference. This resulted in the paradox of misanthropic cosmopolitanism that so captivated the theatrical hypocrisy of the Revolution's *philosophes* – although apparently 'a lover of his kind' Rousseau became a 'hater of his kindred' (WS, VIII: 315).

Whereas Burke accused Rousseau of having promoted the corruption of morals in the *Confessions* in an act of 'wild defiance' against his maker, and at the same time as having undermined all sense of social responsibility by glamorising a life dedicated to 'unsocial independence', in *Emile* and the *Nouvelle Héloïse* he is presumed to have vitiated education and courtship, thus poisoning the germinal components of society (WS, VIII: 314–19). After establishing that the destruction of morals leaves taste as the sole arbiter of behaviour, Burke finally condemns Rousseau for ministering to the perversion of sexual taste by degrading the currency of love in the *Nouvelle Héloïse* (WS, VIII: 316–17). Consequently, with the extinction of the foundations of trust and fidelity, the scene was apparently set for the revolutionary crusade against property and religion. It is this Burkean critique of Rousseau as the patron of a new, self-conceited individualism that was co-opted into later critical accounts of Romanticism. From Ernest Sellière to Irving Babbitt, Romanticism was identified with a kind of rebellious subjectivity, and Rousseau was duly designated as its chief apostle.[23]

Given this process of transmission, there is historical irony in the fact that the German Romantics drew on Burke, in preference to Rousseau, as a source of inspiration. Novalis was famously taken with his 'revolutionary' attack on the Revolution, although clearly he kept his distance from Burke's larger political programme.[24] Schlegel likewise championed him as a prescient diagnostician.[25] What seems to have captivated them is the aesthetic appeal to manners in the *Reflections*, which was absorbed into a Romantic indictment of enlightenment. The terms of this indictment were dramatically enumerated by Novalis in his *Christenheit oder Europa* of 1799. The previous year, in *Glauben und Liebe*, Novalis traced the sources of political obligation to the experience of aesthetic appreciation. On this interpretation, patriotic subjection was secured through the love of beautiful forms rather than on the basis of 'mechanical administration'.[26] Schlegel captured something of the spirit of this distinction in his famous injunction to 'render life and society poetic'.[27] In *Christenheit oder Europa*, Novalis contrasted the poetic impulse with both the faculty of understanding and the soullessness of utilitarian sociability. Poetic sociability, on the other hand, was presented as the harbinger of a post-enlightened religion of humanity – as a restitution at once of mystery and fellowship.[28] It was possible to extract suggestive phrases from Burke in support of this vision, but only by obscuring his enlightenment credentials. Strictly speaking, Romantic aestheticism was a betrayal of the core conviction that guided Burke's campaign against the Revolution in France: it subverted his understanding of the political arena as governed by a conflict between power and interests. The resolution of such conflict could only be attempted on the basis of practical rather than aesthetic judgement.

Burke's relationship to what we now call 'Romanticism' in England is still more complicated; it is also just as remote as it is from the Romanticism of the Germans. In the process of exposing what he took to be a basic inconsistency in Burke's thought, Samuel Taylor Coleridge observed an apparent vacillation between a commitment to expediency and a dedication to benevolence in his writings. As Coleridge saw it, Burke alternately placed calculation and benign feeling at the foundation of morals, whereas in fact neither could serve as an adequate basis for virtue.[29] By way of contrast, in a famous passage added to Book 7 of what was to become the 1850 *Prelude*, Wordsworth celebrated 'the vital power of social ties/ Endeared by Custom' as a core Burkean doctrine.[30] However, a common opposition shared by Wordsworth and Coleridge to calculating expediency as the organising principle of social relations unites them despite these divergent assessments of Burke's significance. For both writers, the moral sympathy that bound agrarian communities together and connected individuals to their natural environment could be evoked and deepened by the spiritual transport that accompanied heightened poetic consciousness.[31] However for Burke, equating spiritual joy with the encounter between mind and nature that we associate with the programme of Coleridge and Wordsworth would have seemed a dangerously poeticised form of religion founded on reverie rather than organised worship. From this perspective, the 'Romantic' imagination represented a surrogate religion whose very indeterminacy allowed its advocates to put it forward as the criterion by which moral and political value should be judged.

Conclusion

Frederick Beiser is right to describe the literary project of the early German Romantics as political in nature.[32] What his account misses is the sense in which their politics were unpolitical. The characterisation of Romantic ideology as 'unpolitisch' is based on a perspective shared by German liberals, left Hegelians, and conservatives since the 1840s.[33] What the charge implied was that their politics were 'aesthetic' in character, in the sense that they equated political preferences with matters of taste. What this equation was assumed to exclude was the normative gravity of political choices together with the historical context in which decisions were made. Burke's purpose through the 1790s was to demonstrate the interdependence between these two components of political judgement: moral value, together with the vicissitudes of political cause and effect, made up the content of public life, and the science of politics aimed to study their relations. Deprived of normative substance, political options were mere fancies; shorn of practicality, they were mere moralising whims. Burke took the 'enlightened' doctrine of the rights of man to exemplify a moralising idiom in politics against which he counter-posed the experience of 'difficulty' as the irremediable condition of political life. 'Difficulty is a severe instructor', Burke commented in the *Reflections* (WS, VIII: 215). Its lessons are continually on display in the medium of politics since the struggle for amelioration is conducted within a context of danger. Enlightenment for Burke was a resource for navigating prospective dangers; as Montesquieu had put it, 'In a time of ignorance, one has no doubts even while doing the greatest evils; in an enlightened age, one trembles even while doing the greatest goods'.[34]

NOTES

1 Edmund Burke and William Burke, *An Account of the European Settlements in America*, 3rd rev. edn., 2 vols. (London, 1760), vol. I, pp. 4–5.
2 For the wider religious and intellectual context in which Burke's intervention needs to be placed, see Hugh Trevor Roper, 'The Religious Origins of the Enlightenment' in idem., *The Crisis of the Seventeenth Century: Religion, the Reformation and Social Change* (London: Macmillan, 1967), pp. 179–218; J. G. A. Pocock, 'Post-Puritan England and the Problem of Enlightenment' in Perez Zagorin (ed.),

Culture and Politics from Puritanism to the Enlightenment (Berkeley: University of California Press, 1980), pp. 91–111; Knud Haakonssen, 'Enlightened Dissent: An Introduction' in idem. (ed.), *Enlightenment and Religion: Rational Dissent in Eighteenth-Century Britain* (Cambridge: Cambridge University Press, 1996), pp. 1–11; Jonathan Israel, 'Introduction' to idem., *Radical Enlightenment: Philosophy and the Making of Modernity* (Oxford: Oxford University Press, 2001), pp. 3–22; John Robertson, *The Case for Enlightenment: Scotland and Naples, 1680–1760* (Cambridge: Cambridge University Press, 2005), pp. 1–51.

3   For discussion, see J. C D. Clark, 'The Enlightenment, Religion and Edmund Burke', *Studies in Burke and the Eighteenth Century*, 21 (2007), 9–38, which treats, inter alia, Isaiah Berlin, Ernst Cassirer, Peter Gay, Russell Kirk, Roy Porter and Peter Stanlis.

4   For criticism, see J. G. A. Pocock, 'Clergy and Commerce: The Conservative Enlightenment in England' in R. Ajello et al. (eds.), *L'età dei Lumi: Studi Storici sul Settecento Europeo in Onore di Franco Venturi*, 2 vols. (Naples: Jovene, 1985), vol. I, pp. 523–62.

5   Alfred Cobban, *Edmund Burke and the Revolt against the Eighteenth Century: A Study of the Political and Social Thinking of Burke, Wordsworth, Coleridge and Southey*, 2nd edn. (London: George Allen and Unwin, 1960).

6   C. E. Vaughan, *The Romantic Revolt*, 3 vols. (Edinburgh: William Blackwood and Sons, 1907), vol. III, p. 131.

7   C. E. Vaughan, *Studies in the History of Political Philosophy before and after Rousseau*, 2 vols. (Manchester: Manchester University Press, 1925), vol. II, pp. 41.

8   Cobban, *Edmund Burke*, p. 75.

9   Henry St. John Bolingbroke, *Letters on the Study and Use of History*, 2 vols. (London, 1752), vol. II, pp. 220.

10   Voltaire, *A Defence of the Late Lord Bolingbroke's Letters on the Study and Use of History* (London, 1753), p. 7.

11   Iain Hampsher-Monk, 'Burke and the Religious Sources of Sceptical Conservatism' in J. van der Zande and R. H. Popkin (eds.), *The Skeptical Tradition around 1800* (Dordrecht: Kluwer, 1998), pp. 235–59.

12   John Toland, *Christianity not Mysterious or, A Treatise Shewing that There Is Nothing in the Gospel Contrary to Reason nor Above It* (London, 1796), p. 6.

13   J. G. A. Pocock, 'Burke and the Ancient Constitution: A Problem in the History of Ideas', *The Historical Journal*, 3 (1960): 125–43.

14   John Leland, *A View of the Principal Writers that Have Appeared in England in the Last and Present Century*, 2 vols. (London, 1754–55), vol. I, p. 248.

15   Robert Lowth, *De Sacra Poesi Hebraeorum* (Oxford, 1753), p 143.

16   Edmund Burke, 'Speech on the Army Estimates' in Ian Harris (ed.), *Burke: PreRevolutionary Writings* (Cambridge: Cambridge University Press, 1993), pp. 309–10.

17   For elucidation, see Richard Bourke, 'Theory and Practice: The Revolution in Political Judgement' in Richard Bourke and Raymond Geuss (eds.), *Political Judgement* (Cambridge: Cambridge University Press, 2009), pp. 73–109.

18   The context for Burke's assault on calculating 'oeconomists' in the name of moral generosity is given in J. G. A. Pocock, 'The Political Economy of Edmund

Burke's Analysis of the French Revolution' in idem., *Virtue, Commerce, and History: Essays on Political Thought and History, Chiefly in the Eighteenth Century* (Cambridge: Cambridge University Press, 1985), pp. 193–211.

19 Anthony Ashley Cooper, Third Earl of Shaftesbury, *An Inquiry Concerning Virtue, or Merit* (1709) in Douglas Den Uyl (ed.), *Characteristicks of Men, Manners, Opinions, Times,* 3 vols. (Indianapolis: Liberty Fund Press, 2001), vol. II, p. 61.

20 Shaftesbury, *The Moralists: A Philosophical Rhapsody* (1709) in ibid., pp. 219–25.

21 On this trajectory, see Iain Hampsher-Monk, 'Rousseau, Burke's *Vindication of Natural Society*, and Revolutionary Ideology', *European Journal of Political Theory* 9 (2010): 245–66.

22 Jean-Jacques Rousseau, *Les Confessions de Jean-Jacques Rousseau* in *Oeuvres Complètes*, ed. Bernard Gagnebin and Marcel Raymond, 5 vols. (Paris: Gallimard, 1959–69), vol. I, ch. 2.

23 Ernest Sellière, *Le Mal Romantique: Essai sur l'Impérialisme Irrationnel* (Paris: Plon-Nourrit, 1908); Irving Babbitt, *Rousseau and Romanticism* (Boston: Houghton Mifflin, 1919).

24 Friedrich von Hardenberg, *Blüthenstaub* (1798) in Paul Kluckhohn and Richard Samuel (eds). *Novalis Schriften: Friedrich von Hardenbergs, Die Werke* 6 vols. (Stuttgart: Kohlhammer, 1960–2006), vol. I, p. 459.

25 Friedrich Schlegel, *Philosophische Lehrjahre* in Ernst Behler et al., (eds.), *Kritische Friedrich-Schlegel Ausgabe*, 35 vols. (Munich: Schöningh, 1959–79), vol. XVII, p. 71.

26 Friedrich von Hardenberg, *Glauben und Liebe oder Der König und die Königin* (1798) in *Novalis Schriften*, vol. II, pp. 494, p 45.

27 Friedrich Schlegel, *Athenäums Fragmente* in *Kritische Ausgabe*, vol. II, p. 182.

28 Friedrich von Hardenberg, *Die Christenheit oder Europa: Ein Fragment* in *Novalis Schriften*, vol. III, pp. 515–18.

29 Samuel Taylor Coleridge, *The Friend,* ed. Barbara E. Rooke, 2 vols. (Princeton: Princeton University Press, 1969), vol. II, p. 124.

30 For Wordsworth's debt to Burke, see James K. Chandler, *Wordsworth's Second Nature: A Study of the Poetry and Politics* (Chicago: Chicago University Press, 1984). For Coleridge's critical appropriation of his thought, see John Morrow, *Coleridge's Political Thought: Property, Morality and the Limits of Traditional Discourse* (Basingstoke: Macmillan, 1990).

31 See, for example, William Wordsworth, 'Preface to the *Lyrical Ballads'* in W. J. B. O'Brien and Jane Worthington Smyser (eds.), *The Prose Works of William Wordsworth,* 3 vols. (Oxford: Clarendon Press, 1974), vol. I, pp. 125, 140–2.

32 Frederick C. Beiser, *Enlightenment, Revolution, and Romanticism: The Genesis of Modern German Political Thought, 1790–1800* (Cambridge MA: Harvard University Press, 1992), pp. 222–7. Cf. Frederick C. Beiser, *The Romantic Imperative: The Concept of Early German Romanticism* (Cambridge MA: Harvard University Press, 2003), Chapter 2.

33 Heinrich Heine, *The Romantic School and Other Essays,* ed. Jost Hermand and Robert C. Holub (New York: Continuum, 1985); Arnold Ruge, *Unsere Klassiker und Romantiker seit Lessing* in *Sämtliche Werke,* 10 vols. (Mannheim: J. P. Grohe, 1847–48), vol. I, pp. 7–11, 248–9; Friedrich Meinecke, *Weltbürgertum*

und Nationalstaat (1907), ed. Hans Herzfeld (München: R. Oldenbourg Verlag, 1962), p. 65; Carl Schmitt, *Politische Romantik* (Berlin: Duncker and Humblot, 1919, 1991), passim.

34 Charles-Louis de Secondat, Baron de Montesquieu, *The Spirit of the Laws*, ed. Anne Cohler, Basia Miller, and Harold Stone (Cambridge: Cambridge University Press, 1989), p. xliv.

3

CHRISTOPHER REID

Burke as Rhetorician and Orator

'Reasonable beings are not solely reasonable'.
(James Boswell, 7 April 1773)

When Thomas Pitt was an undergraduate at Cambridge in the 1750s, he received a series of letters of advice from his uncle William, at the time the dominant speaker in the House of Commons. The orator left him in no doubt about the direction his studies should take: 'You are to be a gentleman of such learning and qualifications as may distinguish you in the service of your country hereafter; not a pedant, who reads only to be called learned, instead of considering learning as an instrument only for action.'[1] As the Elder Pitt, a competent classicist, must have known, the idea that learning should be valued primarily as 'an instrument for action' was a commonplace of Roman thought. It was expressed most completely in the figure of the orator who brings speculative knowledge to bear upon public causes and questions. In the eighteenth century, that idea still meant something to the educated elite. It informs Burke's conception of public life and of the politician as a philosopher in action.[2]

Speech was to be at the centre of Burke's activities for much of his political life. Although he enjoyed the conventional education of the Irish professional classes, his education as an orator was in an important sense self-made. Lacking serious wealth and influence, young Irishmen of his rank knew that without rhetorical skills they would find it difficult to rise in the world. Many looked to Trinity College, Dublin to prepare them for their entry into public life. By all accounts the classical curriculum at Trinity, where Burke matriculated in 1744, was thoroughly taught, and he was able to extend the knowledge of the rhetorical canon he had already gained at Abraham Shackleton's school in Ballitore. Yet we know from his early correspondence that he was frustrated by the rigidity of Trinity's methods of instruction and stifled by its insistence on the study of scholastic logic. In the end, his extra-curricular activities as a youthful speaker in Dublin may have taught him more about the business of persuasion than anything he heard within Trinity's walls.

Three years into his undergraduate studies he established an 'Academy of Belles Lettres' with six of his associates.[3] In the Club, as it was more familiarly known, the young men tested learning's potential as an instrument for action. 'Each may become master of the Theory of Arts and science in his closet', they agreed in their statement of principles, 'but the practice & the benefit & the use of them can only be known and had in Society'. Their common purpose was to seek such improvements of the mind as might make them 'better men' and render them 'fitter, and more agreeable members of the happy community in which we live'.[4] They hoped to refine their powers of discrimination through the discussion of elegant literature and the polite arts. With this in mind, they prepared essays on moral topics, which were read before the assembly and critically assessed. They recited passages from the English classics, evaluated the reciter's performance, and examined each extract for its distinctive beauties and faults. In this way, they hoped to make themselves conversable men who could take an improving role in civil society.

No less important were the debating skills they practised in order to equip themselves for a role in public life. The Club was above all a place of argument, and almost everything said or done there had the potential to initiate a debate. They thought that the clash of opinion would improve their minds as well as make them readier speakers. 'The silver stream runs with the more force, & purifies itself by being opposed, the struggles washing away ye heavy mud that settles at the Bottom', declared Andrew Buck.[5] It was in this spirit that the assembly conducted its business. For all the mock earnestness of its proceedings, the Club had a serious purpose as a small-scale school for orators. Most meetings required the members to take part in extemporaneous debate. It was the president's prerogative to choose the questions and to decide on which side (and sometimes in whose character) they should speak. Sometimes the self-consciously litigious members turned the clubroom into a court of law. In their early meetings, they had agreed on a code of laws that regulated the business of the Club but at the same time provoked disputes and created opportunities for forensic argument. The slightest infringement of the code was enough for the errant member to be brought to trial, and arraigned or defended by his associates. Still more frequent were the occasions when they imagined themselves as the members of a pocket parliament. Impersonating ancient orators in the Roman Senate, or more modern ones in the Irish House of Commons nearby, they learned how to speak on both sides of a question and how to deploy the great deliberative commonplaces of expediency and disadvantage.

When Burke finally entered parliament in 1765, and was able to deliberate for real, he made an immediate impression in debate. With his authorship of the *Philosophical Enquiry* in mind, his opponents sometimes represented him as 'too "refined and Metaphysical"' a speaker, but even they had to concede that he was a man of superior talents.[6] Within months, he established himself as one of the most able and well-informed orators in the House. As one of a small cadre of party spokesmen, he was expected to contest all the major questions that came before the House, and he remained one of the leading speakers there for almost thirty years. Outside the House he gave historically important speeches on the hustings at Bristol, where in 1780 he made a principled defence of his conduct as an MP, and in Westminster Hall, where between 1788 and 1794 he led the impeachment of Warren Hastings. Burke gained his reputation as a speaker at a time when the audiences for oratory were changing. In 1771 the House abandoned its struggle to suppress the publication of parliamentary debates. For the first time, newspaper readers were furnished with regular, if truncated, reports of what their representatives in the House had been saying. Although he sometimes complained that his words were misrepresented in the press, Burke was more willing than most MPs to reach out to the emerging audiences. Conscious of the power of print to influence opinion out of doors, he published a small number of his parliamentary speeches on his own authority, and in much longer versions than any newspaper could carry.[7] Originally delivered, and contested, in the ebb and flow of debate, these epic orations found a new life and purpose as statements of principle and policy for the eyes of a polite reading public. Decontextualised as they are, they do not tell us everything about Burke's day-to-day practice as a parliamentary speaker or the contribution he made to a debate as a rhetorical event.

Speaking and writing were for Burke hardly separable forms of rhetorical action.[8] His oratory was the anvil on which much of his political writing was forged. Arguments and images struck out in the heat of debate found their way into written polemic, sometimes years after the event. At the same time, when circumstances permitted, he drafted his speeches with great care, committing lines of argument, and evidence to support them, to writing and to memory. In all this activity, he was an unremitting rhetorician in the sense that the whole body of his thinking was purposeful, conceived with a view to contesting the ground of opinion, and with particular occasions and audiences in mind. But Burke was not a theorist of rhetoric, and there is no systematic account in his works of the principles that governed his rhetorical practice. Much, however, can be retrieved from his writings and speeches themselves. Burke was often taunted into self-justification. Rebuked for excessive sentiment or heat, he appealed to the occasion (a breach of trust, a crisis of empire, the madness of a king, a revolution) as proof that his words had been fitting. The terms in which he explained and vindicated his rhetorical practice will be considered in the final part of this chapter. But first it will be necessary to establish what in the eighteenth-century context made him so distinctive as an orator.

Burke and Ancient Eloquence

In his important study, *The Fate of Eloquence in the Age of Hume*, Adam Potkay notices a passage in the *Life of Johnson* where Boswell, Johnson, and Mrs Thrale disagree about the validity of what rhetoricians called *actio* (the orator's use of the body, especially gesture) in public speaking. The dispute turned on differing views about the supremacy of reason over the passions and the forms of rhetorical appeal that were most likely to be effective in an enlightened age. Johnson argued uncompromisingly that 'Action can have no effect upon reasonable minds.' Gestures may be useful when we speak to a dog, 'because he is a brute', but 'in proportion as men are removed from brutes, action will have the less influence upon them'. When Mrs Thrale appealed to the authority of the ancients and asked, 'What then becomes of Demosthenes's saying, "Action, action, action"?', Johnson replied, 'Why, Demosthenes spoke to an assembly of brutes, to a barbarous people.' Boswell was puzzled by his friend's intransigence. 'Reasonable beings are not solely reasonable', he reflected. 'They have fancies that must be amused, tastes that must be pleased, passions that must be roused.'[9] Burke was in the minds of the three interlocutors as they entered into this discussion. Two days earlier Boswell had visited the House of Commons, and for the first time he heard Burke speaking. Although he makes no reference to this event in the passage Potkay cites from the *Life*, the version in his journal makes it clear that it was his account of Burke's oratory that sparked off the exchanges.[10]

As Potkay has shown, the conversation at the Thrales' fed into a larger eighteenth-century debate about the nature of ancient eloquence and its applicability to modern life. That debate supplied a set of terms in which the performances of leading orators like Burke could be assessed. Its starting point was David Hume's influential essay 'Of Eloquence' (1742). Hume expressed surprise that the British had failed to produce a single parliamentary speaker of note, let alone one worthy of comparison with Demosthenes and Cicero. A system of popular government seemed to offer powerful incentives for eloquence, yet none of the speakers of his own time, he remarks, 'have attained much beyond a mediocrity in their art [...] the species of eloquence, which they aspire to, gives no exercise to the sublimer faculties of the mind, but may be reached by ordinary talents and a slight application'.[11]

Forty years later, when Burke was at the height of his powers as a parliamentary speaker, Hugh Blair's *Lectures on Rhetoric and Belles Lettres* (1783) echoed Hume's downbeat assessment: 'In every period we have had some who made a figure, by managing the debates in Parliament; but that figure was commonly owing to their wisdom, or their experience in business, more than to their talents for Oratory'. Like Hume, Blair contrasts the 'vehement and passionate' eloquence of the ancients 'by which they endeavoured to inflame the minds of their hearers, and hurry their imaginations away' with the 'much more cool and temperate' style of contemporary speakers, 'which aims at convincing and instructing, rather than affecting the passions, and assumes a tone not much higher than common argument and discourse'. However much this might be regretted, it suited the temper of the times. Modern philosophy had taught the virtues of good sense and had made audiences distrustful of boldly figurative language and passionate appeals to the imagination. The questions that were routinely debated in the House reflected the interests of the commercial people. 'Argument and reasoning must be the basis, if we would be Speakers of business', Blair concluded.[12]

A command of the plainer rhetorical skills of reasoning and narration was indeed indispensable if a speaker was to win a hearing in the House. Reports of Burke's speeches show how accomplished he was when reasoning from circumstances or marshalling information, drawn from an unusually wide range of sources. Without such skills, he could hardly have survived so long as one of the leading speakers in a talented and combative House. The breadth of the canvas on which he reasoned, and his preference for answering the particular questions of the moment (*hypotheses*, as Cicero and Quintilian called them) in the light of the principles (*theses*) of moral and political action, impressed many who heard him.[13] 'Equally in command of the principle and detail', writes F. P. Lock, 'in his best speeches he combines the two.'[14] This is the rhetorical method, and the tone, of his published parliamentary orations, especially the two celebrated speeches on America, when he proposes measures to address the present crisis yet pauses to reflect on the constitution of empires and the methods by which the relations between the subordinate parts and the superintending authority may be wisely and amicably adjusted. This is the Burke of enlarged views who, as Matthew Arnold famously put it, 'saturates politics with thought'.[15]

Yet judging from contemporary accounts, Burke's oratory did not sit squarely within Hume's modern paradigm. Throughout his parliamentary career, observers remarked on the ingenuity, but also the superfluity, of his figures of speech and the boldness of his appeals to the passions. According to the *Gazetteer* (9 November 1776), in a debate on America 'he represented the Solicitor General [Alexander Wedderburn] as the *fallen* Angel; his friend Charles [Fox] as the treader down and *vanquisher* of *sin* and *death*; the House of Commons he likened to *Chaos*, or the *oblivious pool*, its hallowed inhabitants to the *host* of *Satan*; and himself to the poet.' Even in the most statesman-like of his published orations he seemed ready to defy the rhetorical conventions that governed style and arrangement. It was on these grounds that Samuel Romilly found fault with the *Speech on American Taxation*. 'In the very first words of his speech, where an orator ought surely to be very temperate in the use of figures [...] he pursues the metaphor', he complained in 1782, echoing Quintilian's advice on the proper style for an exordium.[16] Both sympathetic and hostile observers judged that this copiousness of discourse set Burke apart. 'It was astonishing how all kinds of figures of speech crowded upon him. He was like a man in an Orchard where boughs loaded with fruit hung arround him, and he pulled apples as fast as he pleased and pelted the ministry', reported Boswell of the speech he discussed at the Thrales'.[17] Varying the metaphor, Boswell's friend, the MP George Dempster, described Burke a month later 'foaming like Niagara' in the House.[18]

Dempster's description suggests a copiousness overflowing with great natural force. He mocks but also elevates Burke's rhetorical abundance. Other accounts play variations on these hints of the sublime. In November 1777 George Johnstone described Burke attacking the solicitor-general, Alexander Wedderburn, 'with repeated flashes of wit like the forked glare of lightning in a thunderstorm under the line. He was shrivelled under it like a blooming tree after a hurricane.'[19] Frances Burney, though an avowed supporter of Warren Hastings, admitted that she had been almost overcome by the speech with which Burke opened the Impeachment. 'At times I confess', she confided in her journal, 'with all that I felt, wished, and thought concerning Mr. Hastings, the whirlwind of his eloquence nearly drew me into its vortex'.[20] Such was his apparently spontaneous grandeur in debate, observed his follower, Sir Gilbert Elliot, that he seemed to be 'transported with the fury of the god within him'.[21] These excited impressions recall the language of ardour, intense sympathetic connection, and irresistible natural force which classical rhetoricians employed when they tried to account for the power that Pericles, Demosthenes, and Cicero exerted over their audiences.

We can trace something of this rhetorical intensity in reports of Burke's involvement in debate in the early 1770s. For much of March 1772 the House was preoccupied with debates on the Royal Marriage Bill. Sponsored by the king, and allegedly drafted by Lord Chief Justice Mansfield, the Bill gave the sovereign sweeping powers to prevent royal marriages of which he disapproved. The measure provoked fierce opposition in the House where it was denounced variously as a despotic assertion of prerogative and a repudiation of the laws of nature. Burke spoke many times in these protracted and often heated debates but by all accounts it was his speech on 16 March that most moved the House. According to Horace Walpole, he had begun his speech 'in a fine rhapsody' of witty rejoinders to the previous speaker (Thomas De Grey) and then quite ranted with eloquent bombast, and then with admirable pathetic, and seeming to see the image of Lord Mansfield, he cried out, '*He has no child* who first *formed this bill*! He was no judge of the crime of following Nature!'[22]

Walpole summarises the speech as a performance that unfolds in several parts. In formal terms it is (like the *Reflections* much later) a mixed and even irregular composition, by turns witty, rhapsodic, bombastic, and pathetic. These shifts in tone seem often to have marked Burke's speaking, not least when he spoke in circumstances of unusual political or personal stress. Responding to fierce criticism of his conduct as paymaster-general in May 1783, he defended himself in a two-hour speech that, the MP Viscount Althorp observed, 'was in some parts full of his usual wit & humour, in some very extravagant, & in others wonderfully fine and pathetick'. Burke reserved the pathetic part for the peroration when, Althorp noted, 'he exerted himself particularly & cried excessively two or three times'.[23]

Burke's 'admirable pathetic' was evidently the rhetorical turning point of the speech on the Royal Marriage Bill. 'Till then I had not conceived what eloquence could do', confessed MP William Burke, one of Edmund's most intimate friends, who had been with him on the benches that night. The House, he recalled, 'was at once in an uproar and dead silent'. One MP 'was ashamed to find himself in tears' until he noticed that around him other men were crying too.[24] According to William, it was the phrase 'he had no children', a quotation from *Macbeth* (iv.iii.216), that electrified the House. Burke was recalling the words spoken by Macduff when he is told of the slaughter of his children. Mansfield, like Macbeth, 'has no children', and hence has no conception of parental affections or filial bonds. But Burke did more than simply quote. According to Walpole, he seemed 'to see the image of Lord Mansfield'. As quotation and exclamation ('he cried out') came together, Burke summoned the shadowy figure of the Lord Chief Justice from his place in the nearby House of Lords and, without quite addressing him, teetered on the brink of an apostrophe, one of the bold and passionate figures that Hume associated with ancient eloquence.

Enlightenment rhetoricians reckoned that apostrophe was a risky figure to employ in a modern senate. Joseph Priestley cautions those who might be tempted to imitate the great Romans who had used it. 'Our hearers', he warns 'have generally more good sense and just discernment, at least they are naturally more *cool* and phlegmatic; both which qualities check a propensity to strong emotions: and marks of great vehemence must appear absurd in a speaker, when the audience is unmoved, and sees nothing to occasion such emotion'.[25] Priestley's term 'vehemence' was a keyword in the vocabulary of rhetorical criticism. It referred to intense and passionate speech 'resulting from, and indicative of, strong feeling or excitement', as the *OED* puts it. In Cicero the term refers to the powerful displays of emotions (indignation, pity, grief) that the orator displays in his voice and on his body, and invites the audience to share.[26] Hume links 'vehemence of thought and expression' with 'the vehemence of action, observed in the ancient orators'. The stamping of feet that seconded their words 'is now esteemed too violent, either for the senate, bar, or pulpit, and is only admitted into the theatre, to accompany the most violent passions, which are there represented'.[27]

It was with these meanings in mind that a parliamentary reporter used the term to emphasise Burke's distinctiveness. 'Mr. *Edmund Burke* next arose, and with a vehemence uncommon amongst our modern Orators, he arraigned, as usual, the conduct of Administration', reported the *General Evening Post* in April 1773.[28] Burke was replying to Lord North who had set out the government's plans for resolving the tangled affairs of the East India Company, and in so doing had raised the question of the Company's right to its territorial acquisitions in India. Burke made North's equivocation, as he saw it, on the question of right the centrepiece of his evidently heated speech. His indignation towards the government was matched by his contempt for the people. Worse than compliant, they were, he thundered, 'a most servile degenerate herd, destitute of capacity to distinguish, or virtue to relish, what was good'. According to the reporter, Burke spoke 'with the *verbum ardens*, or glowing expression of the ancients', a Ciceronian phrase that refers to an excited intensity of speech. We find it in an eighteenth-century rendering of Cicero's last rhetorical treatise, *Orator*, which translates him as saying that 'it is an easy matter to catch a *glowing* expression, (if I may be allowed to call it so) and expose it to ridicule when the fire of attention is extinguished'.[29] The imagery is specifically of flames, the flames of passion that consume the orator, and are communicable to an audience.

The orator's capacity to be himself moved (through willed identification with a cause or as the first audience of his own words) was understood as a precondition of this transfer of emotion and consequently of persuasion itself. This was the principle known as *ipse ardere*, to be oneself aflame, which Cicero elaborates at length in *De oratore*.[30] Years before he entered parliament Burke had similarly explained the manner in which words may work on the affections. 'If the speaker did not call in to his aid those modes of speech that mark a strong and lively feeling in himself', merely verbal description could have little effect, he remarks in the *Philosophical Enquiry*. But when we hear a speaker under the stress of emotion 'by the contagion of our passions, we catch a fire already kindled by another, which probably might never have been struck out by the object described' (WS, I: 319). The principle extends from Burke's oratory to his writings, and most obviously to the *Reflections*. Behind the writer who asks us to share his emotion as he laments the fall of the queen lurks the figure of the orator, appealing to the House, and shedding his tears.

Oratory and Occasion

Once he had finished with Lord North, 'Mr. Burke went out of the House immediately in great warmth', an observer noted.[31] He seems to have felt no need to manufacture the emotions he displayed from the benches. His volatility was well known, and frequently exploited by his adversaries. In the parliamentary debates on the Regency Crisis (1788–9) the indelicacy and fervour he showed in his descriptions of the king's state of mind outraged many in the House and embarrassed his own party. According to a report in *The World* (7 February 1789), when Pitt accused him of displaying an unbecoming warmth in debate, he exclaimed 'on such a theme, 'tis impious to be cool!' This was a misquotation (perhaps a deliberate one) from the poet Edward Young, who in the fourth of his *Night-thoughts* (1743) had written ''tis impious to be calm'. Young was pitting his Christian enthusiasm against the 'cold-hearted, frozen, formalists' of his time whose lukewarm devotion fell far short of the ardour his sense of God's goodness required. 'Think you my song, too turbulent? too warm?', he asks,

> Are *passions*, then, the pagans of the soul?
> *Reason* alone baptiz'd? alone *ordain'd*
> To touch things sacred? Oh for warmer still![32]

The allusion to Young vindicates and elevates Burke's parliamentary conduct. At the same time, it is implicitly a rebuke to his adversary, Pitt, whose frigidity as a public character was as widely noticed as Burke's zeal.[33]

Far from being excessive, Burke insists that his vehemence, not Pitt's coldness, is the appropriate response to the occasion. Their disagreement, which was at once both political and rhetorical, turned on the classical notion of propriety. 'The universal rule, in oratory as in life, is to consider propriety', wrote Cicero in a famous passage. 'This depends on the subject under discussion, and on the character of both the speaker and the audience.'[34] The idea that the language of a speech should not fall below the dignity of the subject or the speaker's standing as a public figure seems straightforward enough. But judgements about propriety are not always so easy to make. The orator may have to adjudicate between the rival claims of reason, experience, taste, and natural feeling in deciding what is fitting, and these judgements involve the three basic variables of the rhetorical situation (speaker, subject, audience), which may be related in very complex ways. In a debating chamber like the House of Commons, where every member of the audience is also a potential speaker, the question of propriety is especially vexed. Rather than simply being invoked, propriety is itself always likely to become a matter for dispute.

Something of this sort happened in a debate on the Hastings impeachment in December 1789 when Burke admonished MP Richard Hardinge for attempting to rouse the passions of the House. He granted that 'he would never condemn those appeals to the heart in favour of the sufferings of innocence [...] because, by magic of eloquence, the remotest sufferings of mankind are thus brought home to our bosoms'. Yet those appeals should always be regulated by the test of appropriateness. 'Let us take care that our appeal to the passions is not rendered rather ridiculous than pathetic, by having no proper relation to the point in question', Burke warned. 'Nothing out of its place and season, is powerful or decent' (WS, VII: 91). Burke answers Hardinge in much the same terms as his adversaries, anxious to undermine the magic of his own eloquence, had long been accustomed to answering him. That does not mean that Burke is inconsistent. Hardinge's pathos may have been 'out of its place and season', but there were places and seasons when such an appeal would be not only timely but imperative.

Burke found many such occasions in the course of his parliamentary career. Sometimes he was wildly at odds with the House in his judgement of what was appropriate. Sometimes his vehemence seemed disproportionate, inexplicable, and perhaps overdetermined, as if it had spoken from some other time or place. But the appeals to the passions he made as an orator expressed something important about his conception of political life, as well his understanding of human nature. Reasoning had its place in the making of political judgements but the emotions were no less sure a guide. The rhetoricians of his own time agreed that it was both useful and legitimate for deliberative orators to move their audiences. 'The coolest reasoner always in persuading addresseth himself to the passions some way or other. This he cannot avoid doing, if he speak to the purpose', wrote George Campbell.[35] At the same time, while admiring the ancient vehemence they characteristically recommended restraint. Burke's difference was the strength of feeling he displayed himself, and asked his audiences to share. 'The people, to be animated, must seem to have some motive to *action*', he told a correspondent in 1789 (C, V: 443). That could never be accomplished by reasoning alone.

NOTES

1 *Correspondence of William Pitt, Earl of Chatham*, 4 vols. (London, 1838–49), vol. I, p. 66.
2 For this idea see WS, II: 317–18.

3 See Arthur P. I. Samuels, *The Early Life, Correspondence and Writings of the Rt. Hon. Edmund Burke* (Cambridge: Cambridge University Press, 1923), which reprints the minute-book of the Club (pp. 255–95); Jean Dietz Moss, '"Discordant Consensus": Old and New Rhetoric at Trinity College, Dublin', *Rhetorica*, 14 (1996): 383–411; F. P. Lock, *Edmund Burke* (Oxford: Clarendon Press, 1996), vol. I, especially pp. 30–52.

4 Samuels, *Early Life*, p. 227.

5 Ibid., p. 275.

6 John Ridge to Edmund and William Burke (March 1766), in C, I: 243.

7 See Ian Harris, 'Publishing Parliamentary Oratory: The Case of Edmund Burke', *Parliamentary History* 26 (2008): 112–30.

8 See Donald C. Bryant, 'Edmund Burke: The New Images 1966', *Quarterly Journal of Speech*, 52 (1966): 329–36.

9 Adam Potkay, *The Fate of Eloquence in the Age of Hume* (Ithaca and London: Cornell University Press, 1994), pp. 48–9. I am indebted to Potkay's work throughout this section.

10 'I gave an account of Burke's speaking on Monday last, and naturally used some action', *Private Papers of James Boswell from Malahide Castle*, ed. Geoffrey Scott and Frederick A. Pottle, 19 vols. (New and York and London: Oxford University Press, 1928–37), vol. VI, p. 95.

11 Hume, *Essays: Moral, Political and Literary*, ed. Eugene F. Miller (Indianapolis: Liberty, 1985), p. 99.

12 *Lectures on Rhetoric and Belles Lettres*, eds. Linda Ferreira-Buckley and S. Michael Halloran (Carbondale: Southern Illinois University Press, 2005), pp. 282–3, 295.

13 *On The Ideal Orator* [*De oratore*], trans. James M. May and Jakob Wisse (Oxford: Oxford University Press, 2001), pp. 134–5; *The Orator's Education* [*Institutio Oratoria*], trans. Donald A. Russell, 5 vols. (Cambridge, MA: Harvard University Press, 2001), vol. II, pp. 41–5.

14 Lock, *Edmund Burke*, vol. I, p. 220.

15 'The Function of Criticism at the Present Time', *Complete Prose Works of Matthew Arnold*, ed. R. H. Super, 11 vols. (Ann Arbor: University of Michigan Press, 1960–70), vol. III, p. 266.

16 *Memoirs of the Life of Sir Samuel Romilly*, 3 vols. (London: John Murray, 1840), vol. II, pp. 213–14.

17 *Private Papers of James Boswell*, vol. VI, p. 83.

18 *Private Papers of James Boswell*, vol. VI, p. 132.

19 Cited by Donald C. Bryant, 'The Contemporary Reception of Edmund Burke's Speaking' in Raymond F. Howes (ed.), *Historical Studies of Rhetoric and Rhetoricians* (Ithaca: Cornell University Press, 1961), pp. 271–93 (p. 284).

20 *Diary & Letters of Madame d'Arblay*, 3 vols. (London: Macmillan, 1904–5), vol. III, p. 448.

21 *The Life and Letters of Sir Gilbert Eliot*, 3 vols. (London, 1874), vol. I, p. 215.

22 *The Last Journals of Horace Walpole*, ed. A. Francis Steuart, 2 vols. (London: John Lane, 1910), vol. 1, p. 56.

23 British Library Add. MSS 75579, Althorp to Lady Spencer, 22 May 1783.

24 William Burke to John Ridge (24 March 1772) in Ross J. S. Hoffman, *Edmund Burke, New York Agent, with His Letters to the New York Assembly and*

Intimate Correspondence with Charles O'Hara 1761–1776 (Philadelphia: The American Philosophical Society, 1956), p. 523.

25 *A Course of Lectures on Oratory and Criticism*, ed. Vincent M. Bevilacqua and Richard Murphy (Carbondale: Southern Illinois University Press, 1965), pp. 113–14.

26 See, for instance, *On the Ideal Orator*, p. 177.

27 Hume, *Essays*, pp. 101–2.

28 The report is reprinted in WS, II: 390–3.

29 E. Jones, *Cicero's Brutus or History of Famous Orators; also His Orator, or Accomplished Speaker* (London, 1776), p. 255.

30 *On the Ideal Orator*, pp. 172–5.

31 British Library Egerton MSS 245, fo. 273.

32 *The Works of the Author of the Night-thoughts*, 4 vols. (London, 1757), vol. III, pp. 90–1.

33 See John Ehrman, *The Younger Pitt: The Years of Acclaim* (London: Constable, 1969), pp. 109–10.

34 Cicero, *Brutus, Orator*, trans. G. L. Hendrickson and H. M. Hubell (Cambridge, MA, Harvard University Press, 1939), pp. 357–61.

35 *The Philosophy of Rhetoric*, ed. Lloyd F. Bitzer (Carbondale: Southern Illinois University Press, 1963), p. 77.

4

PADDY BULLARD

Burke's Aesthetic Psychology

Edmund Burke's *Philosophical Enquiry into the Origin of our Ideas of the Sublime and Beautiful* (1757; expanded second edition, 1759) acts as a sort of midwife at the birth of modern aesthetic theory, but really it belongs to the pre-history of the discipline. Burke never uses the term 'aesthetic', and he is unlikely to have known that the German philosopher Alexander Baumgarten had recently adopted the word to describe the 'criticism of taste' in his treatise *Aesthetica* (1750). The true etymology of 'aesthetic' – the Greek *aisthetikos* means 'pertaining to what the senses perceive' – was much insisted upon by Immanuel Kant in 1781, who pointed out that any such science is by definition empirical, and confined to the mechanics of sensual perception.[1] Modern aesthetics begins with Kant's disappointment at Burke's refusal to move beyond such preliminaries in the *Philosophical Enquiry*. Kant calls for a new *a priori* or 'transcendental aesthetics', one that establishes a synthetic system for how sensible objects ought to be judged, rather than merely reporting how they are judged.[2] Likewise, Hegel declares at the beginning of his lectures on aesthetics that he must break with the old application of 'aesthetics' to works of art 'with regard to the feelings they were supposed to produce, as, for instance, the feeling of pleasure, admiration, fear, pity, and so on'.[3] Burke, for his own part, insists that the most interesting effects of sublime and beautiful objects strike us before we can reason about them or judge them. By the standards of his contemporaries, Burke's *Philosophical Enquiry* was not particularly philosophical.

And yet the *Philosophical Enquiry* is much more than a museum piece, consigned to the footnotes of philosophy by the German Idealists. It demands to be read in the context of its own controversies – even though the polemical nature of Burke's engagement with those controversies is often concealed behind a screen of polite methodicality. The method of Burke's treatise imitates the meticulous inductions of Locke and Newton, as applied to the realm of psychology by their proto-utilitarian followers David Hartley and John Brown. And yet it is arguably a fragmentary text, self-conscious of its suggestive incompleteness. Many of the themes it explores, such as 'taste', 'the sublime', and 'the *je ne sais quoi*', derive from a French neo-classical tradition of criticism that makes witty play on the impossibility of defining its terms.[4] Burke may be suspected of failing to get the joke, but he must be credited with spotting the suggestiveness of this critical language to the emerging British discipline of moral psychology. Neither is it fair to say that the *Philosophical Enquiry* is essentially a treatise on psychology, or that it merely happens to draw most of its examples from the realm of arts, without evincing any real interest in art as such. Two arts are central to Burke's inquiry: those of rhetorical and literary criticism (with reference to the sublime) and of fine art theory (with reference to the beautiful). We will return to the critical context for Burke's discussion of fine art at the end of this chapter, because the category of 'the beautiful' proved surprisingly productive for Burke's later political thought. The concept of the sublime, on the other hand, is closer to the heart of the *Philosophical Enquiry* and raises more pressing questions about the intellectual origins of the treatise.

Tranquility Shadowed with Horror

The *Philosophical Enquiry* belongs to a critical tradition that descends from the Greek treatise *Peri Hupsous* or *On the Sublime*, attributed to a critic of the first century AD called 'Longinus'. *On the Sublime* appeared in its modern *editio princeps* in 1554 under the Latin title *De Grandi Sivi Sublimi Orationis Genere*, but it only came to prominence in European criticism in 1674, when the leading French poet Nicholas Boileau published a translation of the treatise in his *Oeuvres Diverses*. An English translation of Longinus had already appeared in 1652, but it was through Boileau that *On the Sublime* came to have its extensive influence on the poetics of John Dennis, Joseph Addison, Alexander Pope, and on British Augustan literature more generally. Burke cherry-picks ideas from this neo-classical tradition that happen to suit his argument, but he also challenges several of its orthodoxies. The Longinian ideas that Burke finds most useful concern the power of the sublime. For Longinus and his followers, sublime objects manifest an intense energy that sweeps the witness along 'in the forward surge of their current'. Caught up in a rush of excitement and power, the witness cannot perceive the artfulness with which those objects have been created. The sublime is its own second nature.[5] Longinus writes of the suspicion attached to the sophisticated or copious use of figurative language – 'it gives a suggestion of treachery, craft, fallacy' – and recommends the sublime as a way of spinning that suspicion away: 'the artfulness of the trick is no longer obvious in its brilliant setting of beauty and grandeur, and thus avoids all suspicion'.[6] This idea of the sublime's sweeping rapidity crops up often in the *Philosophical Enquiry*: the sublime 'hurries us along by an irresistible force' (WS, I: 230), while 'the mind is hurried out of itself' (WS, I: 234) in a sort of passive inversion of desire, the impulse 'that hurries us on to the possession of certain objects' (WS, I: 255).

Burke is more troubled, however, by suggestions that '[n]o work of art can be great, but as it deceives' (WS, I: 246), and that even 'tragedy is a deceit, and its representations no realities' (WS, I: 223). Although 'sublimity is the echo of a noble mind', as he puts it, and the contemplation of sublime art helps 'develop our natures to some degree of grandeur', it is nevertheless possible to simulate the sublime, to recreate it artificially.[7]

In other words, the sublime can be at once magnificently noble and meanly artful. Burke gets around this problem by insisting, in a way that Longinus and his neo-classical commentators never had, on the pre-eminence of a true sublime in nature over the grandest achievements of human imagination. An audience assembled to watch 'the most sublime and affecting tragedy we have', Burke speculates, will desert the theatre in a minute if they hear that 'a state criminal of high rank is on the point of being executed in the adjoining square', because real sympathy is far more powerful than artful imitation (WS, I: 223). Conversely, the ancient monuments at Stonehenge are sublime because their massive, broken roughness concentrates the witness's mind on the forces required to assemble them, without letting in the mitigating ideas 'of art, and contrivance' (WS, I: 246). In Stonehenge we find an example of magnificent human art that has become sublime through a non-human process of decay and fragmentation. This romantic privileging of nature before art goes to the heart of the *Philosophical Enquiry*'s critical approach. Burke contends that his own discipline of 'philosophy' has a superior dignity to the creative arts, because artists ('and poets principally') are more interested in imitating one another than in going 'beyond the surface of things' to discover the underlying natural principles of the passions (WS, I: 228). Boileau and his neo-classical contemporaries brought to their reading of Longinus the Aristotelian principle of *mimesis* – that our main source of pleasure in art comes from witnessing the process of representation, for which we have an instinct of appreciation.[8] Burke turns this principle on its head. He marks out the sphere of artistic imitation only to describe the true sublime as that which looms beyond its boundaries (WS, I: 224–5).

One measure of Burke's progress 'beyond the surface of things' is that, where his neo-classical predecessors stuck at the process by which art causes pleasure (imitation), the *Philosophical Enquiry* plunges further into the question in a search for the causes of that process. It establishes a new theory for the psychology of pleasure itself. Burke takes the indefinable ideas of pleasure and pain to be the building blocks of human experience, following a philosophical convention established by John Locke in his *Essay Concerning Human Understanding*. Whereas Locke thought of pleasure and pain as opposing sensations that yield to or press upon one another, however, Burke's concern is with their distinctness from one another as qualities, and with the peculiar effects that occur when they do combine. He is especially interested in how we experience some kinds of psychological pain – such as terror and fear – as a species of 'relative pleasure', or (to use Burke's specially assigned key-word) 'delight'. We put a value on the feelings of astonishment, creeping horror, or painful embarrassment that art sometimes evokes not because they gratify us in any immediate way, but because the state of dumbstruck admiration they cause is indirectly 'delightful'. Burke suggests that we seek out this painful delight because it is therapeutic, a sort of exercise for the nerves:

> if the pain and terror are so modified as not to be actually noxious; if the pain is not carried to violence, and the terror is not conversant about the present destruction of the person, as these emotions clear the parts, whether fine, or gross, of a dangerous and troublesome incumbrance, they are capable of producing delight; not pleasure, but a sort of delightful horror, a sort of tranquility tinged with terror; which as it belongs to self-preservation is one of the strongest of all the passions. Its object is the sublime. (WS, I: 288–9)

The language that Burke uses here is almost identical to that of an earlier passage in the *Philosophical Enquiry* in which he describes the feeling of shakenness caused by a narrow escape from great danger: the witness is left 'in a state of much sobriety', says Burke, 'impressed with a sense of awe, in a sort of tranquillity shadowed with horror' (WS, I: 213). In a third passage, the contemplation of infinity 'has a tendency to fill the mind with that sort of delightful horror, which is the most genuine effect, and the truest test of the sublime' (WS, I: 243). Why does Burke keep returning to the phrase 'delightful horror', to this sense of an odd passivity just 'tinged' or 'shadowed' by sublime dread?

The answer here is a literary one, and a clue to it can be found in a fourth passage where Burke talks of 'shadows' and 'terror'. It appears in the new chapter on 'Power' that he adds to the 1759 second edition of the *Philosophical Enquiry*, and its purpose is to introduce a quotation from the didactic poem *De Rerum Natura* by the first-century Epicurean philosopher Lucretius. 'Lucretius', Burke comments, 'is a poet not to be suspected of giving way to superstitious terrors; yet when he supposes the whole mechanism of nature laid open by the master of his philosophy, his transport on this magnificent view which he has represented in the colours of such bold and lively poetry, is overcast with a shade of secret dread and horror' (WS, I: 240). Burke's commentary anticipates the quotation he gives from the start of book III of *De Rerum*, which translates: 'thereupon from all these things a sort of divine delight [*quaedam divina voluptas*] gets hold upon me and a terror [*atque horror*]'.[9] The 'master' Burke alludes to is Epicurus, whose disciples (Lucretius among them) hold that the purpose of philosophy is to raise the subject to a state of *voluptas,* or pleasurable tranquility of mind and body, often produced by contemplation of the subject's escape from discord. This Epicurean phrase 'a sort of tranquility tinged with terror' is so crucial to Burke's argument that it should perhaps persuade us to think of the *Philosophical Enquiry* as belonging to a tradition of the 'Lucretian sublime', rather than to the better-known rhetorical tradition that follows Longinus.[10] The Lucretian sublime is an enlightened sublime. It is produced when scientific knowledge of the natural world has stopped the subject from marveling at trivial (and especially supernatural) things, and has initiated him into the more intoxicating wonders of the material universe. Despite Lucretius's atheism, his ideas had long been absorbed by early-modern Christian thinkers, and put to the same sorts of theological purposes for which Burke reserves it.[11] The context of the Lucretian sublime anticipates the *Philosophical Enquiry*'s striking marriage of disciplined, utilitarian method with pious, and sometimes rhapsodic enthusiasm.

Although the *Philosophical Enquiry* presents itself as tightly organised and methodical, there are several reasons for thinking about it as an unstable, even fragmented text. Burke was so dissatisfied with the 1757 first edition of the treatise that for the second edition of 1759 he wrote twenty-three additional passages – one of them so long that it required an entirely new chapter – together with a new 'Introduction on taste'. These additions were not introduced silently. On the contrary, Burke makes quite a fuss about them in the first paragraph of the revised preface, as though he were presenting something of a work in progress. Further indications of textual instability are the direct allusions Burke makes to an earlier period of composition, apparently complete some four years before the work's publication in 1757 (WS, I: 188). The implication is that Burke established the outline of his argument early in composition, and then looked about for further instances (some literary, some anecdotal and drawn from the world of the literary magazines) to illustrate it – a process of accretion that continued with the 1759 additions. There are also signs that Burke thought of the *Philosophical Enquiry* as the prelude for a much larger project that he never got around to. The book finishes abruptly with no formal conclusion, leaving an impression of open-endedness. Burke insists that the purpose of the work is to fit the reader for 'greater and stronger flights of science' (WS, I: 5), to provide 'a good preparative' (WS, I: 191), to 'lay down [...] principles' (WS, I: 320): 'in an enquiry', he promises, 'it is almost everything to be once in the right road' (WS, I: 228). These remarks all suggest that Burke thought of the *Philosophical Enquiry* as the theoretical foundation for some other, more extensive investigation. Perhaps his plan was to focus on themes that he is careful to exclude from this preliminary work: judgment and reason, for example, or morality and politics.

The Disagreeable Yoke of our Reason

The most obvious difference between the first and second editions of the *Philosophical Enquiry* is that the latter includes a preliminary essay, titled 'Introduction on taste'. The basic purpose of this essay is to clarify Burke's reasons for restricting the scope of his original investigation in the way that he does. Like 'sublime' and 'beautiful', 'taste' was a term associated with the Earl of Shaftesbury, Joseph Addison, and other 'polite' essayist-philosophers who used it to make what they hoped would be an attractive analogy between the aristocratic fashion for acquiring a 'taste' in collectable fine art, and the philosophic cultivation of a 'moral taste'. In a characteristic spirit of controversy, Burke rejects this sort of analogy between art and ethics as misleading. He confines his own definition of 'taste' strictly to 'those faculties of the mind which are affected with, or which form a judgment of the works of imagination and the elegant arts' (WS, I: 197). The implied distinction here between the immediate 'affections' of the sensory imagination and the secondary 'judgments' of the critic proves crucial to Burke's argument. Essentially, Burke wants to keep taste-as-judgment out of the question: 'judgment is for the greater part employed in throwing stumbling blocks in the way of the imagination, in dissipating the scenes of its enchantment, and in tying us down to the disagreeable yoke of our reason' (WS, I: 208–9). As such it can only distort the natural dynamics of sensation and passion. It is impossible, Burke reckons, to say anything about a taste that has been 'acquired' without investigating 'the habits, the prejudices, or the distempers of this particular man', and thus without descending from philosophy to biography. So he ignores what we might call the 'culture of taste' altogether. The purpose of the 'Introduction on taste' is to warn the reader that the *Philosophical Enquiry* has almost nothing to say about 'good taste' in the usual sense of that phrase. This methodological reserve is reasonable, but it leaves Burke begging an important question: is he sure that this new category of purely physiological taste exists in practical terms? Is it not the case that our 'peculiar and acquired relish' for particular objects is so prevalent that we can make only theoretical inferences about what a 'natural' taste might be?

Burke hopes that the examples given in the body of the treatise will bolster his methodological principles. But the main argument of the *Philosophical Enquiry* is itself adjusted in the revised edition of 1759.

Burke altered the character of the *Philosophical Enquiry* in 1759 when he added this new 'Introduction on taste', with its strict contrast between taste-as-sensation and taste-as-judgment. Either by intention or accident a certain quality of conceptual flexibility evident in the 1757 first edition of the treatise has become stiffened in the second. Burke's basic distinction between our experiences of the sublime and beautiful (common, of course, to both editions) depends on an argument laid out at the start of part one of the treatise. The self-directed passions associated with pain and self-preservation are quite separate, Burke argues, from the gentler instincts associated with society and the sociable pleasures. Our experience of the sublime belongs to the former category, whereas the beautiful is associated with the latter. What makes this binary distinction flexible in its original form is Burke's attention to certain irrational impulses that play between the potentially violent sphere of self-preservation and the necessarily more settled sphere of society and conversation. 'Beauty', for example, may belong with the passions of 'sympathy' and 'imitation' in the social sphere, but it is nevertheless 'a *positive* and powerful quality' that operates despite conscious thought (WS, I: 265). 'Imitation' is itself a social passion that urges people to various kinds of compliance with one another 'without any intervention of the reasoning faculty' (WS, I: 224). Ultimately, imitation defines the technical (and therefore rational) scope of representational art. Again the discussion of language in part five of the treatise carries Burke far beyond simple sense impressions into the sociable world of discourse. Even here he identifies an important category of words – what he calls '[c]ompounded *abstract* words … [such as] honour, justice, liberty, and the like' – that have almost no cognitive content in common usage, only a faint emotional charge carried over from earlier associations (WS, I: 312). In each of these cases, Burke finds subrational mental processes, often associated with immediate sensory experience, working obscurely in the sphere of understanding and society. When the 'Introduction on taste' is attached to the *Philosophical Enquiry* in 1759, however, the primary faculties of sense and imagination are put at a distance from the secondary cognitive processes – moral judgment and 'Taste by way of distinction' – in a way that they had not always been in the first edition of 1757 (WS, I: 206). The realm of sensation no longer leaks into the realm of judgment in quite the same way.

Whatever the second edition of the *Philosophical Enquiry* loses in terms of subtlety, however, it gains in the clarity and force of its argument. Above all, Burke realises that the point he should be emphasising is one about the relative power of the impressions that act upon our senses and imaginations. Some impressions are far stronger than others, and those of greatest force are of greatest interest because, uniquely, they offer a means for understanding the psychology of moral obligation. Like several of his contemporaries, Burke felt that the great challenge facing the philosophers of his day was that of explaining how human beings have developed moral sentiments strong enough to counterbalance the natural urges of self-love and self-interest. This was the problem that led Adam Smith, for example, to develop his conjectures about the god-like 'impartial spectator' who lives in every human breast, exerting moral leverage on our otherwise feeble affections of benevolence and sympathy.[12] Similarly, it prompted Burke to insert a new chapter into part two of the *Philosophical Enquiry*, titled simply 'Power'. In the first edition, as we have seen, beauty's '*positive* and powerful' pleasures are given their due, but in the second Burke alters the balance towards pain and the sublime:

> For first, we must remember, that the idea of pain, in its highest degree, is much stronger than the highest degree of pleasure [...] pleasure follows the will; and therefore we are generally affected with it by many things of a force greatly inferior to our own. But pain is always inflicted by a power in some way superior, because we never submit to pain willingly. So that strength, violence, pain and terror, are ideas that rush in upon the mind together. (WS, I: 236)

As we shall see, the idea of an inferior and insinuating 'pleasure' is more relevant to Burke's later politics than the domineering superiority of the sublime. But the *Philosophical Enquiry* has no direct concern with politics, whatever ideological agendas it might happen to serve.[13] The power that interests Burke is ultimately a divine power. It is manifested in the natural magnificence of the created world, in the direct revelation of Bible and church, and in the providential disposition of the human body towards religious awe and astonishment. Adam Smith's theory of the 'impartial spectator' accounts for moral obligation in the expansive terms of a general 'science of man'. Burke's theory lacks the scope and complexity of Smith's, and its focus is much tighter. The *Philosophical Enquiry* searches for the nearest routes of communication between the passive human subject and a universe animated with divine intention.

The Sublime and the Beautiful

So the *Philosophical Enquiry* can be considered an unstable text insofar as Burke composed it in a spirit of open-ended accumulation and revision. But the treatise is fragmentary in another sense: something has been removed from it as well. The central argument of the *Philosophical Enquiry* serves a polemical purpose that seems to have been concealed or written over during the process of composition. This main argument is itself straightforward, if somewhat abstract for an avowedly empirical work. Burke identifies various qualities associated with terror and astonishment that he calls 'sublime', and various qualities associated with love that he calls 'beautiful'. These two classes of qualities are consistent among themselves, he insists, and are absolutely opposed to one another. It is the second point about 'opposition' that seems most important to Burke's argument. The sublime and the beautiful are 'frequently confounded', he complains, and the main business of the *Philosophical Enquiry* is to put them asunder, once and for all (WS, I: 188). Indeed, they 'stand on foundations so different, that it is hard [...] to think of reconciling them in the same subject' (WS, I: 273). But which writers are responsible for this reckless and apparently widespread muddle, this confounding of sublimity with beauty?

Burke never tells us whom he is arguing against. The *Philosophical Enquiry* is a polemic that has been cut away from its controversial background. In 1757, even Burke's closest acquaintances could work out only half of this contextual puzzle. His undergraduate friend William Dennis suggested to his schoolmate Richard Shackleton that Burke had planned the *Philosophical Enquiry* as an answer to the Dublin-born philosopher Francis Hutcheson. In his early work, Hutcheson proposed that humans have a faculty or 'moral sense' attuned to 'the Beauty, Order, fitness and Rectitude of Actions', and Burke (according to Dennis) felt that this theory threatened the cause of established religion, 'by representing Virtue independent of it'.[14] In other words, Burke wanted to prove that humans have no immediate impulse towards that which is morally good, because he believed that divine providence has ordered it so that religion (the Bible, the church) chivvies us towards virtue by the carrot of future rewards in heaven, and with the stick of future punishments in hell. This 'voluntarist' theory of moral obligation belonged very much to the mainstream of Latitudinarian Church of England theology during the mid-eighteenth century, so Dennis's theory is entirely plausible. In part four of the *Philosophical Enquiry*, Burke does indeed argue that 'the application of beauty to virtue' has a 'tendency to confound our ideas of things; and it has given rise to an infinite deal of whimsical theory' (WS, I: 272). But this only accounts for the second half of the title's 'frequently confounded' pairing of the 'sublime' with the 'beautiful'. Dennis's explanation does not tell us about Burke's primary interest in the sublime.

The concealed target of Burke's polemic is in fact the work of Anthony Ashley Cooper, third Earl of Shaftesbury – author of *Characterisitcks*

(1711), and the moralist who had provided the germ for Hutcheson's systematic theory of the moral sense. There is no direct reference to Shaftesbury either in the *Philosophical Enquiry* or in any other relevant document. Nevertheless, there is strong internal evidence that the *Characteristicks* was Burke's chief target, and not the early works of Hutcheson. First, there is the issue (present in the title itself) of Burke's particular concern with the *distinction* between 'sublime' and 'beautiful' objects. These two key-words had already been brought together as a collocation in a much-quoted passage from the fourth part of Shaftesbury's *Characteristicks*, 'An Inquiry concerning Virtue'. The title of Burke's treatise almost certainly refers to this passage. The human mind, says Shaftesbury,

> feels the Soft and the Harsh, the Agreeable and Disagreeable in the Affections, and finds a *Foul* and *Fair*, a *Harmonious* and *Dissonant*, as really and truly here as in any musical Numbers or in the outward Forms and Representations of sensible Things [...] So that to deny the common and natural sense of a SUBLIME and BEAUTIFUL in Things, will appear an Affectation merely.[15]

Using a complicated web of footnotes and internal references, Shaftesbury links the words 'SUBLIME and BEAUTIFUL' to Cicero's treatise *De Finibus*, in which the Roman philosopher argues that 'the honourable' in morality (*honestum*) has a beauty and loveliness (*pulchritudine*) that transcends its practical or conventional functions.[16] In this context, Shaftesbury seems to be using the word 'sublime' to mean something like 'essential' or 'ideal'. He is suggesting, like Cicero, that the 'loveliness' of moral virtue signifies its metaphysical quality. Burke, on the other hand, is committed to explaining our experiences of sublime phenomena only in terms of physical sensation: 'when we go but one step beyond the immediate sensible qualities of things,' he writes, 'we go out of our depth' (WS, I: 283). Burke's empiricism left little room for ideal forms: beauty is palpable or it means nothing.

At the same time, Burke resists Shaftesbury's assumption that our most important experiences of beauty fall within the sphere of human morals – that beautiful things, we might say, make people think about beautiful actions. In an important passage in the 1759 'Introduction on taste', Burke emphasises that the *Philosophical Enquiry* is concerned exclusively with the 'certain, natural and uniform principles' by which the passions operate (WS, I: 207). His treatise deals with art made by humans only insofar as it represents simple, sensible objects, or makes direct 'efforts upon the passions'. The indirect consequences of beauty in the realm of ethics are beyond the scope of his treatise, even though much is made of their roots in the sociable affections. Burke acknowledges, however, that many kinds of art – he might have adduced any modern novel as an example – are concerned primarily with the morality of human actions. As such they involve judgement and reasoning, as well as sensation and passion: 'all these make a very considerable part of what are considered as the objects of Taste', he concedes; 'and Horace sends us to the schools of philosophy and the world for our instruction in them' (WS, I: 106). Burke is referring here to some well-known lines from *De Arte Poetica*, in which Horace recommends a combined course of worldly living and philosophical reading (specifically, the Socratic dialogues of Plato and Xenophon) as the best means for aspiring poets to gather raw material for their work.[17] Once again, it was Shaftesbury who established these Horatian lines as a crux for British literary criticism. They feature largely in his unpublished writings, and he discusses them at length in a crucial passage of the *Characteristicks* while outlining his theory of philosophical dialogue.[18] Where Shaftesbury took this classical reference as a point of departure for his aesthetics, however, Burke uses it to mark out the limits of his inquiry.

Burke's empiricism leads to one further piece of evidence for his targeting of Shaftesbury. It was common in early modern art theory to discuss beauty in terms of spatial proportion, and to illustrate the ratios of proportion using mathematical terms. Shaftesbury deploys this potentially precise vocabulary with all sorts of vague, impressionistic flourishes. He advises his readers to cultivate an instinct for beauty through 'the Contemplation of those *Numbers*, that *Harmony, Proportion* and *Concord* which supports the universal Nature'.[19] Burke has a specific objection to this sort of aesthetic language. Any proper understanding of 'proportion' and 'measurement' requires arithmetical thought, he argues: 'but surely beauty is no idea belonging to mensuration, nor has it anything to do with calculation or geometry' – on the contrary, beauty strikes us with all the immediacy of sensation (WS, I: 256). The point here is that Burke could not have attacked the technical language of neo-classical aesthetics so directly if Shaftesbury had not already pushed it to an extreme of abstraction, using mathematical terms without any reference to the mental actions involved with arithmetic. Throughout the *Philosophical Enquiry* Burke is concerned with the suggestive power of obscurity and indirection. And yet much of the controversial energy that animates the treatise comes from his insistence that the terms of critical debate must be deployed with an accuracy and responsibility for one's meanings to which Shaftesbury did not condescend.

A characteristic irony of Burke's literary career is that it should begin with a treatise dedicated to the clarification of a dysfunctional critical vocabulary and end with radical opponents reading his own political language as mendacious and corrupt.[20] It is tempting to assume that Burke drew upon his youthful speculations to develop a sublime public rhetoric suitable for the age of revolutionary terror. In fact, it is the category of the beautiful that makes the more important contribution to his mature, political thought, and to his post-revolutionary late style. Burke observes in the *Philosophical Enquiry* that the sort of statesmanly charisma or ethical sublimity described by Longinus in his portrait of the Athenian orator Demosthenes is not often the most practicable character for a politician to adopt. Like the Romans themselves, says Burke, we admire Cato but love Caesar: 'it is rather the soft green of the soul on which we rest our eyes, that are fatigued with beholding more glaring objects' (WS, I: 271). This scepticism with regard to the moral grandeur of a certain kind of statesman was particularly useful during the early years of Burke's political career, when William Pitt the elder's parliamentary predominance – 'that glaring and dazzling influence at which the eyes of eagles have blenched', as Burke called it in 1774 – was still regarded with superstitious reverence by the British political classes (WS, II: 441). The limits of Pitt's political effectiveness were defined, paradoxically, by the intensity of his personal power.

As early as 1757, Burke was thinking about the instrumental advantages to be gained by those, like himself, who cannot claim such power. Although Burke stops far short of articulating it, the *Philosophical Enquiry* points towards a political rhetoric of beauty: 'for pleasure must be stolen, and not forced upon us; pleasure follows the will; and therefore we are generally affected with it by many things of a force greatly inferior to our own' (WS, I: 236). A more practical aspect of this politics of beauty can be glimpsed in his first major pamphlet, *Thoughts on our Present Discontents* (1770), when Burke outlines some of the insinuating arts by which 'an individual without authority is often able to govern those who are his equals or superiours; by a knowledge of their temper, and by a judicious management of it' (WS, II: 252). These, we cannot help but infer, are some of the arts that won Burke, the obscure Irish journalist, his seat in parliament and his job as secretary to the prime minister in 1765. By the time of the *Reflections on the Revolution in France* (1790), Burke's politics of the beautiful have developed beyond these prudential considerations. They are absorbed into a far-reaching sense of how the fabric of every political association depends upon the exchange of softer sentiments. Using a Horatian tag that is closely related to the one he contested with Shaftesbury, Burke insists on how crucial it is that states themselves appeal to our relish for that which is morally delectable: 'to make us love our country, our country ought to be lovely', he writes (WS, VIII: 241). This maxim represents the final political development of Burke's aesthetic psychology.

NOTES

1 Immanuel Kant, *Critique of Pure Reason*, trans. and ed. Paul Guyer and Allen W. Wood (Cambridge: Cambridge University Press, 2007), Bxxv–xxvi, pp. 114–5.

2 Immanuel Kant, *Critique of the Power of Judgment*, trans. Paul Guyer and Eric Matthews (Cambridge: Cambridge University Press, 2000), pp. 158–9.

3 G. W. F. Hegel, *Aesthetics: Lectures on Fine Art*, trans. T. M. Knox, 2 vols. (Oxford: Clarendon Press, 1975), vol. I., p. 1.

4 Richard Scholar, *The Je-Ne-Sais-Quoi in Early Modern Europe: Encounters with a Certain Something* (Oxford: Oxford University Press, 2005), pp, 43–59, 196–199; cf. Nicholas Cronk, *The Classical Sublime: French Neoclassicism and the Language of Literature* (Charlottesville: Rookwood Press, 2002), pp. 108–9.

5 'Longinus', *On the Sublime*, trans. W. H. Fyfe, rev. Donald Russell, (Cambridge MA and London: Loeb Classical Library, 1996), vol. XXXII, p.iv.

6 Ibid., XVII.i; cf. XXII.i.

7 Ibid., IX.ii; 1.i.

8 Cronk, *Classical Sublime*, pp. 18–26; *On the Sublime*, XIII.ii.

9 Lucretius, *De Rerum Natura*, trans. W. H. D. Rouse (Cambridge, MA and London: Loeb Classical Library, 1989), III.xxviii–xxx.

10 For Longinus and Lucretius see James I Porter, 'Lucretius and the Poetics of the Void', in A. Monet (ed.), *Le Jardin Romain: Epicurisme et Poésie à Rome. Mélanges offerts à Mayotte Bollack* (Villeneuve d'Ascq: Presses de l'Université Charles-de-Gaulle, 2003), pp. 197–226.

11 Catherine Wilson, *Epicureanism at the Origins of Modernity* (Oxford: Oxford University Press, 2008), pp. 1–38, 88–94; for Pierre Gassendi's influential Christian Epicureanism, see Margaret J. Osler, 'Gassendi on Fortune, Fate and Divination', in Margaret J. Osler (ed.), *Atoms, Pneuma, and Tranquillity: Epicurean and Stoic Themes in European Thought* (Cambridge: Cambridge University Press, 1991), pp. 155–74.

12 See Adam Smith, *The Theory of Moral Sentiments*, ed. D. D. Raphael and A. L. Macfie (Oxford: Clarendon Press, 1979), III.iii.4, p. 137; Burke wrote an admiring letter to Smith after the publication of the *Theory* in May 1759 (C, I: 129–30), but it could not have influenced his revisions to the second edition of the *Philosophical Enquiry*, which had already been published on 10 January 1759.

13 See Terry Eagleton, *The Ideology of the Aesthetic* (London: Blackwell, 1990), pp. 56–7; Tom Furniss, *Edmund Burke's Aesthetic Ideology: Language, Gender and Political Economy in Revolution* (Cambridge: Cambridge University Press, 1993), pp. 31–4.

14 Dennis to Shackleton, March 1758, Beinecke Library, Yale University, Osborn Files 10.213.

15 Shaftesbury, *Characteristicks of Men, Manners, Opinions, Times*, 3 vols. (1711; 2nd ed. 1714), vol. II, p. 29.

16 Cicero, *De Finibus*, (trans.) H. Rackham, (Cambridge, MA and London: Loeb Classical Library, 1989).

17 Horace, *De Arte Poetica in Satires, Epistles, Art of Poetry* (trans.) H. R. Fairclough (Loeb Classical Library 1929). ll.309–22, at 309–11.

18 Shaftesbury, *Characteristicks*, vol. I. pp. 190–209, 192, 195, 205–6.

19 Ibid., vol. II, p. 105.

20 For example, Thomas Paine, *The Rights of Man* (Part 1, 1790) in *Political Writings*, ed. Bruce Kuklick (Cambridge: Cambridge University Press, 1989), p. 59; James Mackinosh, *Vindiciae Gallicae*, ed. Donald Winch (Indianapolis: Liberty Fund, 2006), p. 7; Mary Wollstonecraft *A Vindication of the Rights of Men* (1790) in *Political Writings*, ed. Janet Todd (Oxford : Oxford University Press, 1993), p. 61.

5

SEÁN PATRICK DONLAN

Burke on Law and Legal Theory

Burke's training in, knowledge of, and appreciation for law is generally recognised.[1] Indeed, Anglo-American jurists have been quick to claim him as their own and to employ him as an authority in present debates.[2] But his extensive use of legal language obscures how little he actually said or wrote about legal theory.[3] Burke's comments on the law were typically made in specific and complex, rapidly changing, political controversies. His reflections are often little more than the *obiter dicta* of political and public debates and should not be confused with more formal commentaries on the laws. Pregnant with meaning for the present, Burke's thoughts must, here as elsewhere, be viewed in context. When this is done, his texts suggest a picture that is often at odds with common assumptions about him and his relationship to the law. The Irishman's opinion of English jurisprudence is, for example, complex and not wholly complimentary. Especially in his early pre-political writings, Burke's jurisprudential asides presented a challenge to 'vulgar Whiggism' and insular English and common law histories. His parliamentary statements also suggest that he emphasised the centrality of the legislature rather than, as is often suggested, the courts of common law. Perhaps most importantly, Burke's use of legal terms – contract, partnership, prescription, rights – is often rhetorical, defined against his wider understanding of the relationship of morals, manners, and history.[4]

Laws and Manners

As there was then no place for legal training in his native Ireland, Burke left to study law at London's Middle Temple at the goading of his father, himself a lawyer with the High Court of the Exchequer.[5] The young Burke did not take immediately to his studies. He even flirted with the idea of a literary career before determining that he felt 'comfort that tho a middling Poet cannot be endured there is some quarter for a Middling Lawyer' (C, I: 111). As it turned out, he left his legal studies without entering the Bar. Burke began instead a writing career. His legal studies were no doubt important to his thought and his ideas are consistent with the 'common law mind', the corporate, cumulative development of law over time.[6] But there were similar, equally important sources – the culture of politeness, latitudinarianism, civic thought, and comparative and philosophical histories – that Burke imbibed even earlier. The progressive 'wisdom of the ages' was inherent in contemporary empiricism and what he called, in the *Enquiry*, a 'more extended and perfect induction' (WS, I: 190). This resembles the adjudicative growth of common law, but has as much to do with the corporate growth of science.[7] Here as elsewhere, abstract ideas and general principles played a guiding though falsifiable role, without which 'all reasonings [...] would be only a confused jumble of particular facts and details' (Works, VI: 114). This is not, however, the simple induction of principles from particular cases.[8] Such principles, broader than the rules or rights of law and more adaptable to circumstance, were one of the defining features of European, especially continental, jurisprudence.

Burke developed deep reservations about the narrowness of the legal training of the day and the quality of the public men it produced. Legal education amounted then to little more than attendance in the courts of Westminster and dining with practicing attorneys. It was, he later wrote, a 'narrow and inglorious study' (WS, I: 323).[9] A graduate of the University of Dublin's Trinity College, Burke emphasised instead the importance of a liberal education for those entering the law. In this, at least, he appears to have been in agreement with William Blackstone, whose *A Discourse on the Study of the Law* (1758) made a similar point. As editor and contributor to the *Annual Register*, Burke actually appears to have written a positive review of the *Discourse* (AR, 1758: 452). The *Discourse* served as Blackstone's introduction to his Oxford lectures in 1758, the first in the English common law, and his subsequent *Commentaries on the Laws of England* (1765–9). For Burke, an enlightened jurisprudence had to go beyond law, both pedagogically and philosophically.

By the late 1750s, in addition to his successful publications, Burke had begun to develop a rich web of friendships with many of the leading intellects and artists of the age. Far more important for understanding Burke's thoughts on law and legal theory, he wrote, but never published, two important works on history and law in the late 1750s and early 1760s. Essay towards 'An Essay Towards an Abridgement of the English History' (c1757–62), completed up until the Magna Carta, and a short fragment on English law (c1757) may be the most informative of his texts (WS, I: 338–552; 322–31). Both show him deeply critical of English exceptionalism and insularity.[10] Whatever the virtues of early England, the Saxons were a 'rude and barbarous people' – a trope long in use with the Irish – whose 'liberty' was license and anarchy (WS, I: 430). In a climate that glorified the insular and immemorial nature of English law, Burke wrote that 'the present system of our laws, like our language and our learning, is a very mixed and hetero-geneous mass' (WS, I: 325). Against contemporary party histories, Burke highlighted English improvement through its social commerce or 'commu-nication with the rest of Europe' (WS, I: 453).

It is important to note that Burke's opinion was firmly rooted in the estab-lishment political Whiggism of the mid-eighteenth century. These establish-ment Whigs, like the Rockingham Whigs, sought to undermine the potentially radical histories of Tory writers who had themselves adopted the 'vulgar Whiggism' of the 'ancient constitution'.[11] This latter Whiggism was blink-ered and narrow in its understanding of the English political and legal past, emphasising what many believed to be its exceptionalism. In law, it is asso-ciated with Blackstone and the seventeenth-century English jurist Matthew Hale. But Burke was aligned instead with seventeenth-century jurists like Robert Brady and John Selman. They noted the degree to which English law was importantly European. Burke identified the 'three capital sources' of legal influence on English law as the 'ancient traditionary customs of the North', the 'Canons of the Church, and 'some parts of the Roman civil law' (WS, I: 331). In this and other ways, he is, contrary to superficial analysis of his texts, at odds with both Blackstone and Hale.[12]

By contrast to the ancients, the liberty of the 'moderns' came from the increase of state powers, by the very distance of government from the gov-erned. It eroded the power of local nobility, contributed to the modernisation of many feudal holdovers, led to an increased social mobility and fostered greater levels of social and financial commerce. In jurisprudence, this is seen most clearly in the increasing insistence on a distinction between 'perfect' juridical-political duties (or rights) backed by public sanctions and deemed indispensable for any constituent social order and the 'imperfect' demands and institutions left over, the organs of beneficence (or benevolence). As an important source of self-understanding, the increased universalism of the state suggested a more autonomous, indeed legalistic, concept of the individ-ual. By these developments, those social practices and institutions remain-ing outside the state were thrown into relief. Laws, with their attendant sanctions, were increasingly distinguished from manners and norms.[13] The growing strength of commerce as a 'power' independent of the state only strengthened this tendency.

Where Blackstone, a 'Whiggish' Tory, blamed the Normans for the cor-ruption of English liberty, Burke saw the conquest as joining England with the wider progress of society in Europe. He was specifically critical of Hale for failing to note 'the great changes and remarkable revolutions in the law' over time and for fostering the idea that it was simply 'formed and grew up among ourselves' (WS, I: 323). Burke's account was not a mere jurisprudential history. With the Scots, he maintained that 'the changes […] in the manners, opinions, and sciences of men … [are] as worthy of regard as the fortunes of wars, and the revolutions of kingdoms' (WS, I: 358). Linked to European manners, Burke saw English, and European, law as having progressively improved over time. This modern view was very different from that of many of his contemporaries. Even Montesquieu, 'the greatest genius, which has enlightened this age', was not above criticism (WS, I: 445). Burke suggested, too, that history and the historical method were important elements in a liberal education. He was also, in fact, familiar with a number of leading Scottish jurists and thinkers. With the Scots, Burke exemplifies the most pressing debates and developments – on law, national history, and social change – of the century. His European-wide vision of progressive development rooted in manners would prove to be essential to his critique of the French Revolution.[14]

Burke also spent time in Ireland in the early 1760s, leading to the production of additional texts that shed light on his thoughts on jurisprudence. Burke was active in quieting the reaction of the Dublin government, dominated by the established church, to the so-called 'Whiteboy disturbances'. These agrarian disturbances, mischaracterised as confessional, implicated his own Catholic relatives. Burke was, in fact, nowhere more critical of the laws of Britain and Ireland than in his *Tracts Relative to the Laws Against Propery in Ireland* (c1762–1765) written in the same period. There he recognised that the virtues of a more 'regular, consistent, and stable jurisprudence' – as he put it in the 'Abridgement' – were real, a mark of legal progress and a foundation for social politeness (WS, I: 330). But the abuse of Irish Catholics by means of law struck him as particularly perverse. In the *Tracts*, Burke noted that legal reform was not easy 'because laws, like houses, lean on one another, and the operation is delicate, and should be necessary' (WS, IX: 453). Still, echoing Montesquieu, he wrote that '[t]he Legislature of Ireland, like all Legislatures, ought to frame its Laws to suit the people and the circumstances of the Country' (WS, IX: 650). The *Tracts* also noted the necessity of an 'interior history of Ireland' which would show that Irish grievances were 'not produced by toleration, but by persecution' and resulted 'from unparalleled oppression' (WS, IX: 479). Burke spent considerable time over the next four decades trying to ensure that such histories were written.[15] And while he shared David Hume's scepticism towards England's 'ancient constitution', Burke saw the Scots uncritically repeating the more offensive and prejudicial portrayals of Ireland.

Without appreciating these early texts and contexts, as well as Burke's rich rhetoric, the meaning of his later works may be distorted. In the *Reflections*, for example, Burke wrote that English jurists from '[Lord Edward] Coke [...] to Blackstone, are industrious to prove the pedigree of our liberties', adding that 'if the lawyers mistake in some particulars, it proves my position still the more strongly; because it demonstrates the powerful prepossession towards antiquity' (WS, VIII: 81–2). We can see, however, from these early writings that Burke believed Coke and Blackstone had, with Hale and others, mistaken the particulars. The appeal to the past created a useful continuity necessary for social progress in Europe. But it still remained myth, a point the Irishman would not forget. At its best, the appeal to history was, he said in the *Reflections*, to be 'guided not by the superstition of antiquarians, but by the spirit of philosophical analogy' (WS, VIII: 84). Aware of the virtues of the British constitution, a belief widespread in Europe, Burke was equally conscious of its vices, especially in Ireland, America, and India. And, as will be discussed later, comments of this sort were not a defence of common law adjudication against legislation, but of the British constitution against revolutionary radicalism.

Attempts by critics to link Burke with the so-called Historical School of Jurisprudence of the nineteenth century are also problematic.[16] His influence on German thought is genuine, but simplistically equating his eighteenth-century hostility towards radical revolution with the opposition, especially by Frederick von Savigny, to the nineteenth-century codification of laws is quite seriously misplaced. Like Burke, Savigny emphasised the importance of the past to his present. Both were deeply critical of philosophical rationalism. But Savigny replaced reason with the mystical *Volksgeist*, the 'spirit of the nation or people' linking law and the people. The Historical School was, in fact, linked to the insular nationalism of the nineteenth century and the hope for the creation of a German state. With Montesquieu and others, Burke recognised general differences in national character and culture, but these were extraordinarily fluid. European progress, in both manners and laws, was the result of the 'communication' or interaction of cultures. In the end, the *Volksgeist* resembles nothing so much as the Saxon 'spirit' of vulgar English Whiggism. The often rowdy amalgamation of English and Celts, Protestants and Catholics, Whigs and Tories, that Burke sought to harmonise as a legislator bore little resemblance to such images.

Parliament and the Courts

Not long after returning to England in the 1760s, Burke was working as personal secretary for Charles Watson Wentworth, Lord Rockingham. Shortly afterwards, he entered parliament himself. For nearly twenty years, Burke would serve as the chief ideological spokesman of the Rockingham Whigs. The commercial humanism they sought to maintain was a serious attempt at joining public honour and private interest, balancing the stability and corporate experience of a hereditary aristocracy with the energy and ambition of a 'natural' aristocracy. Their 'civic' languages of critique were very different from the legalist and liberal vocabulary that would come to dominate politics after the Revolution in France.[17] In addition, the reactionary nature of much contemporary populism is especially important to understanding Burke's responses to British radicalism and European revolution. At its best, he saw parliament, as a body, independent of the vagaries of public opinion and the influence of the crown. He spent much of his career engaged in modest, meliorist reform, including unsuccessful economic reforms designed to eliminate feudal holdovers and to reduce crown influence. But Burke championed religious tolerance, spoke against slavery and was critical of many of the more Draconian aspects of contemporary criminal law. The 'true genius' of the British constitution, Burke once confided to Boswell, was 'Tory Language and Whigg [sic] measure' (C, V: 35).

Burke's views on the primacy of the legislature also appear to put him at odds with William Murray, Lord Mansfield, with whom he is often associated. Even though Burke no doubt respected Mansfield's abilities, and the judge was related to Rockingham, the two disagreed on a number of public issues, not least the American war. Mansfield also jailed John Wilkes who was supported by the Rockingham Whigs. Perhaps most damning for Burke, Mansfield was, like Blackstone, a Tory and was linked to John Stuart, Lord Bute. Without descending to the anti-Scottish tirades of fellow Whigs, Burke criticised Bute's influence on the king (as well as the king's on parliament). For his part, Mansfield suspected Burke to be the author of Junius's Letters (1768–72), critical of him and around which another debate on libel arose. Indeed, while the former is credited with creating significant change in English law through the courts, the latter saw legislators rather than judges as the proper agents of legal reform. Given his parliamentary career, this is hardly surprising.

When Mansfield was denying the jury a role in determining questions of law, Burke wrote: 'I have always understood, that a superintendence over the doctrines as well as the proceedings of the courts of justice, was a principal object of the constitution of this House' (Works, VI: 154).[18] The difficult duty of articulating the law – in light of general principles on one hand and the practical limits of local manners on the other – was, in large part, the responsibility of the corporate legislature. Parliament represented, at least 'virtually' and ideally, the public virtue of Britain in a way that the courts could not. In the jury debates, Burke stated that '[t]he Jury are to hear the Judge; the Judge is to hear the Law where it speaks plain where it does not he is to hear the Legislator' (WS, II: 347). Neither English courts nor parliament were alone responsible for institutions like the jury. A development 'so elaborate and artificial as the Jury was [...] brought to its present state by the joint efforts of Legislative authority and judicial prudence' (WS, II: 344). Burke would also continue to emphasise the civic commonplace that it was the rule of men, especially the public virtue of public men, on which justice depended.

Burke's best-known opinion at this stage of his career was his strong opposition to the American war. In debates of the period, he articulated his rejection of legalistic formalism and declarations of abstract right. His objections were both philosophical and political. During the American Revolution, Burke chastised the English parliament's insistence on its formal, theoretical privileges. As with Ireland, what was essential for him were ties of mutual interest and affection.[19] After Rockingham's death in 1782, radical Whigs became more vocal in their demands for extensive constitutional innovations, particularly in representation. British radicals, including religious dissenters, were also critical to the losses of the Rockingham Whigs in the electoral debacle of 1784. The fourteen-year impeachment of Warren Hastings found Burke arguing against any simplistic imposition of British laws and manners on India. Instead, he defended native civilisation and institutions (WS, VII: 168). Burke also noted the 'growing Melioration of the Law' that sought justice beyond legal formalism. Indeed, the close relationship of European culture and commerce 'opened a Communication more largely with other Countries; as the Law of Nature and Nations [...] came to be cultivated; [...] antique Rigour and over-done Severity gave Way to the Accommodation of Human Concerns, for which Rules were made, and not Human Concerns to bend to them' (WS, VII: 163).

The uncertainty of succession in the 'Regency crisis' further exposed the widening divisions over constitutional theory and history. The increasing inflexibility of radical demands in ostensibly 'natural' rights, piqued Burke's hostility. For him, 'abstract principles of natural right – which the dissenters rested on as their strong hold – were the most idle, because the most useless and the most dangerous to resort to. They superceded society, and broke asunder all those bonds which had formed the happiness of mankind for ages'.[20] They threatened, as the revolutionaries would in France, civilisation itself. Burke's focus, he insisted, was instead on the 'civil social man', who in order to 'obtain justice [...] gives up his right of determining what it is in points the most essential to him' (WS, VIII: 110). For him, natural law was expressed or instantiated, however imperfectly, throughout history and a variety of legal orders. This view owed much to both the great pan-European tradition of moral-legal scholarship and contemporary empiricism. But the clarity of claims of natural right were a 'confusion of judicial with civil principles' (Works, III: 109). They were epistemologically unsound and denied the inherently communitarian nature of human association. Politically, they risked the progressive, precarious articulation of political rights in European history.

Burke's doctrine of prescription, which may be seen descriptively as early as the *Abridgement*, became a progressively more important normative requirement in his attempt to pursue and maintain moderate reforms. If Burke's employment of 'prescription' is problematic, it is so because it was unclear how it was to be applied.[21] The legal analogy had little to do with any specific body of law. It may even be universal. And this presumption in favour of established rules and institutions was not uncritical. It was a prudential consideration rooted, in part, on the essentially communal and non-rational nature of human social life and the 'natural' (i.e., naturalistic, basis of human presumption, habituation, etc.). This is related, too, to Burke's critical view, with most of his contemporaries, of any strict doctrine of precedent. With his inherent philosophical-epistemological scepticism towards 'precepts' and 'rules', Burke was always wary of rigid legalism. Neither political nor legal precedent was binding in any simple sense. Indeed, the acceptance of modern *stare decisis*, in which a single decision of a superior court is binding on inferior courts, is a product of nineteenth-century positivism. But '[p]recedents merely as such cannot make Law', Burke wrote, 'because then the very frequency of Crimes would become an Argument of innocence' (WS, IX: 502).[22] Past decisions were persuasive, as evidence of learned opinion of the law and a valuable source of legal stability, but they were not authoritative in themselves.

Reform and Revolution

It was in this context that Burke's response to events in France must be understood. As constitutional reform turned to cultural revolution, the novelty and proselytising spirit of the Revolution became ever more apparent. The *Reflections on the Revolution in France* (1790) was largely aimed at a native audience. Thomas Paine and Richard Price seemed to confirm Burke's belief in important political and philosophical links between British religious radicalism and French revolutionary thought. This revolutionary zeal appeared to him little different from the religious enthusiasm of the British, Irish, and European wars of the previous century. A defender of the modernity of the *anciens régimes*, including his own, Burke did not dread change, but the loss of centuries of European civilisation. It was the slow, fragile development of European manners that ultimately supported both commerce and the laws. In the 'shade' of these manners, 'commerce, and trade, and manufacture, the gods of our oeconomical politicians, are themselves perhaps but creatures; are themselves but effects, which, as first causes, we choose to worship [...] They too may decay with their natural protecting principles' (WS, VIII: 130).[23] Burke's essential concern was for the corporate, mediating, process by which individual and popular will was balanced by public reason.

In what may be his most famous passage, Burke wrote that 'Society is, indeed, a contract' (WS, VIII: 146). But this extract shows, perhaps better than any, the mistake of applying to Burke any narrowly political or jurisprudential reading. It suggests instead the close connections between manners, history, and law in 'a partnership not only between those who are living, but between those who are living, those whose are dead, and those who are to be born' (WS, VIII: 147). Burke's point is precisely to deny that the language of 'contract' is sufficient to understanding or articulating the complexities of human community and history. For Burke, 'society', that is the civil or civilised society, was an entity wider than state or nation. It was the felt sociability and lived associations of men, plural and corporate, enveloping all social practices and institutions. While these were based in natural human dispositions, they were not insignificantly altered by culture and historical circumstance. There are few points more important in understanding Burkean jurisprudence than the recognition that he does not collapse 'civil society' into the state, but sets the state into civilised society. The social practices and manners of a people, not least their economic structures, influenced the character and content of their laws and institutions. Modern legislators must be concerned with manners, and the mediating orders and institutions that moderate them, precisely because he may do so little to alter them.

Burke saw manners as both the source of the laws and practical limits to their efficacy. And manners had, of course, 'natural' sources. For all of the uniqueness of its mechanisms and sanctions, law was ultimately 'beneficence acting by a rule' (WS, VIII: 109). The modern and enlightened cultures of pre-revolutionary Europe were historically progressive, as Burke saw it, precisely because they balanced the inevitable development of relationships of status with those of choice, including contract. This emphasis on manners and beneficence, on nature and culture, is Burke's most serious challenge to the epistemological transparency and ontological subjectivism of the radical Enlightenment, both secular and religious. It also puts him closer to thinkers of the so-called Scottish Enlightenment – and to Irish Catholic historians – than to common lawyers in ultimately prioritising manners (or culture) over law. Law was insufficient without beneficence, just as reason was without sentiment. The 'spirit of our Laws' were founded on 'our own dispositions, which are stronger than Laws' (WS, IX: 110). It is in this sense that manners 'are of more importance than laws' (WS, IX: 242). Burke's jurisprudence is imperfect, in both the general and eighteenth-century senses. For better and worse, he argued that manners and history continually reassert themselves in the face of a more perfect justice that neglected manners, other norms, and the mediating practices and institutions of society.[24]

Conclusion

For Burke, the relationship of law, history, and manners was rooted in the dynamic empiricism of his age, the legacy of the 'culture of politeness', and religious latitudinarianism. What he called, in the *Reflections*, the 'moral constitution of the heart', the formation of individual character, was a sublime amalgamation of native predispositions and cultural influence (WS, VIII: 132). It was on this 'constitution' that the history of European manners and progress was built. In articulating such a view, Burke was working in parallel, if not actually in partnership, with many of the most sophisticated historians and jurists of the day. A 'civil economy' of glory, he believed, continued to provide the social stability necessary for improvement and a link between private and public interest. A commercial humanism provided energy and ambition for social change and 'communication'. Here as elsewhere, the 'civic' traditions, ancient and modern, leavened Burke's faith in commerce and law. Finally, general principles of natural justice, with none of the clarity of revolutionary rights, continued to guide legislators. In the final analysis, law was itself only a highly formal, though critical, method of ensuring public virtue and private beneficence in light of manners and history.

Among the materials in the Burke archives is what appears to be a draft defence of his later, anti-revolutionary writings. There he wrote:

> For the future, I shall stick to my profession. We lawyers do not always make the best hand of a Metaphor. I have burned my fingers with them. In future, I shall avoid all metaphors – I shall stick to my precedent Book ... & my special Pleading ... Oh. Si sic omnia! (NRO, A.xiv.12a–d)[25]

Burke made considerable and colourful use of legal metaphor throughout his life. We must be careful not to burn our fingers. Burke was not, of course, always imprecise. His early comments on law very clearly show him critical of narrow-minded English and common law histories that failed to acknowledge their external debts to the wider progress of society in Europe. We must also be careful with his parliamentary statements, issued in the midst of major public debates, even though he consistently insisted that parliament rather than courts should be at the centre of legal change. More generally, reading his work as a whole suggests that, for Burke, positive law was the imperfect application of natural principles significantly altered by historical circumstance.[26] His use – or misuse – of the language of law was a rhetorical strategy that served as a critique of the thin legalism of revolutionary sloganeering. He defended the modernity of the old regimes, with all of their imperfections, for fear of the loss of centuries of cumulative, corporate progress.[27] Readers, or at least scholars, must be more attentive to these contexts and less determined to rescue Burke for contemporary causes.

NOTES

1 See the posthumous catalogues of Burke's library: S. Deane (ed.), *Sale Catalogues of Libraries of Eminent Persons: Volume VIII – Politicians*, (London: Mansell, 1973) and the Catalogue of the Library of the late Right Hon. Edmund Burke in the Bodleian Library, University of Oxford (Ms. Eng. Misc. d. 722).

2 For a sample of scholarship employing Burke in modern adjudication, especially that of the U. S. Supreme Court, see C. P. Ives, 'Edmund Burke and the Legal Order' in P. J. Stanlis (ed.), *The Relevance of Edmund Burke* (New York: P. J. Kenedy & Sons, 1964), pp. 59–83; Alexander M. Bickel, 'Constitutionalism and the Political Process' in idem., *The Morality of Consent* (New Haven: Yale University Press, 1975), pp. 3–30; B. Schwartz, 'Edmund Burke and the Law', *Law Quarterly Review*, 95 (1979): 355–75; Mark V. Tushnet, 'A Note on the Revival of Textualism in Constitutional Theory', *Southern California Law Review*, 58 (1985): 683–700; J. G. Wilson, 'Justice Diffused: a Comparison of Edmund Burke's Conservatism with the Views of Five Conservative, Academic Judges', *University of Miami Law Review*, 40 (1986): 913–78; Ernest Young, 'Rediscovering Conservatism: Burkean Political Theory and Constitutional Interpretation', *North Carolina Law Review*, 72 (1993): 619–724; Thomas W. Merrill, 'Bork v. Burke', *Harvard Journal of Law & Public Policy*, 19 (1996): 509–24; Stephen B. Presser, 'What would Burke think of Law and Economics?" *Harvard Journal of Law & Public Policy*, 21.1 (1997): 147–54; Steven G. Calabresi, 'The Tradition of the Written Constitution: Text, Precedent, and Burke', *Alabama Law Review*, 57 (2006): 635–88; Cass R. Sunstein, 'Burkean Minimalism', *Michigan Law Review*, 105 (2006): 353–408. See also David Schneiderman, 'Edmund Burke, John Whyte and Themes in Canadian Constitutional Culture', *Queen's Law Journal*, 31 (2006): 579–97.

3 See Christopher Reid, in this volume, and *Edmund Burke and the Practice of Political Writing* (Dublin and New York: Gill and Macmillan/St. Martin's Press, 1985), p. 32.

4 For earlier, more extensive, overviews, see S. P. Donlan 'Beneficence Acting by a Rule: Edmund Burke on Law, History, and Manners', *Irish Jurist*, 36 (2001): 227–64.

5 See Burke's Middle Temple notebooks, (NRO, A.xxx.6).

6 J. G. A. Pocock, 'Burke and the Ancient Constitution – A Problem in the History of Ideas', *Historical Journal*, 3 (1960): 125–43 (reprinted in J. G. A. Pocock,

Politics, Language, and Time: Essays on Political Thought and History [Chicago: University of Chicago Press, 1973] and *The Ancient Constitution and the Feudal law: A Study of English Historical Thought in the Seventeenth Century – a Reissue with a Retrospect* [Cambridge: Cambridge University Press, 1986]).

7   Gerald J. Postema, *Bentham and the Common Law Tradition* (Oxford: Clarendon, 1986), p. 29.

8   Michael Lobban, *The Common Law and English Jurisprudence, 1760–1850* (Oxford: Clarendon, 1991), pp. 1–2.

9   See also C, I: 111.

10   S. P. Donlan '"A Very Mixed and Heterogeneous Mass": Edmund Burke and English Jurisprudence, 1757–62', *University of Limerick Law Review*, 4 (2003): 79–88.

11   Duncan Forbes, *Hume's Philosophical Politics* (Cambridge: Cambridge University Press, 1975), especially pp. 139–50.

12   See, for example, Michael Freeman (ed.), *Lloyd's Introduction to Jurisprudence*, 7th edn. (London: Sweet & Maxwell, 1994), pp. 121–3 and Alasdair MacIntyre, *Whose Justice? Which Rationality?* (South Bend, IN: Notre Dame University Press, 1988), p. 229.

13   See John W. Cairns, 'Blackstone, an English Institutist: Legal Literature and the Rise of the Nation State', *Oxford Journal of Legal Studies*, 4 (1984): 318–60, 345.

14   S. P. Donlan, 'Law and lawyers in Edmund Burke's Scottish Enlightenment', *Studies in Burke and His Time*, 20 (2005): 38–59.

15   S. P. Donlan, 'The "Genuine Voice of its Records and Monuments"?: Edmund Burke's "Interior History of Ireland"' in S. P. Donlan (ed.), *Edmund Burke's Irish Identities* (Dublin: Irish Academic Press, 2007), pp. 69–101.

16   J. M. Kelly, *A Short History of Western Legal Theory* (Oxford: Oxford University Press, 1992), p. 274 and Harold J. Berman, 'The Origins of Historical Jurisprudence: Coke, Selden, Hale', *Yale Law Journal*, 103 (1994): 1651–738, 1737.

17   'Liberalism is', as Pocock has written, the 'child of jurisprudence'. See, J. G. A. Pocock, 'Cambridge Paradigms and Scotch Philosophers: a Study of the Relations between the Civic Humanist and the Civil Jurisprudential Interpretation of Eighteenth-century Social Thought' in Istvan Hont and Michael Ignatieff (eds.), *Wealth and Virtue: the Shaping of Political Economy in the Scottish Enlightenment* (Cambridge: Cambridge University Press, 1983), pp. 235–52, 249.

18   This is contained in the draft speech. The speech as delivered does not contain these lines: see WS, II: 343–9.

19   See S. P. Donlan, 'Little Better than Cannibals: Property and Progress in Sir John Davies and Edmund Burke', *Northern Ireland Legal Quarterly*, 54 (2003): 1–24.

20   'Report of Mr. Burke's speech on 2 March 1790, in the Debates on the Test and Corporation Acts of 1790' in *The Parliamentary Register*, Vol. XXVII, (London: John Debrett, 1790), pp. 178–87, 180.

21   Paul Lucas, 'On Edmund Burke's Doctrine of Prescription; or, an Appeal from the New to the Old Lawyers', *Historical Journal*, 11 (1968): 35–63.

22   See Anthony T. Kronman, 'Precedent and Tradition', *Yale Law Journal*, 99 (1990): 1029–68.

23 See J. G. A. Pocock, 'The Political Economy of Burke's Analysis of the French Revolution' in *Virtue, Commerce, and History: Essays in Political Thought and History, Chiefly in the Eighteenth Century* (Cambridge: Cambridge University Press, 1985), pp. 193–212 and 'Edmund Burke and the Redefinition of Enthusiasm: the Context as Counter-Revolution' in F. Furet and M. Ozouf (eds.), *The French Revolution and the Creation of Modern Political Culture: Volume 3, the Transformation of Political Culture 1789–1848* (Oxford and New York: Pergamon Press, 1990), pp. 19–43.

24 See Garrett Barden, 'Discovering a Constitution' in Tim Murphy and Patrick Twomey (eds.), *Ireland's Evolving Constitution, 1937–97: Collected Essays* (Oxford: Hart Publishing, 1998), pp. 1–10, 4.

25 This last phrase means, roughly, 'oh that it were so'.

26 Peter Stein, *Legal Evolution: The Story of an Idea* (Cambridge: Cambridge University Press, 1980), p. 58.

27 S. P. Donlan, '"Language Is the Eye of Society": Edmund Burke on the Origins of the Polite and the Civil', *Eighteenth-Century Ireland/Iris an dá Chultúr*, 18 (2003): 80–97.

6

RICHARD WHATMORE

Burke on Political Economy

Burke's Fears for the Future of Europe.

Scholars of Burke's writings have sometimes seen his engagement with the French Revolution, towards the end of his life, to have been an 'unkindness of fate', on the grounds that a person 'who has all his life surrounded himself with a mental paradise of order and equilibrium and belief' was forced to confront its antithesis.[1] Such an interpretation correlates with a view of the eighteenth century, and of Britain above any other country, as being characterised largely by equipoise, calm, and order. Burke was laying the foundations for Victorian self-confidence, and was on the side of progress in defining and defending the British constitution, and more particularly the manners it rested upon, as the great bastion against immoderation and excess, whether in the form of atheistic or democratical enthusiasm. Yet Burke's fears about the future, and the future of Europe especially, antedated 1789. Like Gibbon too, he had long been worried about the instability of Europe, because of the gap between the military strength of small and large states, which rested in turn upon the economic ability of bigger states to exploit large markets and to create a public debt, on the basis of anticipated income from taxation, that provided revenues for war. Aspiring imperial powers, always likened to Rome, germinated in such soil, and explained events like the partition of Poland by Prussia, Russia, and Austria in 1772. The event had exercised Burke in a letter to the scion of a prominent Prussian family in 1774, and represented one of many laments for the prospects of Europe's small states. Burke called Poland 'but a breakfast' (C, II: 512–14).

Peace was the overriding goal of politics. Burke proclaimed that it was more important than truth: 'I would, unless the Truth were evident indeed, hold fast to Peace, which has in her company Charity, the highest of the virtues' (Works VI: 99). Arriving at peace, in every sphere of life, entailed the study of political economy, which fascinated Burke from his very first essays on the state of Ireland in his youthful 'Reformer'.[2]

Scholars such as John Pocock, who see the eighteenth century as an age of intellectual crisis, have altered perspectives on Burke's politics and political economy by linking Burke's ideas to the international wars that characterised every decade bar the 1720s, and to the speculation about the future that then dominated political enquiry.[3] Political economy as a subject was significant as it promised to reveal means to domestic economic health. Seen from this perspective, Burke can be associated with distinct approaches to national economics. A great deal of work has been done on Burke's relationship with leading political economists of his time, and above all with Adam Smith. Burke's *Thoughts and Details of Scarcity* (1795) advocated *laissez-faire* policy with respect to the grain trade, agricultural prices, and wages, and equated the laws of the market with Divine Providence. The poor were expected to rely upon the imperfect obligation of charity, and the labouring poor were advised to respect the natural hierarchy of social subordination, enforced by the state-supported national church. Such views are sometimes associated with Smith's opinions, but Burke's defence of a permanent landed aristocracy, and the feudal laws of primogeniture and entail, were at odds with Smith's recognition of the profound injustices of commercial society, and his consistent opposition to corporation, whether clerical or unions of manufacturers seeking to depress the wages of their employees.[4] Burke can emerge as rigid conservative and die-hard economic liberal, devoted to the interests of the landed class, and of the claim that a landed aristocracy was the surest defence against tyranny in modern times.

A different perspective comes when we accept that by 1795 Burke perceived himself to be defending a world being destroyed by international war. The *Thoughts and Details* were above all concerned with maintaining the argument that Britain could remain a stable polity in the face of the French Republican threat. Burke was convinced that economic stability was one of the benefits of the primacy of the landed interest in political life. Smith, by contrast, believed that reform was gradually to be recommended domestically, to ameliorate the injustices of commercial society, but that internationally it was unwise for Britain to play an imperial role long into the future. Burke, in the final years of his life, believed that Britain could both maintain an empire and prevent aspirations to universal monarchy on mainland Europe. This comes to the fore when the meaning of political economy in its eighteenth-century form is recalled. Political economy was the archetypal science of reform, premised on the unavoidability of commercial society as an element of human progress, and encompassing in consequence international relations as the correlate of domestic reform. As Burke put it, the subject dealt with relations between 'war, peace, trade and finances', the key being to 'reconcile national defence with public economy'

(WS, II: 114, 161). Upon applying this definition of political economy to Burke's writings, we see a more consistent figure emerge, one that has a coherent set of attitudes and commitments – to Europe, to the defence of small states, and, in particular, to Ireland. He changed his mind, however, on how to achieve these goals. Although in the 1790s revolutionary France was threatening to wipe away Britain's historic, political culture, Burke had long been aware that Britain could be seen as the revolutionary power with respect to Ireland, with a similarly corrosive effect upon Irish institutions and mores. Burke's interest in political economy arose in part because the discipline promised the pursuit of policies that might prevent Irish culture and manners from being overwhelmed by those of larger states like Britain or France. Such an approach equally reveals a Burke seeking to justify a revolution in political economy at the end of his life, by connecting Britain's political and economic future with the Europe he wanted to defend, and by justifying military intervention and war to prevent new Romes from developing, whether governed by ceasars or by plebeians.

The Context of Burke's Political Economy

For numerous observers, the eighteenth century ought to have been characterised by the continued rise of France, whose Gallicanism and absolutist politics had been asserted so aggressively by Louis XIV, and appeared to provide a model of efficiency and commercial development capable of sustaining an empire founded on dominion across central Europe.[5] Mixed states, and more particularly mixed governments forming part of a composite monarchy, had traditionally been perceived to be incapable of successfully sustaining wars, but England and Wales, in an alliance of Protestant powers after 1688/9, and Britain, after the Anglo-Scottish union of 1707, shocked contemporaries by doing exactly this. Britain's capacity to wage war was sometimes explained by the composite nature of the polity, and particularly the Celtic fringes that were reputed to supply troops who fought like savages, but was more often associated with flourishing national commerce, and with public credit. One major issue was whether Britain could continue to oppose France across Europe. Arthur Young, the travel-writer and agricultural reformer, and a friend of Burke's, consistently reminded his readers that Britain was inferior in national resources, population, size, and civilisation to France.[6] Sooner or later the larger power must defeat Britain, and restore a politics in which international prominence was correlated with national power. Such arguments reflected the extensive jeremiad literature that had developed anticipating Britain's decline. Within such writing, the term 'mercantile system' became commonplace. It signified the unnatural progress of opulence towards anti-competitive forms of trade. The commercial companies that were supported by laws to restrict competitive trade from other nations exemplified the system. The surest illustration of the effects of the policy was the uneven and constrained nature of the trade of Ireland.

Viewed from France, the issue was whether Britain would self-destruct as an empire by war or bankruptcy; whether it could be vanquished by military prowess, or whether it might be challenged by the development of more moral and stable forms of commerce that were nevertheless capable of out-competing their mercantile counterparts. The alternative was that France became mercantile in the manner of the British, and developed a national debt to the same extent. Contemporaries were, however, fearful that armies funded by credit would lead to the rule of new tyrants. Bankruptcy caused by excessive credit was associated with popular rebellion headed by a latter-day Spartacus. Perhaps the most feared possibility was voluntary bankruptcy, whereby an absolute monarch expanded credit to strengthen the military capacities of their state, and then sacrificed the creditors in the name of national survival or imperial glory, creating a potentially all-powerful polity inimical to liberty and addicted to war. The deadly consequences of national bankruptcy, whether unintended or inspired by a corrupt monarch, were likened by David Hume, in his essay 'Of Public Credit', to a cudgel match in a china shop.[7] In an era of experiment with representative government and more general constitutionalism, another danger commonly identified was that the imperative of paying the national debt would lead wealthy creditors to control politicians and statesmen. Alternatively, high taxes would beggar the populace, or at the very least reduce commercial competitiveness, making rich states prey to their poorer neighbours, and necessitating the intensification of mercantile policy.

Such concerns made the eighteenth century an era of acute pessimism about the future of commercial empires. It was also an era of constant innovation with respect to conjectures intended to prevent economic decline and, in the cases of Britain and of France, to secure international supremacy. In the background for British and French authors was the constant fear of a new form of government that required a new coinage, 'oriental despotism', foreseeing the fall of Europe's effeminate and exhausted monarchies before vast marauding slave-based armies from the East. Many observers took an interest in the 'Asiatic' or 'Oriental' despotisms of the East, and pre-eminently Russia, which several authors, and Rousseau most famously in the second book of the *Contrat Social*, believed would invade Western Europe as soon as the commercial monarchies of France and Britain were weakened by war or fell prey to bankruptcy. For Rousseau, as for so many eighteenth-century observers, the salient fact about civilised monarchies was that they were organised for war. The oft-repeated claim that in Britain's case the economy had grown to an 'unnatural' extent and in a dangerous direction, and that France's international status was not in accordance with its underlying power, meant that few authors were phlegmatic with regard to the future of these states. The view was everywhere accepted that security was the product of economic success, even if, because of the low wages prevalent in poorer states, this success was unlikely to be permanent. All of these factors together (the intrinsic instability of commercial empires, the militant nature of civilised monarchies and an emerging Asiatic threat) explained for contemporaries why the long eighteenth century experienced near-constant war across Europe and in the colonies. In turn, this was why so many observers, however uncertain they were about the future of the great commercial empires of Europe, were convinced that the independence of the smaller states was likely to be short-lived. The future-of-Britain question was linked to such concerns because of the expectation that a victorious France would alter the face of Europe, and in all likelihood invade Britain itself either directly or through Ireland.

In every area of intellectual life, Burke prided himself upon the consistency of his opinions. Part of the difficulty with such a claim was the variety of causes Burke championed, particularly within the House of Commons. Another was Burke's sensitivity to place, history, and practicality and his constant opposition to speculators and projectors, whose uniform solutions to the problems of the day forever had to be castigated. As Burke put it, 'Procrustes shall never be my hero of legislation' because his iron bed entailed the cutting of the long limb or 'the torturing of the short into length'. Such was the state-bed of uniformity (WS, II: 176). The resulting difficulty in boiling down Burke's views into a series of 'Maxims and opinions' was evident in the two-volume compilation of the early nineteenth century, whose long citations from Burke's various writings mainly served to underscore the complexity of Burke's response to issues ranging from 'clamour of citizens against monopoly' to 'embassies from individuals to foreign powers'.[8] With regard to political economy, Burke consistently articulated two opinions. These marked him out from the majority of contemporary observers. More importantly, they formed the foundation of his political economy. The first was a constant opposition to 'national despondency'. As he put it in the *Letters on a Regicide Peace*, there was never 'reason to apprehend, because ordinary means threaten to fail, that no others can spring up.' Although Britain's 'pulse seems to intermit, we must not presume that it will cease instantly to beat.' In short, 'the publick must never be regarded as incurable' (WS, IX: 192). The second opinion was that the established identity of Europe had to be maintained. Modern Europe was in a more flourishing state than any historic continent, and enjoyed more liberty even than the ancient republics. Europe had to be protected at all costs (WS, IX: 287).

If maintaining a Europe characterised by a multitude of national varieties was the central goal of Burke's political economy, different means to this end were envisaged during Burke's life. Indeed, his most radical solution was formulated only when, with Gibbon, he was in despair about republican France. The prospects for France, its impact upon Europe, and the resulting relationship with Britain, were the issues that dominated political economy throughout Burke's life.

Burke's View of Britain and of France

The eighteenth century was the great age of comparative study in political economy in part because of the expectation that Europe was on the verge of another decline and fall. That Burke considered himself a contributor to the ongoing debate was clear in the work he co-authored with his close friend William Burke, the *Account of the European Settlements in America,* which appeared on 1 April 1757, and provided an evaluation of the trading strategies of the Spanish, Portuguese, Dutch, French, and British empires, with the intention of revealing 'how our colonies have grown, what their vegetative principle has been, in what vigour it subsists, or what signs of corruption appear in any of them.' As such, it was significant because it offered guidance on British policy during the general conflagration of the Seven Years' War, which saw Britain, Prussia, Portugal, and allied German states pitted against France, Austria, Sweden, Saxony, Spain, and Russia. The *Account* made clear that the most flourishing European power abroad was France, and expressed a desire that Britain learn from the power with which 'we have been engaged for above a century [...] in a noble contention for the superiority in arms, in politics, in learning, and in commerce'.[9]

The Burkes' central claim was that French strength could be traced in part to wise governance of its colonies, through a council devoted to commercial development, and the balanced powers of a colonial governor and the monarch's administrator, the 'intendant', in the region. France was the greatest threat to Britain, being 'vigorous and enterprising', and desirous of the acquisition of the colonies of Spain. The Burkes recommended a moderate tax regime for the colonies and their cultivation 'with tenfold industry', in imitation of the French regime in North America, including a more humane regime towards the treatment of slaves, without challenging slavery itself or the importance of the trade to the British economy. It was their view that the outcome of the war would be determined by the cultivation 'of the

advantages we have with care and judgement'.[10] The value of colonies was
that they provided goods unavailable at the 'mother country', and generated
profits for domestic merchants, which could be balanced against the costs
of import in addition to the effect of strengthening the profits of commercial rivals in competitor nations.[11] Rather than adding to the sum of gold
or silver, perceived to be the Spanish approach to colonies, the key was the
commercial development of the colony and particularly of the commercial
relationship with the mother country:

> Our present intercourse with them is an emulation in industry; they have noth-
> ing that does not arise from theirs, and what we receive enters into our manu-
> factures, excites our industry, and increases our commerce; whereas gold is the
> measure or account, but not the means of trade. And it is found in nations as
> it is in the fortunes of private men, that what does not arise from labour, but is
> acquired by other means, is never lasting. Such acquisitions extinguish indus-
> try, which is alone the parent of any solid riches.[12]

France conducted itself differently with Spain, which was as powerful an
empire as Britain, and as rapacious in its desire for commerce. The Burkes
acknowledged that the ongoing battle between the imperial superpowers
had to be won by Britain: 'we ought to use every method to repress them, to
prevent them from extending their territories, their trade, or their influence,
and above all to connive at not the least encroachment'.[13] The *Account* did
not provide a view of how to defeat France, other than the general policy of
Britain's colonial development.

The literature of jeremiad reached a peak in the aftermath of the Seven
Years' War. It represented uncertainty about Britain's capacity to maintain
itself as the major European power, as articulated by the Treaty of Paris
of 1763. Such a position was doubted in part because the national debt
generated by the war continued to rise. Attempts to reduce it, by taxing the
colonies, had resulted in the kind of rebellion that had manifested itself in
North America against the Stamp Act (1765) and Townsend Acts (1767).
For the followers of George Grenville and John Stuart, 3rd Earl of Bute, the
simple fact was that Britain could not continue to combat France both mili-
tarily and economically. France appeared to be in rude economic health, to
be coping with debt, and to be more confident about its imperial ambition.
The latter was evinced by the French Foreign Minister Étienne François,
duc de Choiseul's annexation of Corsica and of Lorraine to France, which
Britain accepted with barely a murmur. For William Knox, the spokesman
of the Grenvillites, Britain was in decline and in danger of becoming a tribu-
tary to France. Taxes had to be levied upon the colonies and upon Ireland in
order to pay the national debt, and a less prominent position embraced with
respect to international relations.[14]

Burke's response to Knox, in his *Observations on a Late State of the Nation* (1769) and *Thoughts on the Present Discontents* (1770), articulated a perspective on political economy that he was to expound up to the outbreak of war with France in 1792. The first element was that Britain's predicament was not 'piteously doleful'. Rather than suffering from 'radical weakness and constitutional distempers', the current polity was in good health (WS, II: 112). Constitutionally, 'the old building stands well enough, though part Gothic, part Grecian, and part Chinese, until an attempt is made to square it into uniformity. Then it may come down upon our heads all together in much uniformity of ruin; and great will be the fall thereof' (WS, II: 175). Schemes to allow colonies to send members to the House of Commons were impractical, given the need to make trips back and forth across the ocean, in order for any sense of interest to be properly conveyed. Britain's trade continued to thrive. Scotland was undergoing an economic transformation, and Britons were not overtaxed by comparison with subjects of other states, and particularly those of France. Indeed, Burke stated that the size of the French debt was so great that they 'must hourly look for some extraordinary convulsion in that whole system' (WS, II: 151).

Proof of Britain's strength lay in the recent success in war, 'the most prosperous we ever carried on, by sea and by land, and in every part of the globe, attended with the unparalleled circumstance of an immense increase of trade and augmentation of revenue' (WS, II: 116). France remained a dangerous enemy, particularly as during the Seven Years' War 'the whole Spanish monarchy was melted down into the cabinet of Versailles' (WS, II: 129). Burke lamented that colonies had not been acquired during the Seven Years' War, such as Guadeloupe or Martinique, which would have generated revenue through economic development (WS, II: 116–30). But the existing empire was capable of generating income. This could only be done by supporting the colonies and Ireland rather than by taxing them:

> Some establishments pay us by a *monopoly* of their consumption and their produce. This, nominally no tax, in reality comprehends all taxes. Such establishments are our colonies. To tax them would be as erroneous in policy, as rigorous in equity. Ireland supplies us by furnishing troops in war; and by bearing part of our foreign establishment in peace. She aids us at all times by the money that her absentees spend amongst us; which is no small part of the rental of that kingdom. Thus Ireland contributes her part. (WS, II: 176)

Burke attacked opponents of commerce and of luxury, fears about which were epitomised by John Brown in his *Estimate of the Manners and Principles of the Times* (1757–58), which Burke condemned for its utopian attack upon aristocracy. It was foolish, Burke argued, 'to introduce poverty, as a constable to keep the peace' (WS, II: 254). Even if it was accepted that the colonies were 'roots which feed all this rank luxuriance of sedition, it is not intended to cut them off in order to famish the fruit' (WS, II: 254). In sum, removing the colonies in order to restore virtue was as foolish as alienating the colonies through excessive taxation. Burke envisaged the gradual development of the empire through liberal economic relationships.[15] Burke's later *Speech on American Taxation* and *Speech on Conciliation* were developments of Burke's *Speech on Declaratory Resolution* of 1766, and were in accordance with all of the writings against political Jeremiahs (WS, II: 45–51, 429–32, 460–2). Britain could stand against France once a long period of peace had seen economic growth sufficient to pay the debts of the state, so long as this policy was coupled with retrenchment at home, and the prevention of excessive monarchical power in domestic policy. There was no need for another war in Europe, either to vanquish France or to establish further European colonies that looked to Britain. Whereas states like Ireland were characterised by huge economic potential, they needed to be looked to, in order to create a stable imperial polity. Accordingly Burke could declare that he was consistent in his advocacy of 'liberality in the commercial system', because it entailed giving 'all possible vigour and soundness to those parts [of the empire] which are still content to be governed by our councils' (WS, IX: 507–8).

Burke and the Revolution in British Political Economy

When the North American crisis turned into another international war Burke declared himself to be astonished at the economic strength of France, which appeared to have learned from Britain and created a stable system of credit guaranteed by a fierce patriotism (WS, III: 486–90). He was equally worried that 'war, indeed, is become a sort of substitute for commerce', because mercantile schemes for supplying means of war were flourishing, while commerce in domestic necessities appeared to flounder (C, III: 189–96). Yet Burke remained consistent in his vision of a return to peace and of gradual economic development. He believed that the mercantile system, the evils of which he recognised in the person and activities of Warren Hastings, could be combated by adherence to existing laws, and did not require the realisation of grand schemes for the removal of injustice, luxury, and disorder from the world. When the French Revolution broke out, Burke, in his letter to Sir Philip Francis of 20 February 1790, drew a parallel between projectors in France and in Britain, linking by the 'coffee-houses of Paris and the dissenting meeting houses of London'. First among the latter party in Britain was William Petty, 2nd Earl Shelburne, and his circle of intellectuals and dissenters including Joseph Priestley and Richard Price. Burke declared that his intention in writing the *Reflections on the Revolution in France* was not 'controversy with Dr Price, or Lord Shelburne, or any other of their set', but rather a complete refutation of their politics: 'to set in full view the danger from their wicked principles and their black hearts' (C, VI: 188–92).

The French were providing proof that Burke was correct in his politics. Britain was not on the brink of ruin. Britain's constitution was compatible with empire, and with a positive economic relationship, linking political dominion with economic union in the case of Britain's colonies. The mercantile system had to be combated, but economic liberty was only gradually to be instituted, and in circumstances where little damage was going to be done to the interests that formed the polity. The corporations of national life, such as those of the church and government, had to be preserved. The alternative was to erect states without social hierarchies, and with a secular civil religion, causing power to be separated from property, a process that ultimately led atheists to power, and their turning into 'furious' and 'extravagant' republicans (WS, VIII: 174, 369–72). Democratic doctrines everywhere fostered ignorance and cruelty. Democratic government generated tyranny (WS, VIII: 253–9). When the French armies invaded the Austrian Netherlands and opened the river Scheldt to trade in the winter of 1792, war was declared on 1 February 1793, and Britain joined Prussia, Austria, Spain, Portugal, and the Netherlands against France.

Burke did not expect the fusion of atheism and democracy at Paris to generate a state so powerful that it could once more take steps towards European hegemony. He was even more surprised that when the most extensive coalition of princes yet seen in European warfare was established, to combat French imperial ambition, its forces were vanquished in successive military engagements (WS, IX: 55–60). By 1795 the coalition was broken up. All of Holland had by this time been overrun and Frederick William II of Prussia withdrew his forces from the war. In Britain numerous members of the government, including William Pitt, were inclined to make peace with France. This was the background to Burke's final works. The most important, his *First Letter on a Regicide Peace*, was completed by February 1796. Burke called for a moral war to defend the independence of Europe's states small and large, all of which were being annexed, colonised, and domestically transformed, in accordance with the principles of revolutionary government.

Burke had always seen France as a threat to the 'system of Europe, taking in laws, manners, religion, and politics, in which I delighted so much' (C, IX: 307). In the past, however, Burke had not considered it to be necessary for Britain to combat France directly on mainland Europe, to invade France itself, or to become involved in mainland European politics in the sense of directing international relations between fellow states. The French Revolution altered everything. Burke began to argue that it was necessary to restore the French monarchy, its civil and ecclesiastical orders, and their property. The only means to such an end was a revolution in British foreign policy, entailing intervention in Europe in order to keep the peace, to protect the old world, and to maintain it for the economic development of all those states who favoured trade, morals, and religion.[16] As Burke put it, Britain had become 'the great resource of Europe.' Britain could no longer be 'detached from the rest of the world, and amusing herself with the puppet-shew of a naval power.' Rather, Britain had to be 'embodied with Europe' (WS, IX: 196). The resulting war was 'just, necessary, manly, pious.' Its goal was to preserve 'political independence and civil freedom to nations [...] national independence, property, liberty, life, and honour, from certain universal havock' (WS, IX: 238). In short, it was a war for all nations.

Burke did not expect his policy to be embraced. He died worried that revolutionary doctrines were developing both in Britain and in Ireland. With regard to the latter state, he had envisaged a gradual union, initially based on economic ties generated by economic liberty, that would put Ireland in a similar position to Scotland before its own union with England and Wales. The problem was that English politicians were ignorant and uninterested (C, IX: 112–18). The tension in Burke's vision was that his ultimate solution to the problems of protecting the independence and culture of small states, namely union, depended on Britain remaining Burke's ideal polity: one that has seen free commerce gradually realised, and one in which a *modus vivendi* existed between the crown, the aristocracy, and the people, rather than a Spanish-style empire founded on the oppression and forced conversion of minorities. Burke died before he could complete his attack upon any attempt to make peace with revolutionary France. By 1815 Europe had been transformed, but the doctrine of armed intervention to protect the small states of Europe, for the development of commerce and the maintenance of peace, had become an element of British foreign and commercial policy. The doctrine was always to be contested, but was maintained until the international wars that it led Britain to be involved with transformed Britain into a relatively small state, and one incapable of supporting an empire.

NOTES

1 John Morley, *Edmund Burke: A Historical Study* (London, 1867), pp.254–5.
2 F. P. Lock, *Edmund Burke* (Oxford: Oxford University Press, 1998), vol. I, pp. 2–3, 55–9, 63.
3 J. G. A. Pocock, 'The Political Economy of Burke's Analysis of the French Revolution' in *Virtue, Commerce and History: Essays on Political Thought and History, Chiefly in the Eighteenth Century* (Cambridge: Cambridge University

Press, 1985), pp. 193–212; 'Edmund Burke and the Redefinition of Enthusiasm: the Context as Counter-Revolution', *The French Revolution and the Creation of Modern Political Culture. Volume Three. The Transformation of Political Culture 1789–1848,* ed. F. Furet and M. Ozouf (Oxford:, Pergamon, 1990), pp. 19–43.

4 Compare F. Canavan, *The Political Economy of Edmund Burke. The Role of Property in His Thought* (New York: Fordham University Press, 1995), pp. 6, 13–15, 116–17, 158 and D. Winch, *Riches and Poverty. An Intellectual History of Political Economy in Britain, 1750–1834* (Cambridge: Cambridge University Press, 1996), pp. 170–220.

5 S. Pinkus, *1688. The First Modern Revolution* (New Haven: Yale University Press, 2009), pp. 118–78.

6 Arthur Young, *Letters Concerning the Present State of the French Nation* (London: W. Nicoll, 1769), pp. 1–16, 394–425.

7 David Hume, 'Of Public Credit', *Essays and Treatises on Several Subjects,* 2nd edn., (Edinburgh, 1753), vol. IV, p. 119.

8 Burke, *Maxims and Opinions: Moral, Political, and Economical,* 2 vols. (London: C. Wittingham, 1804, 1811), vol. I, p. 41.

9 William Burke and Edmund Burke, *An Account of the European Settlements in America. In Six Parts* 2 vols. (London: R. and J. Dodsley, 1757), vol. II, pp. 47, 284–5.

10 Ibid., vol. II, pp. 22–4, 38–48.

11 Ibid., vol. II, pp. 106–12.

12 Ibid., vol. II, pp. 285–6.

13 Ibid., vol. II, pp. 287.

14 William Knox, *The Present State of the Nation: Particularly with Respect to Its Trade, Finances &c.* (London: 1769), pp. 34–6, 71.

15 R. Bourke, 'Liberty, Authority and Trust in Burke's Idea of Empire', *Journal of the History of Ideas,* 61.3 (2000): 453–71; Iain Hampsher-Monk, 'Edmund Burke and Empire' in D. Kelly (ed.), *Lineages of Empire* (London: British Academy, 2009), 117–36.

16 R. Bourke, 'Edmund Burke and the Politics of Conquest', *Modern Intellectual History,* 4.3 (2007): 403–32; I. Hampsher-Monk, 'Edmund Burke's Changing Justification for Intervention', *Historical Journal,* 48.1 (2005): 65–100.

7

IAN HARRIS

Burke and Religion

Edmund Burke was not a theologian, but a man of letters and a statesman: it was in these capacities that he was deeply interested in Christianity and its importance for society. He did not conceive religion as an activity of body or mind insulated from the rest of life and thought, but rather as a relation between God and people which, in a range of ways, characterised central aspects of their terrestrial lives as well as their eventual destiny. It will be best to turn to specifics in order to understand what Burke had in view.

Early Thought

Burke was educated – whether at home or Ballitore School or Trinity College, Dublin – at places where the truth of Christianity was assumed. By the time he left Trinity, he had an orientation towards religion, improvement, and politics. Ireland at that date was a place where reflective thinking had its main social setting in a small educational elite, much of it connected with the Church of Ireland. This elite contemplated a political class that owned much of the land, and consisted primarily of a gentry and peerage, headed by the king's representative, the lord-lieutenant, but this elite saw too a tiny professional class, and a huge, illiterate, impoverished peasantry. The aim of the educational elite, which it shared with some of the political class, was improvement in the broadest sense, that is to say it connected self-improvement, via the arts and sciences and through the development of intellectual skills, with moral culture and with economic development. The Irish situation suggested a general rationale of practice to those who wished to improve themselves and others: improvement, if it was to spread outside the educational elite, must spring from the guidance and good will of the possessing classes – from the landlord who developed his property, from the priest who instructed and consoled the poor, and from the lord-lieutenant who used his power benevolently. In other words, direction was from above, and it needed to be given in an easily intelligible form.

This was the social role the young Burke attributed to the Christian religion: that is to say, a doctrine that was not only beneficial but also took a form that made it intelligible to all people, even the simplest. The debating society that he founded at Trinity required impromptu speeches. One topic that fell to Burke himself was a 'commonplace' about the Sermon on the Mount (Matt. 5–7). The Sermon on the Mount is at the centre of Christian worship and conduct. Jesus Christ's doctrine was stated there in respect of both prayer to God and conduct towards other people. The prayer is the Lord's Prayer, and the ethics include the injunction to love not only our neighbours but also our enemies. The Sermon thus makes a distinctive statement about both tables of the Decalogue. The Decalogue, or statement of ten laws, embodied the code that God, according to Exodus, delivered to Moses. The Decalogue had come to be divided into two tables. The first table grouped the commandments relating to the worship of God, while the second concerned duties towards other people. The two tables were summarised as 'love [...] God [...] and love thy neighbour as thyself' (Matt. 22: 37–40). The Lord's Prayer offers submission to God's will, and includes a wish that it should prevail upon earth – a wish that implies the wish to love one's neighbour.

Burke emphasised two points about the Sermon on the Mount. One was the implication of the love commandments: that our disposition – which, in the language of his day, included 'the heart' and 'passions' – was addressed and improved by Christian teaching. The other was that its morality, precisely because it was prescribed by Christ rather than reached by the complicated logomachies of reason, was accessible to everyone that heard or read it, even 'the most ignorant'. For these reasons – its moral content and its intelligibility to all – Christian morality tended to sustain and improve society. Let Burke speak for himself. He had

> taken occasion to observe how much the Christian morality excels the Best heathen by refining our passions, not only our acts but [also] their spring, the heart, our divine physician heals the corrupted source, the others but surgeons tampering with the outward sores. very defective in that, when we stand in two grand relations the one to Society & the other to our Creator – it only teaches the first. that nothing Was better for Society & that this its excellent policy insted of being an objection to it, was one of the greatest proofs of its divinity. that the Heathens even the wisest & best were employ'd a long time in searching what was good or Virtue & consequently lost a good deal of practice – that the most learned were much puzzled in their enquiry & the ignorant could know nothing at all. But the Gospel by substituting faith which the most ignorant can have gives us the preceptor & leaves us immediately to the practice. that the morality inculcated in this ecellent sermon conduced so admirably to the improvement of society that had its rules been observed we

should have a heaven upon earth. but since men are so wicked that this cannot be[,] those who do may be sure of finding it in a better place.[1]

We see Christian teaching underwriting society. Christian churches were capable of contributing directly to the cohesion and improvement of society.

Burke presumed the truth of Christianity – as we see in his presumption that 'we stand' in relation to God, and that Christian morality implies 'heaven upon earth' – but he did not recommend Christian morality firstly because it was true or even implied a life 'in a better place', but because 'nothing Was better for Society'. In other words, he recommended it in terms that were independent of its truth. What were the bearings of his claims?

Christianity versus deism

Theology in Western Europe during Burke's lifetime was understood to have two forms, natural and revealed. A fundamental question about natural theology was its sufficiency for human welfare – or, to put the question in another way, whether a revealed theology was necessary for that end. We have just seen Burke answer that it was necessary, and the matter we need to pursue is the effects of this conclusion on his early thought. In order to do this, we must first examine the other side of the question, for Burke's scepticism about it was an important feature of that thought.

What is natural theology? It is the set of propositions about God and His ways that can be reached by any human mind from the resources provided by its own equipment – its senses and reason – unaided by any other resource. Revealed theology is the set of propositions about God and His ways that can be collected from sources that God is reckoned to have disclosed directly. Christian theology proceeds from the revelation provided by God through Jesus Christ and recorded in the New Testament, as well as in some sense fulfilling the earlier revelation God had provided, recorded in the Old Testament. But Christian theology (so the argument ran in the eighteenth century) was not independent of natural theology, for neither Old nor New Testament demonstrates the existence of God or His attributes. Rather they assume Him. Christian thinkers therefore took natural theology and revealed theology to be complementary: the former provides indications of God's existence and His attributes, whereas the Testaments provide information about His actions. In this sense, nature and revelation point to the same conclusion. But, one can add, one feature of revealed theology is that it happens to have been communicated to a very limited number of people, and spread by them to a larger, but still limited number: revealed theology was not, in Burke's time, known to all human beings.

This is where we encounter the position taken by the deists. They held by natural theology, but eschewed Christianity. They thought that if God was good, His goodness would lead Him to exert His concern for human welfare in a way that made salvation accessible to all. But revelation had not been accorded to all. It had been given, in the first place, to the Jews only, and then, through Christ, to a small fraction of humanity. Even if one supposed, contrary to fact in those days, that Christianity was accessible to the whole world, what of the welfare of all who had perished without it in earlier times? The deists' point was made in two propositions:

> That Rule which is necessary to our future Happiness,
> ought to be generally made known to all men. [...]
> Therefore no Revealed Religion is necessary to future
> Happiness.

The first proposition would be true if we assumed that

> Our Future Happiness depends upon our obeying, or
> endeavouring to fulfil the known Will of God.
> But that Rule which is not generally known, cannot
> be generally obey'd.
> Therefore that Rule which is not generally known, cannot
> be the Rule of Happiness.

The second proposition was that it was a

> matter of Fact, and uncontrovertible, that no Religion
> supernatural has been conveyed to all the World[2]

From this it followed that revelation was not necessary to salvation. Burke was sceptical of this position, noting that there was 'a Set of Men not infrequent in this City [Dublin], who tho' they allow of Morality, cry down reveal'd Religion, yet in their Practice, they make them equal, neglecting both'.[3] It is hardly surprising that his early thought includes a component which implies the inadequacy of deism.

The logic of the Christian position supposed that natural theology and revealed theology cohere, which implies that nature and revelation are patterned in analogous ways. The latter, indeed, was precisely the logic developed by Joseph Butler in his *Analogy of Religion*. Butler's argument was that whatever difficulties appeared in revelation were paralleled by those in nature.[4] Burke held this work 'greatly in [...] estimation.'[5] He also developed an argument about the logic of deism and its effects upon society.

Burke, in his *A Vindication of Natural Society*, published in 1756, assumed the *persona* of Viscount Bolingbroke, who in life had figured most prominently as a politician but in death stood forth as a deist with the publication of his *Works* in 1754. Burke's pseudo-Bolingbroke was made to see a parallel between revealed religion and civil society – or, as he was made to call them, artificial religion and artificial society. Both were riddled with evils, it seemed, and the evils of the former went along with the evils of the latter. In their stead, this pseudo-Bolingbroke held up for admiration natural religion, of course, but also natural society. The latter consisted of people living lives resembling those of the beasts of the field. The logic is plain: natural religion is the counterpart of 'natural society', whereas revealed religion and civil society match each other – or, if one prefers, deism and civil society imply different logics.

The reader of *A Vindication* is not invited explicitly to choose between these two logics, and it was only in the second edition, after the book had been taken by some to be a genuine product of Bolingbroke's mind, that Burke declared that his object was to observe that 'the same Engines which were employed for the Destruction of Religion, might be employed with equal Success for the Subversion of Government' (WS, I: 134). But it can hardly be doubted that Burke was not arguing in favour of deism and 'natural society'. Both his earlier treatment of the Sermon on the Mount, and his later declarations – that 'the state of civil society [...] is a state of nature; and much more truly so than a savage and incoherent mode of life' and that 'man is [...] never perfectly in his natural state, but where reason may be best cultivated, and most predominates' – point in the other direction (Works, III: 86).

Burke's implied argument about the anti-social or anti-human implications of deism was succeeded by an explicit argument to the effect that nature, properly understood, implied a God who acted in the manner disclosed by the Old Testament. Burke's *Philosophical Enquiry into the Origin of Our Ideas of The Sublime and Beautiful* of 1757, as its title implies, accents sublimity. Sublimity was taken to imply power, and the exercise of power through nature was described in terms that invoked Job and the reader is reminded that 'the scripture alone can supply ideas answerable to the majesty of this subject. In the scripture, wherever God is represented as appearing or speaking, every thing terrible in nature is called up to heighten the awe and solemnity of the divine presence' (WS, I: 240). Thus to a justification of Christian morality was added a corroboration by natural reason of part of a Judaeo-Christian regime.

This account of religion suggests an account of society. For deism was a form of primitivism, and primitivism can be developed as a view of society. Thus, if the deist's primitivism implies that human nature in its earliest, least cultivated form is capable of discovering the truth about religion, it can be argued that the earliest form of human existence discloses its true character, which is obscured or corrupted, wholly or partly, by later developments. Burke made the pseudo-Bolingbroke find the best form of society in the earliest and least cultivated state of man. Burke, in attributing this position to his deist, appears to have had in view at least some features of Rousseau's *Discourse on the Origin and Foundations of Inequality amongst Men*.[6] He certainly produced an anti-Rousseauian account of the natural origins and character of society. Rousseau had argued that mankind, as it came from the hand of nature, was incurious, free at once of vice and knowledge, and had lived in a state of material equality. Freedom from vice had been ended by the development of mind, comparison, and a desire to excel, which had generated an unequal society and unhappiness – not that Rousseau supposed that there was any alternative to the exercise of the human mind. Burke, by contrast, supposed not only that curiosity was entirely natural but also that so were ambition and imitation. Here was an anti-primitivistic account of the natural character of society: for these natural passions produced society of another sort. Ambition caused improvement, which Burke desiderated earlier. For ambition 'drives men to all the ways we see in signalizing themselves', imitation 'prompts us to copy' what others do. In fact, God was reckoned to have implanted ambition to prevent people from remaining as 'they were in the beginning of the world', and Burke added that imitation caused them to follow a lead: in other words, nature tended to produce a progressive and hierarchical society (WS, I: 224–6). Social primitivism, evidently, was unnatural.

Burke's ways of thinking in *A Vindication* and *A Philosophical Enquiry* brought aid to Christianity. They support Burke's earlier endorsement of Christian morality. Yet it should be recognised that his terms are those of literature and a philosophy not obviously framed on Christian assumptions, not of Christianity itself. That the grounds for supposing that Christianity was beneficial were philosophical permitted Burke's thought to develop and expand the scope of his claims about religion in ways that his literary and political engagements admitted and encouraged. We should turn to these features now.

Religion, Society and Politics

The years between *A Philosophical Enquiry* of 1757 and *Reflections on the Revolution in France* of 1790 saw Burke engage in a range of literary and political enterprises. Literature and politics were not wholly distinct, for political writing, and parliamentary speaking which turned into publication were instruments of Burke's thinking. One literary mode that Burke pursued prior to entering parliament was historiography. This pursuit figures in its own right in *An Abridgement of English History*, which he wrote before becoming heavily involved in practical politics, and appears also as a strand in the works he wrote later. What appears throughout this period is a strong sense of religion as a feature of civil society and the need to cultivate it properly for social benefit. What appears also during this period is an expansion of Burke's claims about the Christian religion into claims about revealed religion more widely.

All this was possible because Burke, in his writings, considered religion from a philosopher's perspective. Thus, natural theology, which after all is the branch of theology that the human understanding generates, was not a way of thinking that he discounted on account of his attitude to deism. What he had satirised in *A Vindication* was the inadequacy of natural theology to the purposes of civilised life, and what he had implied in *A Philosophical Enquiry* was that nature and revelation disclosed the same God. At least two further implications can be drawn from the position these works implied, namely that if nature and revelation belonged together, revelation also carried people much further towards the gains needed for civil society.

One implication was that Christianity generated benefits not only to the individual's soul (as Burke had stated in 1748) but also to political arrangements. For example, when Burke came to embody his philosophical conceptions in a highly specific form, in historiography, the medieval church was represented as a contributor to English liberties. That is to say, Archbishop Langton instructed the barons who were alienated by King John, and guided them towards the content of Magna Carta. Thus, *An Abridgement* showed that England's liberties arose from the action of a Roman Catholic prelate (WS, I: 539–41, 548). In a like way, *An Account of the European Settlements*, to which Burke contributed, represented Jesuit missionaries as the agents of civilisation, raising Americans from savagery to decency.[7] Thus, historiography translated general conceptions into particulars, and showed the good effects that Christian agency could have.

Another implication was that because benefits were judged by standards of civilisation and liberty – in other words by the standards of eighteenth-century philosophy – it was possible to envisage that Christianity could generate disadvantages. This, in fact, was how Burke judged arrangements in Ireland. He considered that nothing was so clear as the proposition that the members of civil society (or at least a majority of them) should enjoy its 'common advantages' – nothing, not even 'the truth of our common Christianity' (WS, IX: 464). Accordingly, he heavily criticised the laws that penalised Roman Catholic belief, because these laws violated natural law. This friendliness to the oppressed of Ireland may make Burke sound like an advocate for Roman Catholicism. Yet one should not suppose that Burke endorsed this in its civil aspects. Burke urged a firm control of Catholic priests in Ireland by the king's representatives because a '*popish Clergy, who are not restrained by the most austere subordination, will become a Nuisance, a real publick Grievance of the heaviest kind in any Country that entertains them*' (WS, IX: 578). In other words, his yardstick for judging the effects of religion on civil society remained social benefit or the reverse.

Burke's position, then, is that a specific revealed religion brings considerable social benefits to a specific place, namely Britain and (as he hoped would be true more fully) Ireland. Thus he gave historical examples of how a revealed religion had generated good consequences, and through these examples embodied his general view that the proper development of nature implied the agencies of revealed religion. Burke came to think of revealed religions besides Christianity as productive of benefits in the societies where they were to be found.

For his position is capable of expansion. That is to say, it admits of a generalising move from species to genus: if this specific revealed religion is socially beneficial, it may be that revealed religions as a genus can have the same character. That, in fact, is what Burke explored in speaking and writing about the Indian sub-continent. He affirmed that 'wherever the Hindoo Religion has been established, that Country has been flourishing', and also that to 'name a Mahometan Government is to name a Government by law', indeed one that supposed 'law is given by God, and it has the double sanction of law and of religion' (WS, VI: 305, 353). Indeed, priests helped to secure prosperity (WS, V: 422). The practical effect of this interpretative move is not far to seek, namely that because Burke was attributing guilt, he needed to show that his alleged villain, Warren Hastings, had been a disruptive force: this presupposed there was a civilisation to be disrupted. Perhaps, without this medium of thought, Burke would not have made his generalising move. But it was available to him intellectually because his mind was not bounded by the terms of a specific religion.

This endorsement of other revealed religions does not imply that Burke forewent Christianity nor that he entertained relativism about religious truth. As to the former, Burke was discussing the social role of these religions, not their truth, still less his personal beliefs. As to the latter, it was not his business in pursuing Hastings to ask whether Hinduism or Mohammedanism were true. His point was that these religions were correlated to social benefits, and that Hastings had reduced these gains significantly. Burke, in any case, was clear that the civilisation which had a Christian component had produced at least some results that were superior to those found in India. For instance, eighteenth-century Britons enjoyed *guarantees* of their civil liberties, which were not present in India, and Burke did *not* say of oriental religions, as he said of Christianity, that they were agents of progress (WS, V: 141; VIII: 127).

Rather, a different sort of relativism was present: that the religion which has become bound up with a society is the one that suits it. This follows from Burke's historiography. If people, their actions, and their institutions embody the benefits of revealed religion, then their society and their religion are intertwined and, perhaps, tend to become indistinguishable. Hence, that 'form of Religious Institution connected with Government and Policy that makes a people happy and a Government flourishing' was to be recommended for that setting (WS, VI: 305). So, though Burke thought that priests might need to be restrained for the good of civil society, he was equally clear that a civil society needed its religion: thus, he declared of the England of 1792 that 'in a *Christian* commonwealth the *Church & the State* are one & the same thing; being different *integrant parts* of the *same whole*' (NRO, A.xxvii.102).

We should not suppose, however, that Burke's connection of revealed religion and civil society implied perfection in the latter. Indeed, the progressive orientation of Burke's thought suggests otherwise, and his observations of particulars confirm it. In *A Vindication*, Burke made his pseudo-Bolingbroke comment adversely on the plight of miners, and in *Reflections*, writing in his own persona, he made similar criticisms (WS, I: 177–8; VIII: 209). His observations imply that the civil society of his day was far from perfect. But, as we shall see, it was clear to Burke in 1790 that Christianity and Western society should go together, and that an attack on the former was likely to produce retrogression in the latter.

Religion and the French Revolution

The French Revolution is the most famous object of Burke's enmity, and that enmity had features relating to religion. We need not suppose that these were at all times the same features, but all originated in the mental orientation that we have explored, as ways, first to interpret, and then to respond practically to the developments the Revolution presented.

The interpretation that Burke gave in *Reflections* concerned primarily political thought and practical results. The book is not primarily about religion. Rather, it continued Burke's view that revealed religion is an integral feature of a civilised society: indeed, it expanded this claim. It presented Christianity as a source of the distinctive civilisation of Europe, rather than merely as a source of English polity or a means of raising savages to a civilised condition. Burke made this move by emphasising how intertwined Christianity had become with the European social order. Indeed, it was the combination of the two that produced the order Burke saw before him. For to him:

> Nothing is more certain, than that [...] our civilization, and all the good things which are connected with [...] civilization, have, in this European world of ours, depended for ages upon two principles; and were indeed the result of both combined; I mean the spirit of a gentleman, and the spirit of religion. (WS, VIII: 129–30)

If this was what the Revolution threatened, the threat emanated in part from the enemies of Christianity, namely the deists. Burke accordingly exhumed the objects of his earlier enmity in order to imply that the French had been gulled by an intellectually naïve religion:

> I hear on all hands that a cabal, calling itself philosophic, receives the glory of many of the late proceedings; and that their opinions and systems are the true actuating spirit of the whole of them [...] It is not with you composed of those men, is it? whom the vulgar, in their blunt, homely style, commonly call Atheists and Infidels? If it be, I admit that we too have writers of that description, who made some noise in their day. At present they repose in lasting oblivion [...] Who now reads Bolingbroke? Who ever read him through? (WS, VIII: 140)

Reflections, in other words, linked ecclesiastical allegiance, social order, and clear thought to each other, and presented the Revolution as the enemy of all three. This development is a fairly obvious way to extend Burke's earlier opinions in order to make sense of what was happening in France – obvious, that is to say, to Burke. What is not obvious to the reader is that just as his political claims preceded the Terror and Napoleon so also he anticipated the de-Christianisation that became more powerful as the Revolution proceeded. The Civil Constitution of the Clergy of July 1790 had alienated many priests, besides Louis XVI himself, before *Reflections* was published, but their responses to that Constitution and the rise of the Jacobins had yet to give extensive scope for an assault on Christian life and for an attempt to make a Rousseauvian analogue of deism the official religion of France. So Burke in 1790, by linking revolution, de-Christianisation and deism, by supposing that 'the philosophical fanatics' intended 'the utter abolition [...] of the Christian religion', remembered the future (WS, VIII: 197).

He did not in 1790 anticipate that the Revolution, far from being just a misjudged attempt to substitute a constitutional monarchy and a constitutional church for the *ancien régime*, would turn into a continuing system of internal and external war, in which Paris sought to subdue both provincial resistance and the monarchies of Western Europe. Although in one sense this was the last thing Burke wanted, in another it provided him with an astonishing opportunity. From the Spring of 1792, when the Revolution turned decisively against both church and monarchy, Burke figured as the prophet of a realised apocalypse, and enlivened his last years by denouncing a revolutionary aggression based on '*doctrine and theoretick dogma*' as irreconcilable with Christian, constitutional and monarchical polities (WS, VIII: 341).

That is to say, Burke understood the Revolution to have a religious aspect. Because this aspect was anti-Christian, it was possible for Burke to denounce it as '*Atheism by Establishment*' (WS, IX: 241). This was an integral feature of his interpretation of the Revolution.

For Burke both understood the Revolution in terms of his conception of religion and supposed that it had religious features. Burke had understood revealed religion as a means of developing civilisation, and, conversely, had understood natural religion as inadequate to that purpose. He therefore found it easy to think of an exclusive preference for natural religion as a component in an assault on civilisation. To see deism as a component in political aggression is to attribute to the latter a religious force: the excessively simplified thinking of the revolutionaries was an error with a positive charge, a charge to do with saving people's souls – or rather the opposite. Hence Burke thought of the Revolution in its international aspect as no mere exercise in extending French rule, but instead as a crusade to destroy Christianity in Europe. Burke went so far as to say that the 'temporal ambition' of the revolutionaries was 'wholly subservient to their proselytizing spirit in which they were not exceeded by Mahomet himself' (WS, IX: 278). He thought '*it is a religious war*', for 'through this destruction of religion that our enemies propose the accomplishment of all their other views', and so their ends required them to 'persecute christianity throughout Europe with fire and sword' (WS, VIII: 485).

Thus, the Revolution figured as an exercise in religiously inspired destruction of civilisation, analogous to Protestant oppression of Irish Catholics, but far more radical in its scope and much more energetic. So the Revolution had to be met by a counter-crusade, not by wars limited to diplomatic and economic goals; religious war called for religious counter-revolution. Hence, Burke's later years witnessed the most uncompromising opposition to the Revolution. Correspondingly, his plans for a new order among the French called not only for 'breaking their strength' but also for '*civilizing* them', by means of a 'corps of instruments of civilization', by which 'I mean the clergy' (WS, VIII: 468, 469).

It is possible that the energetic character of Burke's claims owed something to a tactical need to whip up British enthusiasm for a long and costly war, but this implies that the claims themselves had a rationale. Something of the latter is recorded about Burke's deathbed, where he read William Wilberforce's *View of the [...] Religious System of Professed Christians*. That book, the work of another practical politician, was received cautiously by some. For instance, a prominent man of affairs, writing to the author as 'a wisher' to be one amongst 'good Christians', found the book 'alarming' at first, and thought Wilberforce 'must risk much in point of fame' by writing about revealed religion.[8] But Burke 'derived much comfort from it', and said 'that if he lived he should thank Wilberforce for having sent such a book into the world'.[9]

Thus, we end where we began – with Burke's acceptance of the truth of Christianity and its importance for the soul. His earliest views about society and his latest about the French Revolution alike implied the inadequacy of natural religion not only to salvation but also to civilised society. Burke emphasised the social benefits of Christianity, rather than its truth, in his political writings, and latter he extended his embrace from Christianity to Hinduism and Islam in their own social ambit. Thus, he developed a cor-relation between revealed religion and society, and at the same time par-ticularised it, by suggesting that specific religions suited specific societies. If philosophical thinking and historiographical expression were vehicles of this development of mind, Christianity was identified as a distinctive feature of the progress of society, just as deism and its like, whether in England or in France, implied retrogression.

NOTES

1 Edmund Burke, *Pre-Revolutionary Writings*, ed. Ian Harris (Cambridge: Cambridge University Press, 1993), p. 3. I have here silently expanded the con-tractions in the original, and added a word and a comma (in square brackets) for the sake of intelligibility.

2 'A.W.', 'To Charles Blount, Esq.', in *The Miscellaneous Works of Charles Blount* (London, 1695), p. 198.

3 *The Reformer*, no.11 (7 April 1748), (WS, I: 115).

4 See esp. *Analogy*, 'Introduction', p.13, in J. H. Bernard, (ed.), *The Works of Bishop Butler*, 2 vols. (London, 1900), vol. II, pp. 9–10.

5 Frances Anne Crewe, 'Extracts from Mr. Burke's Table Talk', no. 50 'Religion', repr. *Burke Newsletter*, 5. 2 (1963), pp. 276–92, ed. Jeffrey Hart, at 290.

6 R.B. Sewall Jr., 'Rousseau's Second Discourse in England from 1755 to 1762', *Philological Quarterly*, 17 (1938): 97–114.

7 [William Burke and Edmund Burke], *An Account of the European Settlements*, 2 vols. (London, 1757), vol. I, pp. 275–6.

8 David Scott to William Wilberforce, 31 October 1797, C. H. Phillips, (ed.), *The Correspondence of David Scott*, 2 vols. (London: Offices of the Royal Historical Society, 1951), vol. I, pp. 119–20.

9 R. I. Wilberforce and S. Wilberforce, *The Life of William Wilberforce*, 2nd edn., 5 vols. (London: John Murray 1839), vol. II, p. 208 (from Mrs Crewe).

8

DAVID CRAIG

Burke and the Constitution

To all intents and purposes, Burke's connection with the Whig party was over by May 1791. An emotional debate in the House of Commons indicated the final severance from Charles James Fox, and brought to a head disagreements that went back to early 1790. Thereafter, Burke was to suffer increasing sniping and criticism from other Whigs. In *Appeal from the New to the Old Whigs* he offered a sort of unapologetic valedictory in which he restated his understanding of Whiggism and vindicated his political consistency. He had reason to be concerned about both because he had done more than anyone else to provide a cogent intellectual justification for the party. He had joined the connection led by the Marquess of Rockingham in 1765 and quickly rose to become a leading advocate for its causes both in parliament and in print. He gave system and policy to their belief that the power of the Crown was increasing and ought to be diminished, and also provided firmer grounds for the connection cohering as a party. Hence, when by the early 1790s he was charged with abandoning everything he had held dear, it was essential to show that he at least remained true to Whig convictions even if those around him were losing theirs. This chapter examines Burke's thinking about the constitution: its ideal forms, the threats it was exposed to, and the solutions proposed between the 1760s and 1780s.

The Mixed and Balanced Constitution

The constitution in the eighteenth century was the subject of persistent self-congratulation. The central leitmotif was provided by William Blackstone's *Commentaries*. The separate systems of monarchy, aristocracy, and democracy were all liable to various disadvantages, but 'happily' Britain had mixed them together. The executive power was lodged in one man and so provided the strength associated with absolute monarchy. The legislature, however, was entrusted to 'three distinct powers, entirely independent of each other'. The king was matched with the Lords who were selected for piety, birth, wisdom, valour, and property and with the Commons who were 'freely chosen by the people from among themselves, which makes it a kind of democracy'. Together these formed parliament, in which no single branch could inconvenience the other as each was given a negative. These were familiar pieties, as was Blackstone's argument that the balance between these elements protected English liberty.[1] In addition, Blackstone was also a proponent of the idea of the 'ancient constitution', arguing that it had been established by the laws of Alfred and Edward the Confessor, and the Norman Conquest had overridden but not destroyed it. By stages, beginning with Magna Carta, the ancient constitution was restored, and finally perfected in the late seventeenth century.

This sort of 'vulgar whiggism' – to use Duncan Forbes's phrase – was common currency, but it was not uncontested.[2] Hume, for instance, opposed conventional interpretations of the Glorious Revolution and was unconvinced by the contrast between English liberty and French slavery. A central aim of his work was to show that the civilised monarchies of Europe were just as capable of providing justice – 'the liberty and security of the individual under the rule of law' – as England.[3] Hume saw the development of civilisation as intimately connected to the benefits of modern politics. For the same reasons, he was also dismissive of the ancient constitution, for which there was no historical evidence. Magna Carta was one of many documents wrung from a largely despotic monarchy by powerful feudal lords. In the *History of England*, an ironic footnote noted that there had been an ancient constitution under the Stuarts, and a more ancient one in the late medieval period, and then a further ancient constitution before the barons or the people had special privileges. Hence the English constitution 'like all others, has been in a state of continual fluctuation'.[4]

Burke also shared an interest in the new science of political economy, and a belief in the benefits brought by commercial society.[5] Nevertheless, it initially seems that there were many 'vulgar' aspects of his Whiggism. Pocock has influentially argued that he supported appeals to the ancient constitution, and that affinities with seventeenth-century common lawyers – especially Matthew Hale – underpinned his traditionalism.[6] Burke argued that the constitution was prescriptive and that its 'sole authority is that it has existed time out of mind' (Works, VI: 146). He wrote in the *Reflections* of how it was constitutional practice 'to claim and assert our liberties as an *entailed inheritance* derived to us from our forefathers' (WS, VIII: 83), and invoked the authority of common lawyers from Coke to Blackstone who claimed that Magna Carta was a reaffirmation of 'antient standing law' (WS, VIII: 82). However, as Donlan argues in this volume, such commitments can be overstated. In earlier writings, Burke was more ambiguous.

In the *Abridgment of English History*, he agreed that Magna Carta was the 'foundation of English liberty' (WS, I: 543), but opposed the historians and lawyers who saw it as a restatement of the laws of Edward the Confessor (WS, I: 544). Even in *Reflections* he chose his words carefully. The lawyers were right 'for the greater part' but 'perhaps not always' (WS, VIII: 82). What really mattered was the more general point about a predilection for antiquity and the widespread belief that rights and franchises were an inheritance. This was part of Burke's broader assault on radical interpretations of the Glorious Revolution. The Revolution was justified by necessity and in fact 'was made to preserve our *antient*, indisputable laws and liberties and that *ancient* constitution of government which is our only security for law and liberty' (WS, VIII: 81). He was not, however, aligning himself with those who wished to 'restore' the constitution to some earlier, purer form, but rather stressing continuity through evolution. The idea of inheritance provided a basis for conservation and transmission but 'without at all excluding a principle of improvement' (WS, VIII: 84). The constitution had developed according to 'the peculiar circumstances, occasions, tempers, dispositions, and moral, civil and social habitudes of the people [...] It is a vestment, which accommodates itself to the body' (Works, VI: 147).[7] This was not a uniquely Burkean idea. William Paley, for instance, could be found arguing against the idea of a planned constitution. It had grown out of 'occasion and emergency; from the fluctuating policy of different ages; from the contentions, successes, interests, and opportunities, of different orders and parties of men in the community'.[8]

Burke was also a defender of the mixed constitution. He explained how the constitution was composed of 'three very different natures' and that its 'whole scheme' was to prevent any element from being taken to an extreme (Works, III: 25, 110). It followed that a constitution made of 'balanced Powers must ever be a critical thing', requiring continual compromise between each branch (WS, III: 70).[9] This was a useful argument, because it enabled Burke to defend himself against the charge of inconsistency in criticising the power of the crown in the 1760s, and defending it in the 1790s (Works, III: 24–5). The idea of balance was not, however, suitable parliamentary language, and he was particularly incensed by the king's speech in 1784 which urged parliament to consider the 'just balance' of every branch of the legislature. Such language was not 'safe' and was likely to stir 'improper discussions' and create 'mischievous innovations' in the constitution (Works, II: 256). Nevertheless, even though the idea of balance was necessarily imprecise, and could be used by any of the three branches for polemical purposes, it remained a staple of constitutional thought.

The central and recurring debate, however, was really about the relationship between crown and parliament. The eighteenth century saw an enormous expansion in the size and cost of the state because of the needs of war. Politicians from the 'country party' like Bolingbroke railed against the erosion of parliamentary independence by a vast network of government patronage, which provided places, pensions, and offices to ensure the compliance of parliamentarians. The solution was to end the public debt, remove placemen and contractors from parliament, and to create free and frequent elections. The independent MP would ensure liberties could be restored and the influence of the executive ended. The opposing case was made best by Hume who argued that the institutional structure that had developed since the Revolution was in fact necessary. Because of its fiscal authority, the Commons possessed by far the greatest power of any of the branches of the mixed constitution, and a more independent parliament could easily suborn executive power if it wished. What preserved the delicate mix of republican and monarchical features was influence. The fact that a good number of parliamentarians supported the crown ensured that its authority was maintained, and so demands for more independence were misplaced.

Burke's contribution to these debates occurred within the political context of the 1760s. George III desired to break the 'old corps' of Whigs who had dominated government and parliament, and who, he thought, unsettled the balance of the constitution.[10] The effect was to fracture the political landscape and lead to a series of weak ministries until 1770. Some groups tried to remain close to the king, while others spoke a popular language of patriotism and independence. The Rockinghamites, meanwhile, were 'a sort of patrician elite with a presumptive right to power'.[11] Their brief spell in office between 1765 and 1766 was unhappy. Many of the 'king's friends' voted against the government's measure to repeal the Stamp Act, and the king's refusal to discipline them seemed proof that he was working against his own government. Over the next two and a half decades, this 'party' struggled with how to react to its new-found opposition to the king, how to endure as an aristocratic elite, and whether to seek new political support inside and beyond parliament. Burke's reputation in his pre-revolutionary phase was partly to rest on the answers he proposed to these questions. After *Reflections*, *Thoughts on the Causes of the Present Discontents* was probably his most influential work. Although written with a polemical purpose, it was also intended to be 'the political Creed of our Party' (C II: 136). The ideas that informed it were to remain crucial to his political thinking into the 1780s.

The Causes of the Present Discontents

As well as the divided and unstable nature of parliamentary politics, the 'present discontents' also referred to the agitation surrounding John Wilkes's disputed election for Middlesex in 1768. Despite being elected three times, he was expelled from the Commons, and the seat was awarded to his opponent the following year. To critics, this was a step too far, and seemed to show the contempt with which an increasingly authoritarian government viewed the rights of electors. It provided Burke with a valuable opportunity to outline the Rockinghamite analysis of the underlying causes of discontent. The general features of his argument about influence would have been familiar to readers, but he went further in speaking of an organised system pioneered by a 'cabal' of the king's friends which had the intention of creating a new type of arbitrary government. Rather than trying to attack parliament, as in the seventeenth century, the 'cabal' had realised that the forms of free government could be maintained if they could turn the House of Commons from being an 'antagonist' to an 'instrument' of government (WS, II: 258). The 'king's friends' were depicted as shadowy figures who were distributed with 'art and judgment' throughout government departments and the royal household (WS, II: 273). They formed what Burke called a 'double cabinet' – a controversial idea that suggested they could manipulate or frustrate any ministry through the control of the votes of placemen. Eventually, they would turn against the government and secure its collapse, but not before they had persuaded many junior members to remain in place. They were also pioneering an ideological assault that tried to alarm the people with 'an affected terror' of aristocratic power, which was supposedly crushing the independence of the king and destroying the balance of the constitution (WS, II, 267). In the place of party, there was to be 'public spirit' – the king would choose his ministers from among the very best men irrespective of their connection. The court, in other words, was cynically clothing its ambitions in a language of virtue and patriotism in order to appeal to those enamoured of 'country' sentiments, and at the same time to discredit all forms of party as nothing more than selfish, factious behaviour.

The dangers that Burke anticipated from this new system tell us much about the ideal relationship he envisaged between king, parliament, and people. What mattered most to him were the chains of trust that existed between these elements and that were crucial to the effectiveness of government. The new 'system' of arbitrary government ultimately destroyed trust and paralysed the constitution. This was because of the need to ensure oversight of the executive. Even though the Revolution prevented the king from overturning law, numerous discretionary powers remained: the execution of laws, appointment of magistrates and officers, the conduct of peace and war, and the ordering of revenue. It was essential that these '*be exercised upon public principles and national grounds*' (WS, II: 277). Most commonly in free states this was ensured by the popular election of magistrates, but the constitution did not allow for this. In fact, Burke argued, it provided something better – at least while the 'spirit of the constitution' was preserved – by enabling the election of representatives upon whose support government depended (WS, II: 278). This produced all the benefits of popular election with none of the mischief. The power to refuse support for ministers was what kept them in awe of parliaments and ensured ultimately that government was acceptable to the people. If the king had complete freedom to appoint ministers, there was little likelihood that worthy and trusted men would be chosen. Even if the letter of the law was not violated, the spirit of the constitution was. Moreover, this had a cumulative logic: once ambitious men realised that the best way to preferment was through the court, they would no longer bother to cultivate opinion in the country, and so the connection between people and government would become ever weaker. Once that was gone, 'every thing is lost, Parliament and all' (WS, II: 279).

The new 'system' had similarly disastrous effects on parliament. Here Burke was concerned more with the 'spirit' of the Commons rather than its legal forms, and he found it necessary to clear up some confusions. It was not the popular origin of the Commons that made it the voice of the people. All parts of the constitution – King, Lords and Commons – were representatives of the people in the sense of holding their power as a trust for the people. Instead, the 'virtue, spirit and essence of a House of Commons consists in its being the express image of the feelings of the nation.' Arising from the people and close to their concerns, it emerged as a body of control on the government. 'A vigilant and jealous eye over executory and judicial magistracy; an anxious care of public money, an openness, approaching towards facility, to public complaint: these seem to be the true characteristics of an House of Commons' (WS, II: 292). Since the Revolution, however, this function of control on government had been eroded, ironically, because of the need for a more regular legislature. A growing habit of authority and infrequent elections had helped transform the Commons into a standing senate, and hence to lose some of its original purpose. This was being worsened by the enormous amount of patronage in the hands of the court, which could not only gratify the vanity and avarice of many MPs, but could also prevent the less corrupt from assisting their constituents. In addition, the 'cabal' vaunted indiscriminate support for ministers as a sign of loyalty, made moves against the right to free election, and discouraged genuine parliamentary debate and dissent. Taken together, this increasingly made parliament simply an adjunct of the executive with very little relation to its former role as a control for the people.

Clearly, Burke's analysis was different to that of Hume. In the late 1760s and early 1770s, Hume was to be found despairing at how many powers government had given up, and at the excesses of liberty. He looked for 'vigorous measures' to resist the march to republicanism which would lead first to anarchy and then to despotism.[12] Burke also worried about the consequences of popular discontent, but mapped an alternative source. The king's friends were ironically undermining the power of government. The foundation of government was in the confidence of the people, and they were systematically eroding those foundations. The people could already see that the Commons was increasingly an alien body, and that their representatives could only do what the court allowed them. As it became an arm of the government, and ceased to be a '*corrective and controul*' so it lost their confidence and veneration' (WS, II: 294). As public bodies became 'dead and putrid' so the people became indifferent to the constitution. In time the love of peace and order slipped away, and demagogues emerged to stoke up further discontent. The sword was increasingly required, and that provoked further disorder until the sword was given special protection by the state. 'Anarchy predominates without freedom, and servitude without submission or subordination': these were to be the ultimate results of stripping away parliamentary control of government and breaking the chains of trust that held the mixed system together (WS, II: 287).

Representation and Reform

In putting forward arguments about independence resonant of the 'country' ideology, it might be thought that Burke would also propose familiar solutions. Certainly he discussed them: place and pension bills, shorter parliaments, a more virtuous electorate. The Rockinghamites, however, had to proceed carefully in case they stirred up excessive expectations about the kinds of political reform they patronised. The furore over Wilkes's election galvanised reformers and led to the establishment of various reform societies, some of which went as far as annual parliaments, seat redistribution, and an extended franchise. The County Association movement revived interest in reform in 1779 – a time of dire concern about the war with America – and proposed administrative reform, triennial parliaments, abolition of rotten boroughs, and the creation of more county members. While trying to ride on the coat-tails of this movement, most of the Rockinghamites committed themselves only to administrative or 'economical' reform. On many occasions, Burke explained why he did not support extensive parliamentary reform, and these reasons are consistent with his understanding of the relationship between people and parliament.

One of the aims of *Present Discontents* was to defend the rights of electors – principally those of Middlesex – to elect a representative of their choice (WS, II: 295–303).[13] Nevertheless, Burke is famed for his defence of 'virtual representation' and of the need for the independence of the representative from his constituents. In the early 1770s, reformers were trying to popularise the idea of constituent instructions, and hoped to secure support for it at the 1774 election. Burke tackled the issue at his election for Bristol in that year. He praised close links between constituents and their representative, and argued that their opinions would always carry weight with him (WS, III: 69).[14] This was completely different, however, from instructions to which the member was 'bound blindly and implicitly to obey, to vote, and to argue for'. Burke opposed this because of his conception of the role of parliament. In a well-known passage, he spoke of it as a '*deliberative* Assembly of *one* Nation' where the general good resulted from 'the general Reason of the whole'. It was therefore essential that a representative could exercise reason and judgment in deliberating, and ought not to be expected to sacrifice 'his unbiassed opinion, his mature judgment, his enlightened conscience' (WS, III: 69). Indeed, it was patently absurd to view representatives simply as proxies, because it meant that decisions preceded the discussion, thereby undermining the whole point of parliament. Instead, electors should choose persons whom they could trust, and allow them to exercise that trust on their behalf. At the time of re-election they were free to reject a representative, but they ought to consider the '*whole tenour*' of his conduct, not whether they agreed with this or that position. If electors insisted on constraining and directing his judgment, there was little chance he would ever be able to take on the responsibilities of statesmanship. The irony was that in instructing members, the reformers would create more opportunities for the crown to monopolise the seats of power (WS, III: 634, 626).

This was a theme Burke stressed in his more general opposition to parliamentary reform. As well as consistently opposing arguments based on abstract rights, he also criticised the more moderate reformers. A concern often repeated was the disorder of elections. Some form of popular election was essential to ensure government was in the interests of the people; nevertheless, it was a 'mighty Evil' that had led to the destruction of many free states (WS, III: 590). Their cost, and 'the prostitute and daring venality, the corruption of manners, the idleness and profligacy of the lower sort of voters' ruled out increasing the incidence of elections (WS, II: 177). All that mattered was that they were frequent enough to maintain the confidence of the people (WS, III: 590). Beyond that, any reduction in the length of parliaments had to directly counteract the influence of the crown. Burke – unlike most proponents of such reforms – thought that the opposite was more likely. First, more frequent elections would not decrease corruption: electors might find their rewards lowered, but corruption itself would still continue. Even if there were too many electors in larger boroughs, the court would simply transfer its attentions to the 'leading man' in a constituency who would generally tend to bring supporters with him (WS, III: 594). Second, triennial parliaments would increase exorbitantly the costs of elections – treating, corruption, disorder – and sooner or later independent gentlemen would either retire from the field or seek financial aid from the government (WS, III: 595; II: 308–9). In both cases, more elections equalled less independence. The hints that Burke did throw out did not satisfy the new breeds of reformers.[15] There needed to be a reduction in the number of voters so that 'weight and independency' counted for more, and so that 'integrity and publick spirit' could counteract the corruption among the lower class of voters (WS, II: 177; III: 592).

Burke's real interest was in measures that directly attacked the influence of the crown, without conceding parliamentary independence to popular influence. A staple of the 'country party' had been bills to remove placemen, pensioners, and contractors from parliament. In *Present Discontents*, he attached some significance to such measures, but it is notable that he was sceptical about stripping all government interests from parliament. While these had grown substantially over the preceding century, they were made up of men of 'weight, ability, wealth, and spirit'. They were interests that needed to be recognised rather than forcing them to find other less open avenues to power (WS, II: 310). Ten years later, when Burke tried to capitalise on the County Association movement, it was necessary to ground 'economical reform' in principles. He proposed the abolition of all offices, estates, and jurisdictions that served no useful function. The separate administration of Wales, Cornwall, Lancaster, and Chester would be scrapped, various hereditary offices removed, the civil list controlled and pensions limited to £60,000 a year. However there must also be sufficient means to reward public service; otherwise, there would be no incentive to 'virtuous ambition' (WS III: 528). Indeed, he was quite clear that *useful* offices must be properly remunerated, and that holders should be forbidden from refusing the salary: depending on 'rare and heroic virtues' for service was more likely to breed corruption (WS, III: 530–1).[16] These reforms were designed to peel away only those unnecessary offices that bolstered influence; they would leave behind a more efficient and effective state.

An important point made in *Present Discontents* is often neglected. Burke expressed scepticism towards the idea that 'laws and regulations' were the best cure for public 'distempers' (WS, II: 310). He questioned whether the solution to discontent could even begin in parliament, and suggested that until confidence in government was restored, what was needed was more virtue among electors. This meant much more attention to the conduct of representatives. To this end, he suggested that county and corporation meetings should establish formal standards by which to judge a member, and that more accurate division lists be made available to the public. The existing electorate would then better be able to scrutinise the conduct of their representative, and to discover which had lost 'integrity and confidence' and thereby weakened the frame of government (WS, II: 312). The electors were urged not only to reject MPs who took office under weak governments, but also those who even offered votes of support to them: 'The notorious infidelity and versatility of Members of Parliament in their opinions of men and things ought in a particular manner to be considered by electors in the enquiry which is recommended to them' (WS, II: 314). Ultimately, the best solution to corruption was increased public spirit.

Party

Burke's defence of party has long been the subject of commentary. It is true that there was deep suspicion of 'faction' throughout the eighteenth century, and it could easily be depicted as unpatriotic and selfish. Nevertheless, the ideas of the 'country party' formed in opposition to Walpole between the 1720s and 1740s provided some legitimation. It was argued that when the constitution was being endangered by wicked ministers, it was a duty for true patriots to come together and oppose them. However, this argument could also be used against party connection, because the stress was on 'measures not men'.[17] Burke drew on 'country party' arguments to support opposition to the crown, but also provided a powerful defence of connection more broadly. Party was a thing 'inseparable' from free government, and the ideal of personal independence – much vaunted in this period – was in fact fatally flawed and deeply irresponsible (WS, II: 110). No matter how much such a man acted according to his conscience and supported his country's interest, he fell 'miserably short' of a proper conception of public duty, because the business of a politician was not simply to detect evil but to defeat it (WS, II: 315).

Burke's famous definition was that party was 'a body of men united, for promoting by their joint endeavours the national interest, upon some particular principle in which they are all agreed' (WS, II: 317). Unlike traditional country party arguments, however, this was not primarily about otherwise unconnected men coming together at a moment of crisis. Crucially, Burke grounded his conception of party in personal honour. Endorsing Cicero, he argued that the Romans believed 'private honour to be the great foundation of public trust' and that 'friendship was no mean step towards patriotism'. Here the public and the private were harmoniously combined and grew out of each other in a 'noble and orderly gradation, reciprocally supporting and supported' (WS, II: 316).[18] The private virtues were assumed to be a security for and a promise of a disinterested public life. The Whigs of Queen Anne's reign were exemplary: 'They believed no men could act with effect, who did not act in concert; that no men could act in concert, who did not act with confidence; and that no men could act with confidence, who were not bound together by common opinions, common affections, and common interests' (WS, II: 317). This kind of party was not a confederacy of narrow and big-oted men fixated on power, but men who had cultivated their minds and reared to perfection 'every sort of generous and honest feeling that belongs to our nature' (WS, II: 315, 320). What mattered was less that Burke was providing a defence of the existence of party as such, and more the terms of honour and character in which he grounded it.

Was this an aristocratic conception of party? Burke accepted the nat-uralness of aristocracy, and certainly he was eulogising the virtues of the Rockinghamites, but he did so in terms that tried to show merited public affection for this elite. It was not simply that peers had influence because of their possession of property – 'its natural operation' – but because they had also deserved trust by 'uniform, upright, constitutional' conduct and by 'their public and their private virtues' (WS, II: 268). Similarly, the Rockinghamites were indeed from the greatest families in the nation, but 'infinitely more distinguished' because of their 'untainted honour public and private, and their zealous but sober attachment to the constitution' (WS, II: 209). Of course, in a polemical pamphlet these were prudent things to say, but Burke did also make clear his absolute opposition to pure sys-tems of aristocracy (WS, II: 268). Indeed, this defence of popular trust in an honourable connection was crucial to restoring confidence to the con-stitution. The election of more representatives independent of the court would once again make the Commons a control on the executive. It would then prevent men who lacked confidence and connection from occupying high office, and, in time, the court would realise that effective government was best provided by those who were recommended by the opinion of the country. 'This, with allowances for human frailty, may probably be the gen-eral character of a Ministry, which thinks itself accountable to the House of Commons; when the House of Commons thinks itself accountable to its constituents' (WS, II: 322).

In the short term, none of this was achieved, and, if anything, it appeared that influence increased. In 1783, the king secured the collapse of the Fox-North ministry by effectively making it known that he was opposed to his government's East India Bill. The subsequent election in 1784 endorsed the king's new ministry, and in the new parliament Burke again warned of the danger of the Commons becoming 'a mere appendage of Administration' (Works, II: 261). In private, he despaired that twenty years of labour to make the Commons independent had been destroyed. Worst of all, 'The people did not like our work; and they joind the Court to pull it down. The demolition is very complete' (C, V: 154). Slowly thereafter Burke became absorbed in Indian and then French affairs and became more distant from his party. It was the preceding years on which a good part of his nineteenth-century reputation rested. Even if Whig Liberals could not forgive his role in the 1790s, they found much of value in these constitutional writings. Burke was the defender of parliament who understood its deliberative functions and its need to represent the interests of the nation, and he provided a template for parliamentary government and a role for party. Only in the twentieth century – with the decline of Whiggism itself – was he fully abandoned to conservatism.

NOTES

1 William Blackstone, *Commentaries on the Laws of England*, 4 vols. (London, 1765–9), vol. I, pp. 50–1.
2 Duncan Forbes, *Hume's Philosophical Politics* (Cambridge: Cambridge University Press, 1975), pp. 142–9.
3 Ibid., p. 154.
4 David Hume, *The History of England*, 8 vols. (London, 1767), vol. V, p. 472.
5 J. G. A. Pocock, 'The Political Economy of Burke's Analysis of the French Revolution', *Historical Journal*, 25 (1982): 331–49.
6 J. G. A. Pocock, 'Burke and the Ancient Constitution: a Problem in the History of Ideas', *Historical Journal*, 3 (1960): 125–43.
7 See also WS, I: 321–37.
8 William Paley, *The Principles of Moral and Political Philosophy* (London, 1785), p. 465.
9 See also (Works, III: 110).
10 See John Brewer, *Party Ideology and Popular Politics at the accession of George III* (Cambridge: Cambridge University Press, 1976).
11 Ibid., p. 12.
12 Cited in Forbes, *Hume's Philosophical Politics*, p. 191.
13 See also WS, II: 228–30.
14 See also WS, III: 590–2.
15 E.g., Catherine Macaulay, *Observations on a Pamphlet, entitled Thoughts on the Causes of the Present Discontents* (London, 1770).

16   See N. C. Phillips, 'Edmund Burke and the County Movement, 1779–80', *English Historical Review,* 76 (1961): 254–78.

17   Brewer, *Party Ideology,* ch. 4.

18   See A. D. Kriegel, 'Edmund Burke and the Quality of Honor', *Albion,* 12 (1980): 337–49; Richard Bourke, 'Edmund Burke and Enlightenment Sociability: Justice, Honour and the Principles of Government', *History of Political Thought,* 21 (2000): 632–56.

9

CHRISTOPHER J. INSOLE

Burke and the Natural Law

When Burke attends to wrongs committed by the state, as he does in relation to British actions in Ireland and India, he reaches for the notion of an 'immutable, pre-existent law' (WS, VI: 350) that cannot be trumped by positive laws or human authority. Similarly, when facing down the philosophical zeal of the French revolutionaries, he makes appeal to a normative conception of nature that he claims the *philosophes* violate. Burke's resort to natural law language is neither frequent nor systematic. Nonetheless, a treatment of the theme is warranted, because of the dramatic role such references play in what Burke considers to be extreme situations of state-sanctioned injustice or immanent European chaos.

Recent commentators on Burke can be forgiven for giving this topic a fairly wide berth. More heat than light has emerged from recent exchanges about the importance or otherwise of natural law thought in Burke's writings. Tribal loyalty or hostility to 'natural law' or 'Thomist'[1] readings of Burke can take the place of more nuanced and differentiated evaluations. More recently, the terms of the older debate as to whether Burke is a 'natural law' or 'utilitarian' thinker, tend to be seen as redundant, with a consensus that the complexity of Burke's work is not unlocked but distorted by using the lens of a single philosophical system, whether that be utilitarian or Thomist. Rather, the task for Burke scholars is more commonly conceived to be that of tracing a large number of diverse discourses and influences, with a tendency to emphasise the lack of any systematic theory in Burke.

Without presenting Burke as a systematic natural lawyer, it must still be a valuable exercise to track the genealogy and significance of Burke's use of natural law language. In truth, to call any figure in the eighteenth century a 'natural law thinker' is in any case not yet to say very much. The tendency of thinkers in this period to express normative or pragmatic commitments in terms of what conforms to the 'laws of nature' is so pervasive that it serves more to obscure profound differences than to illumine genuinely common commitments or intellectual genealogies. In fact, as will become clear, diametrically opposed positions are put forward in this period as foundations of, or implications from, the 'laws of nature'.

To say something more informative and nuanced about any thinker's use of natural law language, it is necessary to differentiate *conceptually* between the commitments that can underlie and explain various natural law references. There is a tendency in the literature to determine the content of natural law references in terms of epochs (ancient, medieval, or modern) or alliances (Thomist, Lockean, or Hobbesian). To an extent this is helpful, unavoidable even, but there are dangers in the exclusive use of such an approach. By only asking whether or not Burke's use of natural law language is 'medieval', 'Thomist', or 'modern', we can import fraught and prejudged schemes for fixing these categories; it is also worth asking whether and where the natural law reference is eudaimonistic, cosmological, teleological, reductionist, empiricist, voluntarist, or intellectualist (these terms will be explained). These are the live, precise, and contested options that would have been available to Burke when drawing on natural law language, rather than the categories of 'Thomist' or 'early modern'. On some of these contested issues, Burke takes a clear and unambiguous position; on others, he remains inscrutably vague. For example, it is simply not possible to tell from Burke's actual pronouncements whether he has a fundamentally voluntarist or intellectualist conception of the natural law, or even that he is very clear about the difference. This sort of vagary is in itself an indication of the limitations of describing Burke as a 'natural law thinker': natural law thinkers, such as Pufendorf and Grotius, are hardly so unaware and vague about such things, even if they can be inconsistent or unpersuasive.

Burke's Use of Classical Natural Law Language

From the classical period, Burke shows detailed knowledge of Aristotle, Cicero, and Philo, with the genealogy picking up again in the modern period with Suarez and then Hobbes, Grotius, Pufendorf, Locke, and Vattel. The curriculum at Trinity College Dublin included seventeenth-century text books of scholastic philosophy, written by Sanderson, Baronius and Eustachius,[2] which Burke is perhaps referring to when he writes to Richard Shackleton in 1746 that he is "deep in metaphysics" (C, I: 67–8). There is no evidence of direct knowledge of medieval sources such as Aquinas, although Hansard reports a speech given in the Commons in 1780 by 'Mr Burke', where he 'quoted the opinion of Thomas Aquinas, in the twelfth century, against breaking the law of nature … and said the darkness of the twelfth century rose against the light of the eighteenth' (PH, 21: 7). That Burke places Aquinas in the wrong century, and that there are no references to

Aquinas elsewhere in Burke's writings or speeches, suggests that it is unwise to make too much of this line when determining how 'Thomist' Burke might be. Nonetheless, when tracking the meaning of early modern natural law, it is essential to say something about Aquinas, if only to show significant ways in which early modern writers departed from Thomism.

For Aquinas, natural law is the appropriation by rational creatures of the eternal law that is embodied in the divine nature.[3] Nature, or *natura* ('creation'), is a purposive realm ordered by intrinsic teleological dispositions that find their ultimate fulfilment in God. So Aquinas precedes his discussion of natural law with a description of the beatific vision – the contemplation of the divine nature – which constitutes the ultimate telos of human beings. In the early modern period, we find a quite different mood among natural law thinkers. Although both God and intrinsic purposes play various roles in different thinkers, natural law seems to be more a theory based upon the empirical observation of human nature, and less a theological treatise arising from a doctrine of creation. Characteristic of the natural lawyers of early modernity is a search for a deductive system of truths, acceptable to all rational people. Such a system need not be based upon the virtuous discernment of a transcendent end, but can be built up from self-evident or empirically observed first principles: inasmuch as the notion of a 'purpose' is admitted into the system, it is one that is more modestly derived from the observation of pervasive features of the human condition, such as that human beings desire self-preservation, or that they need to live in society.

This disappearance of a strong theological framework can happen even with an explicitly theistic thinker such as Grotius. Grotius grapples with our 'unsociable sociability': that we have 'a certain inclination to live with ... our own kind',[4] but that we are quarrelsome and prone to conflict. By empirical observation of our human nature, Grotius aims to derive universal moral norms which would be valid even if we 'grant, what without the greatest wickedness cannot be granted, that there is no God, or that he takes no care of human affairs'.[5] Where God does play a role in natural law thought in this period, it tends to be in terms of supplying the element of command required to make principles normative laws. Suarez considers that even though moral rightness and wrongness are independent of God's will, the divine command is needed to render these *law,* as a 'law cannot actually bind, unless it is externally promulgated'.[6] Pufendorf's universe is fundamentally corpuscularian, with a non-purposive realm of atoms in motion, upon which God imposes physical and moral order. For Pufendorf, although what is rationally prudent is independent of divine command, moral rightness and wrongness needs God's command: 'law' is simply 'a decree by which a superior obliges a subject to adapt his actions to his former's command'.[7]

Burke is certainly capable of using natural law language with a similar detachment from any theological worldview: particularly at times in his discussion of revolutionary France, or in his use of Vattel and Grotius and the 'laws of nations', that is, the law of nature as applied to international relations (WS, VIII: 340). Nonetheless, it is striking that, in other places, Burke's references to natural law are framed within a construal of the universe as being saturated in a divine order and mindfulness that is largely absent from Grotius, Pufendorf, and Hobbes.

When prosecuting Hastings for his malpractice in India, Burke comments that if he were to keep 'faith' with the East India Company, he would 'break the faith, the covenant, the solemn, original, indispensable oath, in which I am bound, by the eternal frame and constitution of things, to the whole human race' (WS, V: 425). In the opening speech of Hasting's trial Burke insists that we are born in subjection 'to one great, immutable, pre-existent law prior to all our devices, and prior to all our contrivances, paramount to our very being itself, by which we are knit and connected in the eternal frame of the universe, out of which we cannot stir' (WS, VI: 350). It is not just, as with Vattel, that certain laws for sovereign states have universal application, but rather that the universe as such is framed by law, meaning that 'the laws of morality are the same every where' and 'there is no action which would pass for an action of extortion, of peculation, of bribery and of oppression in England, that is not an act of extortion, of peculation, of bribery and of oppression in Europe, Asia, Africa, and all the world over' (WS, VI: 346).

It is passages such as these that have encouraged Thomist readings of Burke, but, in truth, there is nothing in the preceeding passages that Burke could not get directly from Cicero. This is a much more likely source, given that Cicero is explicitly cited a number of times, in relation to natural law, in the speeches concerning India. Cicero tells us that the 'supreme Law' had 'its origin ages before any written law existed or any state had been established',[8] such that when people obey this law, they are 'members of the same commonwealth', obeying 'this celestial system, the divine mind, and the God of transcendent power'.[9]

We find similar allusions to the order of the universe in Burke's comments on France. God is the 'supreme ruler ... wise to form, and potent to enforce, the moral law' (Works, III: 79). 'I love order', he tells us, 'for the universe is order'.[10] God is the 'awful Author of our being' and 'the Author of our place in the order of existence' (Works, III: 79). He declares that we are all bound by the law that God has prescribed for us, the 'great immutable, pre-existent law' that connects us with the 'eternal frame of the universe',[11] such that 'each contract of each particular state is but a clause in the great primeval contract of eternal society, linking the lower with the higher natures, connecting the visible and invisible world, according to a fixed compact sanctioned by the inviolable oath which holds all physical and moral natures, each in their appointed place' (WS, VIII: 147). The parallels with Cicero are suggestive. Cicero denies that 'the principles of Justice were founded on the decrees of peoples, the edicts of princes, or the decisions of judges.'[12] Rather, 'Justice is one, it binds all human society, and is based on one Law',[13] where law 'is not a product of human thought, nor is it an enactment of peoples, but something eternal which rules the whole universe'.[14]

By drawing on Cicero, Burke attaches himself to a conception of natural law as constituted by the teleological structure of a divinely framed universe, in conformity to which human beings need to orient themselves. In other ways, Burke also associates himself with aspects of classical strands of natural law thought. These strands have their seminal expression in Aristotle, but become common to the later classical tradition. Burke would have been acquainted with these aspects of classical thought both from his reading of Aristotle (see WS, III: 157; IV: 174) and through his knowledge of Cicero. Within the Aristotelian tradition, virtues are construed as those habits or dispositions by which we stretch out to our perfection: a perfection that is oriented to an objective conception of what constitutes human flourishing within a wider order. When natural law is constituted by a teleological conception of the universe, with an objective conception of human perfection, reflection on virtues can be an intrinsic part of reflection on natural law. This will not be the case with other conceptions of natural law, where the only reference point is the satisfaction of our desires, whatever they may be (Hobbes), or obedience to divine commands (Pufendorf). Burke sets out an Aristotelian conception of the virtues: describing, accurately, an Aristotelian account of temperance (WS, IX: 359), fortitude and its corresponding vice, pussillanimity (WS, IX: 301), in the context of British reluctance to go to war with post-revolutionary France.

Of most relevance to the natural law tradition is Burke's conception of prudence, 'the first in rank of the virtues political and moral ... the director, the regulator, the standard of them all' (Works, III: 16). In his statements on prudence Burke clearly aligns himself with thinkers such as Hutcheson[15] and Smith[16] in construing the virtue normatively as that which discerns the correct course of action in order to achieve a (morally legitimate) end, rather than simply as a guarantor of rational self-interest (as it is in Hobbes). Hobbes could conceive of a prudent (skilful) burglar, but for Burke the 'rules of prudence ... are formed upon the known march of the ordinary providence of God' (WS, IX: 269). Prudence, as practical reason, is oriented 'to good or evil' (Works, III: 81), and 'God forbid that prudence, the first of all the virtues, as well as the supreme director of them all, should ever be employed in the service of any of the vices' (WS, VI: 396). Aristotle's divine mind is engaged with contemplating its own perfection, and is not providentially concerned with the course of history. To the extent that Burke associates the virtue of prudence with a providential God, it distances Burke from Aristotle, bringing him closer to a position that is more aptly described as a Christian appropriation of Cicero.[17]

An adequate conception of classical strands of natural law thinking also enables us to cut through some unhelpful dichotomies that have at times plagued the debate around Burke and natural law. Whenever it is suggested that Burke's interest in utility, history, tradition, custom, or necessity pulls him away from natural law, it needs to be understood that all of these can be understood by an author such as Cicero as aspects of the natural law, and of its mediation in history (about which, see Chapter 10 in this volume).

Furthermore, Burke's critique of the 'abstract' and geometrical conception of natural rights, far from pulling Burke away from 'natural law' thinking, is a particular application of the Aristotelian distinction, which he could also have found in Cicero,[18] between scientific knowledge (*epistêmê*) and prudence (*phronēsis*). Prudence is concerned with 'human concerns', 'things open to deliberation'[19] in relation to that which is 'good or bad for a human being';[20] scientific knowledge (*epistêmê*) involves certain and necessary demonstrations derived from *a priori* first principles.[21] The geometer who successfully constructs a triangle exercises *epistêmê*, rather than prudence. Burke criticises the 'geometrical' paradigm applied to politics, complaining that 'pure metaphysical abstraction does not belong to these [moral] matters', as 'the lines of morality are not like ideal lines of mathematics' (Works, III: 16). Aristotle would agree that the paradigm of geometry and the intellectual virtue of *epistêmê* are not appropriately applied to politics,[22] as 'prudence is not science'.[23] On this point, Burke is on a clear collision course with early modern thinkers such as Hobbes, Grotius, and Pufendorf, who aspire to model natural law on geometry, deriving certain truths from self-evident axiomatic principles: as soon as the geometrical 'Figure is drawn, the Consequences, and Demonstrations are plain and clear', reflects Pufendorf, 'just the same it is in *moral* knowledge'.[24]

Limitations of the Natural Law Interpretation of Burke

We might distinguish between different types of 'limitation' to the natural law interpretation of Burke: limitations to the interpretation of Burke as a natural law thinker, limitations with Burke's own understanding or comprehension of the tradition, and limitations that attach themselves generically to natural law approaches and that Burke suffers from by association. Whether one thinks of a particular limitation as a problem depends upon one's wider expectations from a field of knowledge. It is a 'limitation' of mathematics that it does not concern itself with how human beings can achieve happiness, but it could hardly be said to be a 'problem' with mathematics. For this reason, it is preferable to speak of 'limitations' with reference to the natural law interpretation of Burke, rather than of 'problems'.

Considering first of all the scope and ambition of interpretations of Burke as a natural law thinker, there is the obvious point – made earlier – that Burke's writings and speeches are porous cites for a wide range of discourses and strategies. Burke is not a natural law thinker, if by that we mean one who places this category at the centre of his thought; rather, Burke draws – strategically and sparingly – upon the natural law tradition. As we have seen, most of Burke's more theologically ambitious references to the natural law can be unpacked in terms of Aristotle, Cicero, and Philo. That Burke was himself a Christian – and placed a high value on revelation (see Chapter 7 in this volume) does not itself baptise the discourses that he draws upon, and so does not necessarily mitigate the non-Christian nature of Burke's natural law references.

If this is a problem for a Christian appropriation of Burke's natural law commitments, it is a 'problem' with the relationship between natural law thought and Christianity as such. The natural law strand of theology, even within the Christian tradition, is supposed to be accessible to rational human beings independently of special revelation or distinctively Christian doctrines, such as the Creation, Fall, and Incarnation. For this reason, there is considerable hostility to the natural law tradition from some strands of Protestant theology, where it is considered that independently of revelation and grace, human beings have a severely impaired access to moral truth.

Those in search of more distinctively Christian aspects of Burke's particular appropriation of natural law language might be drawn to Burke's defence of casuistry, a characteristically Catholic and Thomist way of mediating the universality of the natural law to particular and changing circumstances. Burke approves of the 'moral science called *casuistry*', in situations where 'duties … sometimes cross one another', cautioning that it 'requires a very solid and discriminating judgment, great modesty and caution, and much sobriety of mind in the handling' (Works, III: 81). It is true that of Burke's known early modern sources for natural law thought, only the Jesuit thinker Suarez has an extensive defence of casuistry,[25] giving a nice edge to the contemporary caricature of Burke in the biretta and cassock of a Jesuit priest, which Burke earned not for reading Suarez, but for defending Irish Catholics. The evidence here for a specifically Christian appropriation is ambiguous though, as Cicero also has a discussion of casuistry – weighing up conflicting duties in specific situations[26] – to which Burke makes explicit reference (Works, III: 81). Possibly, here as elsewhere, Burke can sound Thomist because he, like the Thomists, has read his Cicero.

Of more universal and unambiguous appeal to Christian theologians would be that Burke draws on the doctrine of the Incarnation amidst one of his most significant and cosmological uses of natural law language, in the conclusion to the opening speech of the Hastings trial. Christianity, comments Burke, is 'a religion which so much hates oppression, that, when the God whom we adore appeared in human form, he did not appear in the form of greatness and majesty, but in sympathy with the lowest of the people' so making it 'a firm and ruling principle that their welfare was the object of all Government, since the person who was the Master of Nature chose to appear himself in a subordinate situation':

> These are the considerations that influence them, which animate them, and will animate them against all oppression; knowing that He who is called first among them, and first among us all, both of the flock that is fed and of those who feed it, made Himself The Servant of all. (WS, V: 459)

That Burke combines scriptural allusions (to Philippians 2: 6–9) with natural law language does not in itself settle the underlying issue of their real compatibility, which for both secular and Christian thinkers remains a controversial topic. Burke's contribution here neither further complicates nor helps to resolve a perennially fraught topic.

We have already seen that Burke makes some clear and informed choices in relation to natural law language, associating himself with a eudaimonistic and teleological construal of natural law, which orients human nature in relation to a lawful and purposive universe, and which gives a strong role to virtue, history, custom, and prudence. Where we might find a significant limitation with Burke's own understanding or comprehension of the natural law tradition is in his lack of clarity about whether the laws of nature have a fundamentally voluntaristic or intellectualist grounding. The issue has the shape of the Euthyphro dilemma, where we ask whether something is good because God commands it, or whether God commands something because it is good. If the very act of divine command renders a maxim lawful/morally right, then at a fundamental theological level, we have a voluntarist construal of natural law. If God commands something because the divine intellect comprehends that it is lawful/morally right, then we have a theologically intellectualist construal of natural law.

For Burke's early modern sources, this is an issue of high importance, and extensive explicit discussion. Suarez is intellectualist about the nature of created essences – God can decide whether to create a human being, but not what constitutes human nature, where such a being is created.[27] Accordingly, Suarez follows Aquinas in being intellectualist about moral rightness and wrongness, but differs from Aquinas in insisting that for something to be *law* (over and above moral rightness) there must be a divine command. Grotius is more robustly intellectualist, arguing that natural right proceeds 'from the internal principles of man',[28] so that to establish the natural rightness or wrongness of something we have to show its 'necessary fitness or unfitness' to 'reasonable and social nature'.[29] Grotius tells us that 'the Law of Nature is so unalterable, that God himself cannot change it ... as God himself cannot effect, that twice two should not be four; so neither can he, that what is intrinsically evil should not be evil'.[30] This indicates an intriguing way in which Grotius's suggestion that natural law holds even if 'there is no God' does not exist, is an implication of what started out as theological intellectualism.[31] Pufendorf is more clearly voluntarist, lamenting efforts to 'establish an eternal rule for morality of the actions without respect to the divine injunction or constitution',[32] and so even the 'forms and essences of things' must proceed from the 'free will' and 'good pleasure of the Creator'.[33]

Burke refers to both the reason and will of God when invoking natural law language, but is conspicuously vague about the relationship of priority between them. In the context of revolutionary France, Burke explains that legitimate authority 'must be according to that eternal, immutable law, in which will and reason are the same' (WS, VIII: 145). In Aquinas's doctrine of divine simplicity, there is indeed a strict *identity* between divine will and reason that is supposed to cut off the sort of Euthyphro dilemma (will *or* reason) that dominates the later tradition. This notion of divine simplicity seems to be more or less absent from the early modern period, and it would be fanciful to ascribe it to Burke here. Again, it seems more likely that Burke's untroubled and elusive running together of divine reason and command might owe more to Cicero – 'Law is the primal and ultimate mind of God, whose reason directs all things' – and perhaps a lack of systematic reading around, or concern with, more contemporary issues.[34]

At moments Burke can seem more theologically voluntarist, with an interesting twist. With thinkers such as Hobbes and Pufendorf, a theological voluntarism that grounds law in divine command tends to be mirrored at the political level with a voluntarism about law in relation to human sovereigns. Similarly, intellectualism can go alongside a hostility to voluntarist and positivist accounts of law (as it does, for example, in Cudworth[35]). In Burke, though, there are moments where he seems to imply a fundamental theological voluntarism about law, which is used to counter and subvert voluntarism and positivism at a human level. Because God has 'disposed and marshalled us by a divine tactic, not according to our will, but according to his ... we have obligations to mankind at large, which are not in consequence of any special voluntary pact' (Works III: 79). Because law arises from the divine will, the 'exercise of authority' is a 'holy function' not to be exercised according to 'sordid, selfish interest' or 'arbitrary will' (WS, VIII: 145). At other points though, human voluntarism is opposed by a statement of the order in the universe – the 'great immutable, pre-existent law' – that could equally be construed along intellectualist lines, as a structure of lawfulness that binds and disciplines all voluntary decisions (WS, VI: 350).

On the issue of voluntarism and intellectualism Burke is less clear than his modern sources. There are other areas where the limitations are not so much with Burke's particular appropriation of the natural law, but with natural law thinking as such: these problems surface in Burke when he draws upon a strand of natural law thought. The issue can be set out fairly schematically.[36] When framing natural laws, we can either aim for very general statements or attempt to frame very particular injunctions for specific circumstances. In either case, we have associated difficulties. We can try first of all to frame general statements. If we formulate general statements in an uncontroversial way, such as Aquinas' 'good is to be done and evil avoided', or 'act in accord with reason', then we have not determined in any particular situation *what* would constitute avoiding evil, and acting in accord with reason. If we are still determined to deliver general statements, we might deliver content by stipulating in concrete terms what in *any* situation avoiding evil would consist of. Where the purpose of natural law is reduced to self-preservation, things can seem more straightforward. For Hobbes, the general law of nature that we need to obey in all particular situations is to obey the sovereign. Pufendorf tells us that 'the common and important precepts of natural law are so plain and clear that they meet with immediate assent, and become so ingrained in our minds that they can never thereafter be wiped from them'.[37] If we are unhappy with the crudity of such blanket – albeit concrete – commands, then we can attempt to frame specific injunctions that take into account all the circumstances of a particular situation; but then we hardly have a general rule at all.

Strands of the tradition are aware of this issue, and attempt to mediate the generalities of natural law to circumstances through the application of prudence. Himself drawing on Aristotle and Cicero, Aquinas concedes that some conclusions from the highest principles of natural law hold only usually and have exceptions: 'the more you descend into details the more it appears how the general rule admits of exceptions'.[38] Suarez explains that the higher principles of natural law are not really violated in such a case, because the possible exceptions are 'implied' in the general law, as it is not possible to 'draw up a complete statement of all points involved' in the 'shape of a law humanly drawn up'.[39] Burke again has some clear preferences, leaning towards Aristotle, Cicero, Aquinas, and Suarez, rather than Hobbes and Pufendorf, when he tells us that it is 'metaphysically mad' to neglect the particularities of a situation when applying general principles (Works, VI: 101). This is such an explicit theme of Burke's work, that we might even say that it is a general principle that particular circumstances are carefully attended to. The lines of morality are 'broad and deep as well as long', they 'admit of exceptions; they demand modifications', to the extent that 'nothing universal can be rationally affirmed on any moral, or any political subject' (Works, III: 16). We find a particularly strong example of Burke attempting this balancing act between the universal and the particular in the context of India, with a universal maxim to protect the local laws, manners and religion, and to govern upon 'British principles, not by British forms' (WS, VI: 345).

When this option is taken, of prudentially framing and adapting general principles to particular situations, we no longer have the problem of neglecting specificities, but now the issue of epistemic access to the correct application of principles becomes problematic. How do we know which circumstances are relevant, and by what criteria do we determine whether a particular course of action is the correct application of a principle in a certain situation? To say that the 'prudent' person will know the correct application just repeats the problem on a different level: by what criteria can we determine who is a prudent agent? This generic problem with natural law approaches that attempt to respond to particularities maps out problematic features of Burke's work, where Burke's judgements about what constitutes 'natural law' can seem rather arbitrary and shifting: in particular with reference to just war theory (the law of nature as applied to international relations) and the rights of resistance. On the former issue, Burke shifts his position, from the view that states cannot intervene in cases of internal injustices in other states, to the view that intervention and regime change is justified, implausibly claiming the support of Vattel's 'law of nations' for both positions (see Chapter 16 in this volume).

On the issue of the rights of resistance, there is similarly something of an arbitrary shift in Burke's thought. Hobbes identifies Aristotelian philosophy as a subversive influence, which can undermine obedience to the sovereign. There is something to be said for this view, in that strongly eudaimonistic and teleological natural law perspectives tend to have in view a higher purpose for human beings, to which temporal power is answerable. There are more criteria by which a state is judged than its capacity to keep the peace;

we might also require the state to promote, or at least not endanger, a range of rational and social goods that enable human flourishing. It is therefore no accident that the strands of natural law thought that Burke more closely identifies with tend to have some space for legitimate resistance against tyrannical rule. Suarez, for example, explains that 'if a lawful ruler is ruling tyrannically, and if the kingdom has available no other remedy for defending itself ... the whole commonwealth, acting on the public and common advice of the cities and leaders, will be allowed to depose him'.[40]

Suarez's resistance theory became notorious in seventeenth-century England and France, and so it is striking to find Burke reflecting and endorsing Suarez in the context of Ireland, writing in the 1760s that the 'essence of Law' requires that it 'be made as much as possible for the benefit of the whole' (WS, IX: 457), 'and so that ... all forms whatsoever of Government are only good as they are subservient to that purpose, to which they are entirely subordinate' (WS, IX: 464). This is sometimes referred to as Burke's Lockean moment, and it is consistent with Locke's account of government as a trust to secure the common good; but it is worth noting that it is actually Suarez whom Burke quotes here, 'it is inherent in the nature and essence of law that it be enacted for the sake of the common good' (WS, IX: 457).[41]

In the context of France, Burke seems to reverse this position, explaining that the multitude have no right of resistance, in that independently of the state, they have no existence as a *people*: 'when men ... break up the original compact or agreement which gives its corporate form and capacity to a state, they are no longer a people; they have no longer a corporate existence ... They are a number of vague, loose individuals, and nothing more' (Works III, 82). Here – as Hampsher-Monk sets out in Chapter 16 of this volume – Burke uses a Hobbesian strategy, which flies in the face of Suarez's assertion that from a 'moral point of view' a 'multitude of human beings' are a 'mystical body' who by 'common consent' appoint a 'single head', presupposing a political community without actual government.[42] All of which helps to illustrate that when the content of natural law is vague until concretely worked out in specific circumstances, a lack of clear epistemic criteria can lead to apparent arbitrariness.

It is hard not to see this limitation of natural law approaches as problematic, but it is worth pointing out that to identify it as a problem requires certain presuppositions about the sort of thing natural law ought to do. The epistemic difficulties of ascertaining the content of natural law look especially troubling if we primarily expect natural law to be a transparent *method* for working out the content of morality, where we must have access to the process of reasoning. Arguably, this reflects the preoccupations and concerns of early modern thinkers such as Hobbes and Grotius: to find a transparent method, where the reasons for conclusions must be internally and explicitly accessible. The language of natural law in a thinker such as Cicero or Aquinas is not so much a transparent method, as a way of expressing a conviction about what it is for something to be morally right or wrong, when it is right or wrong. To be morally right is to be oriented to the structure and movement of the universe. That we know what it is to be morally wrong does not tell us what is morally wrong: for that we need to draw on a variety of sources and capacities, some more internally transparent (prudence about how to achieve an end), others reliable without our knowing how (our grasp of what our proper end is, revelation and authority). Perhaps in this, as before, Burke shows that he is closer to the classical sources than he is to the early modern innovators.

NOTES

1 The standard 'natural law' readings are those provided by Francis P. Canavan, *The Political Reason of Edmund Burke* (Durham, N. C.: Duke University Press, 1960), and Peter J. Stanlis, *Edmund Burke and the Natural Law* (Ann Arbor, Michigan: University of Michigan Press, 1958).

2 For these details I am indebted to Canavan, *The Political Reason of Edmund Burke*, pp. 197–211.

3 For a recent discussion and defence of Thomistic natural law, see Jean Porter, *Nature as Reason: A Thomistic Theory of the Natural Law* (Grand Rapids, Michigan and Cambridge: William B. Eerdmans Publishing Company, 2005).

4 Hugo Grotius, *On the Rights of War and Peace,* ed. Richard Tuck, from the edition by Jean Barbeyrac (Indianapolis: Liberty Fund, 2005), prol. VI, p. 79.

5 Ibid., prol. XI, p. 89.

6 Suarez, *Tractatus de Legibus ac Deo Legislatore 1612,* in ed. and trans. Gwladys L. William, Ammi Brown, and John Waldron, *Selection from Three Works of Francisco Suarez S. J.* (Buffalo: William S. Hein & Co, 1995), II.iv.7–10, pp. 172–7, II.iv.10, p.177. For a discussion of Suarez's thought, to which I am indebted in this chapter, see Terence Irwin, 'From Suarez to Rousseau' *The Development of Ethics, A Historical and Critical Study,* vol. II, (Oxford: Oxford University Press, 2008), chs. 30–31.

7 Samuel Pufendorf, *On the Duty of Man and Citizen,* ed. James Tully (Cambridge: Cambridge University Press, 2006), I.ii.2, p. 27.

8 Cicero, *On the Laws,* I. vi. 19.56, in *De Republica, De Legibus,* the Loeb Classical Library, trans. Clinton Keyes (London: William Heinemann, 1928), p. 319.

9 Ibid., I. vii 23.33, p.333.

10 Burke, 'Letter to the Archbishop of Nisobi' (1791) in H. V. F. Somerset, 'Edmund Burke, England and the Papacy', *Dublin Review,* 202.404 (1938): 138–48, 141.

11 Ibid., p. 141.

12 Cicero, *On the Laws,* I. xi. 42, in *De Republica. De Legibus,* p. 345.

13 Ibid.

14 Ibid. II. iv. 8–10, p. 381.

15 Francis Hutcheson, *Logic, Metaphysics, and the Natural Sociability of Mankind*, eds., James Moore and Michael Silverthorne (Indianapolis: Liberty Fund, 2006), pp. 9–10.

16 Adam Smith, *The Theory of Moral Sentiments* (Cambridge: Cambridge University Press, 2009), pp. 249–55.

17 For this point, I am indebted to a discussion with Lewis Ayers.

18 Cicero, *On Duties*, in the Loeb Classical Library trans. Walter Miller, (Cambridge, MA: Harvard University Press, 2001), I. xliii–xliv, pp. 157–65.

19 Aristotle, *Nicomachean Ethics*, VI.VII §6, 1139b15–30, trans. Terence Irwin (Indianapolis: Hackett Publishing Company, 1999), p. 91.

20 Ibid., VI.v.4, p. 89.

21 Ibid., VI.iv.1, p. 88.

22 Ibid., VI.v.3, p. 89.

23 Ibid. VI.v.3, p. 89.

24 Pufendorf, *Of the Law of Nature and Nations*, trans. B. Kennett (London, 1729), I.ii.6, p. 6.

25 See, for example, Suarez, *De Legibus* II.xiii.6–8, pp. 261–3. See Irwin, *The Development of Ethics*, pp. 48–57 for an account of Suarez's casuistical method.

26 Cicero, *On Duties*, the Loeb Classical Library, trans. Walter Miller (Cambridge MA: Harvard University Press, 2001), I.xliii.152–5, p.155–9.

27 See, for example, Suarez, *de Legibus*, II.xiii.2, pp. 258–9. I am indebted here to Irwin's account of Suarez, *The Development of Ethics*, pp.10–21, 38–48.

28 Grotius, *On the Rights of War and Peace*, prol., XII, p. 91.

29 Ibid,. I.i.12, p. 159.

30 Ibid., I.i.10, p. 155.

31 Ibid., prol. XI, 89.

32 Pufendorf, *Of the Law of Nature and Nations*, trans. B. Kennett (London, 1729), I.ii.4, p. 17.

33 Ibid.

34 Cicero, *On the Laws*, II.iv.8, p. 381.

35 Ralph Cudworth, *A Treatise Concerning Eternal and Immutable Morality with a Treatise of Freewill*, ed. Sarah Hutton (Cambridge: Cambridge University Press, 1996), I.ii.4, p. 19.

36 In my formulation here I am indebted to Irwin, *The Development of Ethics*, 49–57.

37 Pufendorf, *On the Duty of Man and Citizen*, I.iii.12, p. 37.

38 Aquinas, *Summa Theologiae*, I-II.94.4, ed. Thomas Gilby (Cambridge: Cambridge University Press, 2006), vol. XXVIII, p. 89.

39 Suarez, *De Legibus*, II.xiii.6, p. 262.

40 Suarez, *Defensio Fiedei Catholicae*, VI.iv.15, in *Opera Omnia*, ed. C. Berton, 28 vols. (Paris: Vivés, 1866), vol. XXIV, cited and discussed by Irwin, *The Development of Ethics*, p. 66. I am indebted to Irwin, pp. 64–7, in my discussion of Suarez and resistance theory.

41 The Suarez reference is *De Legibus*, I.vii.1, p. 90.

42 Suarez, *Defensio Fiedei Catholicae*, III.ii.4, cited and discussed in Irwin, *The Development of Ethics*, p. 66.

10

DAVID DWAN

Burke and Utility

In an early fragment, Burke drafted 'A Plan for Arguing' in which he listed key strategies of debate: arguments from 'justice' were of fundamental importance, but crucial too were appeals to 'interest' and 'convenience' (N, 46–7). These would remain important rhetorical principles throughout Burke's career as a statesman, but it is difficult to determine how justice, interest, and convenience exactly relate – or, indeed, if their relation is systematic or largely arbitrary – in his moral universe. This issue is central to an understanding of 'utility' – a key, but much disputed theme, in Burke's political thought. He repeatedly insisted that the utility of a proposal was central to deciding its merits, but it was not always clear if this utility was independent or, in fact, constitutive of its justice. In 1765 he presented 'utility' – alongside 'equity' – as one of the two pillars of law (WS, IX: 456). Fourteen years later, however, utility seemed to have become not just a necessary legal principle, but a sufficient criterion of justice for lawmakers: 'only the utility and convenience of the community as it happens by accident to be constituted' were, he insisted, proper grounds for legislation (WS, III: 432). Somewhere down the line justice, interest, and convenience appeared to have merged.

Partly for these reasons, Burke is often considered to be a 'utilitarian' thinker.[1] Clearly, much depends here upon the meaning of the word 'utilitarian' (a term that seems to have been first deployed by Jeremy Bentham in a letter in 1781) and the extent to which this represents a distinctive and systematic doctrine.[2] Some might suggest that to attribute any systematic theory to Burke is already to distort his intellectual practice. It is worth reiterating that his major political writings were triggered by specific events and were practical responses to them; they were not offered as a comprehensive system of morals – and it is often the systematic character of utilitarianism (its 'all-comprehensiveness and consistency', as Bentham put it) that its adherents endorse and its critics disparage.[3] But there are more interesting and intellectually substantive reasons why Burke cannot be considered a utilitarian – at least in the way that doctrine was later expounded by

Bentham or J. S. Mill. This chapter explores some of these reasons and situates them within a broader discussion of Burke's moral and political views.

The emphasis Burke placed on utility reveals some of his most basic moral commitments and methods of political reasoning; at the same time, utility could only enjoy this foundational role by remaining a broad – even trivial – principle in its own right. It implied that 'usefulness' was a criterion of value. But this was an entirely empty standard without some way of determining what ends or ultimate goods should determine our sense of a useful means, for utility was either a circular or incoherent ideal if it made 'usefulness' the only good. Burke provided scattered descriptions of humanity's ultimate ends, and, however incomplete, they say important things about the nature of happiness and virtue and the role these ends should possess in public decision-making. But, as I shall argue, his account of these goods had little in common with what utilitarians would later judge to be of ultimate value or with their methods for arriving at such judgements.

Consequences and Intrinsic Goods

Burke frequently invoked the principle of utility, but like many of his eighteenth-century contemporaries from David Hume to Adam Smith to John Millar, he did so in a very broad sense. In *A Philosophical Enquiry*, he defined utility as the fitness of means for certain ends (or 'a part's being well adapted to answer its end') and dismissed this as an adequate criterion for determining beauty (WS, 1: 266). However, in the teleological universe of the *Enquiry*, all aspects of human life were oriented towards certain ends and thus might appear to have a functional value. His account of the 'purposes of our being' in the *Enquiry* was fairly spare and was restricted to two recognisably Grotian principles: self-preservation and sociability (WS, I: 220). With reference to these ends everything had a relative use. But here Burke's 'utilitarianism' is so wide that it tends to disappear. If, as Hume suggested, utility or usefulness is 'only a tendency towards a certain end', then all teleological theories are utilitarian in a trivial sense; they presume that properties are useful with reference to certain ends, but they can remain indeterminate about the content, number, and range of such ends.[4] Bentham worried about this latitude and recognised that utility was often interpreted as 'conduciveness to an end, whatsoever be that end'.[5] For Bentham, however, the only ultimate goal to which humanity could rationally aspire was happiness or – what was tantamount, in his eyes, to the same thing – pleasure.

Thus, Benthamite utilitarianism is often judged to combine two elements: a consequentialist theory of right action and a hedonistic account of value. It is consequentialist insofar as it holds that the rightness of any action always lies in the value of its consequences, and it is only with reference to these outcomes that actions, practices, and institutions can be justified. Of course, no consequentialism can be absolute, for this would lead to an eternal regress: something in the end must have intrinsic worth for any estimation of the value of consequences to be possible. For classical versions of utilitarianism, the only property that has intrinsic value is a type of well-being that was reducible to pleasure. As Bentham put it, 'pleasure is in *itself* a good: nay, even setting aside immunity from pain, the only good: pain is in itself an evil; and indeed, without exception, the only evil; or else the words good and evil have no meaning'.[6] However, it is very difficult to identify this hedonistic consequentialism with the principles espoused by Burke. He repeatedly argued on consequentialist lines and judged 'that to be good from whence good is derived' (WS, VIII: 220). But this formula simply meant that an action was right if it produced a good state of affairs. Since it left the definition of the good entirely open, the goodness of a state of affairs might include a whole series of non-consequential values – actions, practices and virtues that were right in themselves. The same holds true for Burke's 'standard of expedience': that 'which is good for the community, and good for every individual in it' (Works, VI: 149). A consequentialism so broad commits Burke to very little.[7]

Like any sane politician, he stressed the importance of consequences for assessing the merits of a proposed action, policy, or law: as he put it, the 'practical consequences of any political tenet go a great way in deciding upon its value' (Works, III: 81). However, this did not mean that *everything* depended on consequences or that there were no intrinsic values. He appeared to condemn the violation of such values by the French revolutionaries and often emphasised the moral insanity of their consequential reasoning, 'weighing, as it were in scales hung in a shop of horrors, – so much actual crime against so much contingent advantage' (WS, VIII: 132). However, he would also attack the French and their English supporters for their utter neglect of consequences: 'They are sublime Metaphysicians; and the horrible consequences produced by their Speculations affect them not at all' (C, VII: 63). Such men prided themselves on their methodical rigour, but the logical consistency of a system was not the only test of its merits; it must also have practical benefits: 'Political problems do not primarily concern truth or falsehood. They relate to good or evil. What in the result is likely to produce evil, is politically false: that which is productive of good, politically true' (Works, III: 81). Burke never precisely defined what goodness was – indeed, he may have regarded precision in such matters as either unattainable or unnecessary – but judged across the whole sweep of his writings, it is clear that it was not identical to pleasure.

In *A Philosophical Enquiry*, he subscribed in part to a hedonistic theory of motivation. Here he described pleasure and pain – in Lockean terms – as simple ideas incapable of definition; they were a fundamental constituent of our passions and gave them their motivating force (although these feelings were also orientated towards final causes that were valuable in themselves; pleasure, therefore, was not the only intrinsic good). However, this was an explanation of our passions, not a justification of them. God, in his wisdom, often allowed our duties to be tracked by our desires, but pleasure was not the ground of obligation. Later he went further: human beings had no right to 'act any where according to their pleasure, without any moral tie' (WS, IX: 249). Nor should they confuse their well-being with the satisfaction of desire or the gratification of the will. 'Neither the few nor the many', he declared, 'have a right to act merely by their will, in any matter connected with duty, trust, engagement, or obligation' (Works, III: 76). Some interpreters might claim that these duties, trusts, and moral ties, for Burke, ultimately derive from pleasure and are instrumental to the satisfaction of higher-order or more sustainable desires. But this risks extending the semantic remit of 'pleasure' – at least as it was used by Burke – until it ceases to say anything specific about the nature of goodness and becomes a simple synonym for the good as such. Moreover, it is notoriously difficult to distinguish between lower and higher-order pleasures from within the category of pleasure itself. If an independent evaluative criterion is required, then hedonism has been left behind.

Burke was not a hedonist, but he did ascribe an important justificatory role to happiness – a form of well-being that was not reducible to hedonic feelings and presupposed other intrinsic values. 'The object of the state', he declared, 'is (as far as may be) the happiness of the whole' (Works, VI: 116). This objective could be abused – 'the great inlet, by which a colour for oppression has entered into the world, is by one man's pretending to determine concerning the happiness of another' (WS, IX: 463). Nevertheless, government remained for him 'a practical thing, made for the happiness of mankind' (WS, III: 317). The consequentialist structure of his ethical views might suggest that traditional virtues such as benevolence, prudence, or courage had a purely functional value for Burke: they were means to happiness, but were purely external to that end. Nevertheless, his writings and speeches often assume that virtues were valuable in themselves; they 'perfected' our nature and were expressive of that perfection. This could also lead to a demanding conception of the state: it was 'a partnership in every virtue, and in all perfection' (WS, VIII: 147–8). It is not clear how the goals of perfection and of happiness were related in Burke's eyes, and it is easy to see how they could diverge. Yet he tended to assume that they were compatible ends: that which made us 'better and happier', he wrote in his youth, should serve as a moral standard (N, 72). Late in life he rued the fact that the French had failed 'to recognize the happiness that is to be found by virtue in all conditions' (WS, VIII: 87). Here he may have assumed that happiness and virtue were intrinsic but independent goods, while occupying a purely instrumental relationship to each other; or he may have concluded, like many classical writers before him, that virtue was a constituent, not just an external cause, of happiness. Either way, the good – or happiness – incorporated a range of different and irreducible moral values, even if this might seem to put a unitary concept of goodness under some strain.

Partly because moral life involved a diversity of values, the good was not simply an aggregative matter. Bentham liked to insist that all values could be reduced to a common denominator of felicity or pleasure and thus could be compared and aggregated; 'on every occasion happiness is ... a subject-matter of calculation, of profit and loss, just as money itself is'.[8] Burke, however, never subscribed to this calculus – indeed, the pursuit of geometrical exactitude in moral affairs compromised the principle of 'mutual convenience' (WS, II: 457). He did admit that politics aimed for a virtuous mean between different and rival interests and to this extent it had a calculative dimension, but here he enlisted arithmetical metaphors only to rule out a quantitative approach to ethical questions. 'Political reason,' he explained, 'is a computing principle; adding, subtracting, multiplying, and dividing, morally and not metaphysically or mathematically, true moral denominations' (WS, VIII: 112–13). Thus, calculations of interest are an intrinsically moral affair; they are so, not simply because it is a moral obligation to harmonise or to optimise interests, but because those interests – or the ones that should matter – are themselves constituted by a series of commitments to what is right and important. Such 'moral denominations' are irreducible and cannot be converted into some non-moral state of affairs such as pleasure – or, if pleasure is a moral property, it is not the only one. What makes political calculation difficult, for Burke, is that there are plural values – or what he calls 'differences of good' – which are not reducible to a common currency, except that on the most abstract basis they are all deemed 'good' (WS, VIII: 112).

Burke wished to maximise the good in the trivial sense that he wanted the best outcome in moral and political affairs. But he never openly subscribed to Francis Hutcheson's belief that 'that action is best, which procures the greatest Happiness for the greatest Numbers'.[9] The 'greatest happiness principle' would become one of the fundamental tenets of utilitarianism under Bentham and J. S. Mill, although it could mean different things: the demands to produce the 'greatest happiness' and to benefit the 'greatest number' could pull in different directions. Burke never invited this problem upon himself, partly because he never regarded happiness as an aggregative matter, but also because he was critical of naïve bids for its maximisation. In writings on France and Ireland, he argued that 'universal benevolence' was self-undermining (WS, VIII: 318). The 'comprehensive system of universal fraternity', extolled by the French, bred sympathy for everyone and for no one and alienated us from the little platoons that were the ground of our public affections (WS, IX: 303). In Burke's eyes, 'benevolence so displaced' was virtually the same thing as benevolence destroyed (WS, IX: 461). Rousseau – 'a lover of his kind, but a hater of his kindred' – was an embodiment of this perverted charity, but these criticisms could also incorporate, at least in principle, the maximising ambitions of later utilitarianism (WS, VIII: 315).

'Of the greatest happiness principle', Bentham announced, 'application cannot be made upon too large a scale: it cannot be carried on too far'.[10] Of course, Bentham was aware of the problem of diminishing marginal returns, but he felt that there was no intrinsic reason why utility should not be fully maximised; indeed, it was immoral not to do so. Burke recognised no such imperative. Charity, he believed, began at home and should be extended outwards, but it did not function as an abstract programme to be universally applied and impartially administered. Moreover, by privileging 'home-bred connections' over 'foreign affections', he allowed individuals to put a special emphasis on their own projects and concerns and to prioritise their families and friends over unfamiliar albeit more numerous others (WS, IX: 461). Superficially, at least, this defence of humanity's 'partial affections' is at odds with the apparent 'agent-neutrality' of classical utilitarianism – its attempts to prescribe to all individuals the same moral aim irrespective of their particular identities, relationships, and commitments (WS, IX: 303). Demands to abandon our personal loyalties and moral projects and to incorporate them within some general plan of optimised utility or universal benevolence were, from Burke's perspective, an assault on our moral characters.

Justice, Rules and Manners

Burke is not easily situated within classical utilitarianism, but he did present 'utility' as a key principle of justice. In a public letter in 1791, he cited some lines from Horace's *Satires*, which concluded with the following resonant phrase: '*Atque ipsa utilitas justi propre mater et aequi*' – 'utility itself, mother of justice and equity' (WS, VIII: 318). Back in 1765 he had described 'equality' as the mother of justice, although even then he declared utility to be an equally fundamental principle. But in his Horatian moment of

1791, utility had assumed priority, and equity appeared to be a secondary or derivative value. By insisting on the utility of justice, Burke was mainly emphasising its practical character (the lines from Horace were offered as a rebuke to Rousseau whose doctrines were 'inapplicable to real life and manners'), but he was also taking up – perhaps inadvertently – a controversial position in an ongoing debate about the nature of justice (WS, VIII: 318). Grotius and Pufendorf, the great modern exponents of natural law, had criticised Horace's line as a mistaken interpretation of right; they acknowledged that the rules of justice were useful, but this was not the reason why they were instituted or should be observed.[11] On the other hand, David Hume – for whom utility was 'the sole origin of justice' – endorsed Horace's phrase and argued that if Grotius and Pufendorf were properly consistent, they would have done the same.[12] Years after Burke's death, Bentham would invoke Horace's 'correct' observation, while outlining the origins of his own utilitarianism.[13]

The provocation of Horace's phrase is that it seems to deny that justice has an objective foundation, which is independent of what humans simply deem to be just. Moreover, it implies that their claims about justice are always derived from their interest or sense of benefit. To ground law on utility was, for some interpreters, to make it a purely contingent affair as well as a mercenary matter; it undermined the real and universal or so-called natural properties of justice and thus negated its very essence. According to Cicero – another of Burke's favoured authors – 'there is no justice at all if it is not by nature, and the justice set up on the basis of utility is uprooted by that same utility'.[14] Elsewhere Cicero was even more emphatic: 'if equity, honesty and justice have not their source in nature, and if all these things are only valuable for their utility, no good man can anywhere be found'.[15] Modern thinkers usually entertained different conceptions of nature than those held by Cicero, but they often shared his assumption that justice was 'natural': its laws were universal and unchanging, existing prior to and independent of humanity's particular moral practices and legal institutions. For some, this necessarily precluded utility from enjoying a foundational role in the constitution of justice; at most, utility was the child of law, never its mother. When Burke concluded in 1765 that utility was a pillar of law, or when he suggested in 1779 and in 1791 that it was a sufficient condition of justice, he was potentially occupying a highly contentious position.

But the more provocative features of this position disappear when one considers what utility means for Burke: it means 'useful' with reference to certain ends. He sometimes used the words 'utility', 'interest', 'advantage', or 'benefit' as synonyms for humanity's ends, but he clearly believed that a concern for virtue was a constitutive feature of human interests. Thus, our moral commitments provided us with criteria for calculating benefits or good outcomes; they were not just an external means to these results. Moreover, an interest in the welfare of others was – to some degree at least – internal to any assessment of our own advantage. The utility he sponsored, therefore, 'must be understood, not of partial or limited, but of general and publick utility, connected in the same manner with, and derived directly from, our rational nature; for any other utility may be the utility of a robber, but cannot be that of a citizen' (WS, IX: 456). This, Burke proclaimed, was the only utility that was agreeable to nature and he added that it was a conception of justice that Cicero had endorsed. In *De Officiis*, from which Burke quoted, Cicero had maintained that utility, properly regarded, was not opposed to or even separate from justice (the utility he had criticised was one that appeared to be logically independent from honour and right, while also operating as their cause and justification). As Cicero argued: 'nothing is beneficial that is not also honourable, and nothing honourable that is not also beneficial.'[16] Human beings were constrained by the law of nature to pursue both honour and benefit and there is no necessary reason for Cicero – or indeed for Burke – why these should be viewed as opposed ends. 'Men of Virtue', Burke explained, 'will require no other Incentive to doing Good than Virtue itself; but as if that was not sufficient, Providence often joins Honour and Interest in rewarding it' (WS, I: 84).

Burke's emphasis on the 'natural' constitution of law (namely its objective and universal properties) is perfectly consistent, therefore, with his sense of its utility. Some of the noisier discussions of Burke in recent decades, however, have depended on a strong distinction between an attachment to 'natural law' on the one hand, and a subscription to the principle of utility on the other.[17] As we have seen, there are passages in Cicero, which seem to support this dichotomy. Modern thinkers such as Grotius, Pufendorf, and Locke also distinguished between natural law and utility, whereas Bentham's spirited assault on the arbitrariness and vagueness of natural law in the name of the more rational methods of utilitarianism further entrenched the distinction.[18] However, there is no necessary reason why natural law should preclude utility as a normative principle, and Burke was arguably part of a long tradition in which both were compatible and even co-dependent ideas. He placed his trust 'in political convenience, and in human nature' and saw both as perfectly harmonious principles (Works, III: 109). Thus, from Burke's teleological perspective, human beings were naturally oriented to pursue the good and the happiness this yielded. The content of that happiness was dictated by the nature of things in general and by humanity's own nature in particular: all human beings, for instance, sought self-preservation and society (and as we have seen, he sometimes cast these as prerequisites for humanity's pursuit of moral perfection). Whatever the precise content of human ends, the laws of nature could be construed as the necessary rules for their acquisition. Natural laws, therefore, were both universal and useful, and could not be abrogated for more local or short-term conceptions of utility or convenience (WS, VII: 317).

However, to the extent that Burke was a teleological thinker, the 'good' would seem to have a logical and even moral priority over the rules that we must observe to acquire it: namely law (unless, of course, lawfulness is itself a constituent of that good – a possibility that Burke raises but leaves indeterminate). He declared that 'law itself is only beneficence acting by a rule' in ways that suggested that rules had an instrumental relationship to a more general good. He also maintained that rights acquired their normative force from the benefits that they guaranteed. Civil society, he proclaimed, was made for the advantage of man and 'all the advantages for which it is made become his right' (WS, VIII: 109); or, as he also put it, 'the rights of men in governments are their advantages' (WS, VIII: 112). Thus, for Burke, rights sometimes seem to have only a contingent value that derives from the welfare they promote. When they fail to yield general benefits, they appear to relinquish their moral force. Similarly, when a law ceases to be an instrument of beneficence, it loses its obligating power. Some laws could be abrogated, therefore, in cases of extreme emergency – cases of 'public necessity, so vast, so clear, so evident, that they supersede all laws'. After all, laws were 'only made for the benefit of the community' and should not be deployed to undermine that end – or as he put it, 'no law can set itself up against the cause and reason of all law' (WS, III: 527).

But the suspension of law could only happen in the most rare of cases, for not only were some rules universally beneficial, there were universal benefits in general rule-following. Thus, Burke tended to stress the utility of laws rather than individual actions, although, presumably, these evaluative criteria converged at some point downstream (the usefulness of rules might be ultimately derived from a utility assessment of the actions they engendered). Nevertheless, Burke wished to stress the consequential value of rules against those who would jeopardise that utility by basing their sense of right on the direct benefits of discrete actions. Justice should not be a matter of individual decision-making and to prioritise the immediate benefits of specific actions over the indirect utility of general rules was to undermine the very concept of law and the collective benefits it guaranteed. In his 'Speech on Foreign Troops in Ireland' (1776), he maintained that actions must be legal and to be legal they must conform to general principles: 'They can never be tried by the *Special* and particular *utility* separately taken of each *act*. For this is so far from establishing a Rule of Law;

that this is the manner in which we must act if there were no Law at all in being. It is to prevent this discussion and the utility of *each* act, taken separately, that Laws have been made' (WS, IX: 502). But if rules were necessary, they were also, as we have seen, secondary, derived, as they were, from the principle of goodness itself. They were also incomplete, for social practices could not be entirely reduced to rules, and laws could only do so much to guarantee public well-being.

In this context, Burke would often stress the utility of manners. As he famously put it: 'Manners are of more importance than laws. Upon them, in a great measure the laws depend. The law touches us but here and there, and now and then. Manners are what vex or sooth, corrupt or purify, exalt or debase, barbarize or refine us, by a constant, steady, uniform, insensible operation, like that of the air we breathe in' (WS, IX: 242). Hume and Smith would argue that the spread of commerce improved public mores – a point that Burke accepted. But he also maintained that economic life was itself dependent on 'antient manners': 'commerce, and trade, and manufacture, the gods of our oeconomical politicians, are themselves perhaps but creatures; are themselves but effects, which, as first causes, we choose to worship' (WS, VIII: 130).

Here Burke also gestured towards an ancient paradox of moral thought: those who would base everything on utility would find that utility undermined by that same token. He made this point about religion in his youth ('If you attempt to make the end of Religion to be its Utility to human Society ... You make it an Engine of no efficacy at all'), and he put forward a similar argument in his defence of manners and prejudice in later life (N, 67). Manners were useful, but they would not survive in a society of vulgar utilitarians, who would derive all worth from narrow calculations of interest. For the utility of manners depended on the fact that their operation was non-calculative or quasi-intuitive; moreover, they often seemed to be built upon an assumption that some things were valuable or honourable in themselves. He hinted that the intrinsic worth of some of our customs may be illusory, but the utility of these values depended on everyone being taken in. Manners would not survive in a world in which the value of everything was purely consequential or necessarily deducible from self-interest.

Burke had always maintained that the collective pursuit of self-interest brought significant public benefits. In this harmonious arrangement, he saw some evidence of the invisible hand of God – 'the benign and wise disposer of all things, who obliges men, whether they will or not, in pursing their own selfish interests, to connect the general good with their own individual success' (WS, IX: 125). Against those who would demand a self-sacrificing form of virtue as a guarantor of public well-being, he was prepared to defend the 'love of lucre' and the benefits that derived from the selfish enterprises of 'monied men' (WS, IX: 347). He did not advocate a society of angels, but he did maintain that there could never be an alliance of devils, for it was 'an indubitable truth written in the essence of things, that good cannot be extracted from bad men by any human device' (C, VI: 319). There could be no 'tie of *honour*' and no 'tie of common *interest*' in a society of rapacious individuals: some minimal commitment to the welfare of others was required (WS, IX: 269). Moreover, this welfare could only be vouchsafed if people assumed, on some level, that virtue and honour were valuable in their own right.

The revolutionaries of France made no such assumptions. They had triggered a revolution in manners, partly because they tried to ground them on narrow principles of self-interest – an approach 'founded in a knowledge of the physical wants of men; progressively carried to an enlightened self-interest, which, when well understood, they tell us will identify with an interest more enlarged and public' (WS, VIII: 197). For Burke, this was a recipe for barbarism, pronounced by those who would subtilise us into savages. In the *Reflections*, he mourned the loss of those manners that he associated with an ancient chivalric code. 'But the age of chivalry is gone,' he famously complained; the era 'of sophisters, oeconomists, and calculators has succeeded' (WS, VIII: 127). The code of honour that Burke lamented was in many respects a competitive ethos: as Montesquieu had argued, people often competed for honour out of self-interest, although this competition served the public good.[19] Nevertheless, this moral economy seemed to depend on the collective assumption that some actions were intrinsically honourable and that honour was something worth having. The economists and calculators of enlightened self-interest, Burke argued, were incapable of acknowledging such goods. Their utility would ultimately prove to be self-undermining.

Here utility may have remained a key criterion for Burke, but if it did so, it operated on an extremely indirect basis – via a system of rules, manners, and ethical dispositions that were necessarily regarded by their practitioners as valuable in themselves. Individuals might attempt to abstract themselves from this ethical system, in order to judge its general utility. From this transcendental perspective, our ethical practices might appear to be hollow, while their practical benefits might be seen to be real. Burke adopted this position when he presented manners as 'pleasing illusions' from which we received inestimable returns (WS, VIII: 128). But he generally assumed that a transcendental viewpoint was not a very good view to adopt, for it risked alienating us from our everyday moral feelings. And it was largely through such feelings that our moral relationship to the world was given to us.[20]

They had a key role to play in political deliberation, while 'that sort of reason which banishes the affections is incapable or filling their place' (WS, VIII: 129).

Conclusion

Burke's defence of feeling exposes the limits of moral rationality in general and of utilitarian calculations in particular. Many of our deepest moral responses, precede any utilitarian assessment of value. This was why the principle of utility was ill-equipped to understand our aesthetic attitudes – a point that he made at some length in *A Philosophical Enquiry*; nor could the principle do justice to our everyday moral feelings, for some things were just felt to be wrong prior to any deliberation about their consequences. For Burke, some things were too monstrous to expect a rational justification of them; indeed, there was a moral obscenity in any attempt to provide such reasons. The consequentialist reasoning deployed by the French, for instance, was utterly grotesque:

> In the theatre, the first intuitive glance, without any elaborate process of reasoning, would shew, that this method of political computation, would justify every extent of crime ... Justifying perfidy and murder for public benefit, public benefit would soon become the pretext, and perfidy and murder the end; until rapacity, malice, revenge, and fear more dreadful than revenge, could satiate their insatiable appetites. Such must be the consequences of losing in the splendour of these triumphs of the rights of men, all natural sense of wrong and right. (WS, VIII: 133–4)

Burke's own argument is itself consequentialist to the extent that it worries about the results of losing our moral sense. But this reveals once again how vanishingly broad his consequentialism is: it assumes what human beings generally or 'naturally' assume – that some things are wrong or right in themselves and that these deontological commitments are criterial for any estimate of good outcomes.

Burke was a utilitarian in the extremely trivial sense that he wanted good outcomes for people. He believed that this goodness was often indirect and presupposed a range of rules, practices, manners, and dispositions that had, at least for their participants, a distinctly non-utilitarian character. This might be a sophisticated utilitarianism, but it is probably better viewed as a rebuttal of any such theory. For judged by most of the classical features of that doctrine – its hedonistic, aggregative, maximising, agent-neutral, and ratio-calculative perspective – Burke in the end seems to present himself as one of utilitarianism's harshest critics.

NOTES

1 This tradition has nineteenth-century origins – see in particular: John Morley, *Edmund Burke: A Historical Study* (London, 1869) and *Burke* (London, 1879). Interpretations of Burke as a utilitarian prospered throughout the twentieth century. The most persuasive – because highly qualified – was offered by J. R. Dinwiddy, 'Utility and Natural Law in Burke's Thought: A Reconsideration', *Studies in Burke and His Time*, 6 (1979): 105–28.

2 Jeremy Bentham, *The Correspondence of Jeremy Bentham*, ed. Ian R. Christie, 14 vols. (London: Athlone Press, 1971), vol. III, p. 11.

3 Jeremy Bentham, *The Collected Works of Jeremy Bentham: Deontology Together with a Table of the Springs of Action and Article on Utilitarianism*, ed. J. R. Dinwiddy and Amnon Goldworth (Oxford: Clarendon, 1983), p. 318.

4 David Hume, *An Enquiry Concerning the Principles of Morals*, ed. Tom L. Beauchamp (Oxford: Oxford University Press, 1993), p. 109.

5 Bentham, *Article on Utilitarianism*, p. 321.

6 Jeremy Bentham, *The Collected Works of Jeremy Bentham: The Principles of Morals and Legislation*, ed. J. H. Burns and J. L. A. Hart (Oxford: Clarendon, 1996), p. 100.

7 Thus, Dinwiddy's discussion of Burke's consequentialism does little to prove that he was a utilitarian. See Dinwiddy, 'Utility and Natural Law in Burke's Thought', pp. 111, 121, 126–7.

8 Bentham, *Article on Utilitarianism*, p. 297.

9 Francis Hutcheson, *An Inquiry Into the Original of our Ideas of Beauty and Virtue*, ed. Wolfgang Leidhold (Indianapolis: Liberty Fund, 2004), p. 125.

10 Bentham, *Article on Utilitarianism*, p. 318.

11 Hugo Grotius, *The Rights of War and Peace*, ed. Richard Tuck, 3 vols. (Indianapolis: Liberty Fund, 2005), vol. 1, p. 93. Samuel Pufendorf, *On the Law of Nations*, trans. Basil Kennett (London, 1729), Bk II.iii.10, p. 128.

12 David Hume, *The Letters of David Hume*, ed. J. Y. T. Greig, 2 vols. (Oxford: Clarendon, 1932), vol. 1, p. 33. On this issue see James Moore, 'Natural Law and the Pyrrhonian Controversy' in *Philosophy and Science in the Scottish Enlightenment*, ed. Peter Jones (Edinburgh: John Donald, 1988), pp. 20–38, 33, 38.

13 Bentham, *Article on Utilitarianism*, 321. On this point See Frederick Rosen, *Classical Utilitarianism from Hume to Mill* (London and New York: Routledge, 2003), p. 15.

14 Cicero, *On the Laws*, in *On the Commonwealth and On the Laws*, ed. James E. G. Zetzel (Cambridge: Cambridge University Press, 1999), I.xv.42, p. 121.

15 Cicero, *De Finibus Bonorum et Malorum*, ed. Johan Nicolai Madvig (Cambridge: Cambridge University Press, 2010), Bk. V, p. 244 [my translation].

16 Cicero, *On Duties*, ed. M. T. Griffin and E. M. Atkins (Cambridge: Cambridge University Press, 1991), III.vii.34, p. 112.

17 See Peter. J. Stanlis, *Edmund Burke and Natural Law* (Ann Arbor: University of Michigan, 1958); Francis, J. Canavan, *The Political Reason of Edmund Burke*, (Durham: Duke University Press, 1960); Joseph L. Pappin III, *The Metaphysics of Edmund Burke* (New York: Fordham University Press, 1994).

18 Grotius, *Rights of War and Peace*, vol. 1, p. 93; Pufendorf, *On the Law of Nations*, vol. II, p. 128; John Locke, *Essays on the Laws of Nature*, ed. W. von

Leyden (Oxford: Clarendon, 1954), p. 205; Bentham, *Introduction to the Principles of Morals and Legislation*, pp. 26–9.

19 Montesquieu, *The Spirit of the Laws*, trans. and ed. Anne M. Cohler, Basia Carolyn Miller, and Harold Samuel Stone (Cambridge: Cambridge University Press, 1989), p. 26. On this point see, Richard Bourke, 'Edmund Burke and Enlightenment Sociability: Justice, Honour and the Principles of Government', *History of Political Thought*, 21.4 (2000): 632–56.

20 For a fuller discussion of the role of feeling in Burke, see David Dwan, 'Edmund Burke and the Emotions', *Journal of the History of Ideas*, 72.4 (2011): 571–93.

II

JENNIFER PITTS

Burke and the Ends of Empire

The politics of empire and conquest were among Burke's most intense and abiding preoccupations throughout his life as a writer and legislator. He took up these themes in some of his earliest published writing, his contributions to *An Account of the European Settlements in America*, written with his friend William Burke and first published in 1757, and he continued to dwell on Indian and especially Irish affairs until his death.[1] Burke's career spanned a period widely seen at the time, as well as by later historians, as one of imperial crisis.[2] Before entering parliament, Burke returned to his native Dublin in the early 1760s as an aide to William Hamilton, chief secretary in Ireland, during the early phase of the Whiteboy disturbances, when Protestant landlords and the Irish government were savagely suppressing Catholic peasant unrest with reprisals, mass arrests, and judicial murders.[3] By the end of the Seven Years' War in 1763, Britain had acquired substantial new territories, with diverse and seemingly alien populations, including Quebec, with its large population of French Catholics, and in India, after Robert Clive's decisive defeat of French ambitions there. British efforts under the Grenville ministry to recoup the costs of the war in America, most infamously through the 1765 Stamp Act, opened the breach with the American colonies that Burke struggled in vain to repair with his policy of conciliation. The crisis in the American colonies dominated Burke's early years as a member of parliament, especially after he began in 1774 to represent Bristol, the 'second city in the British dominions', and a trading city whose prosperity was bound up perhaps more than any other in Britain with colonial commerce.[4] Soon after the break with America, Burke began his fourteen-year campaign to stem the corruption and despotism of the British East India Company, the work for which he claimed near the end of his life to value himself the most (WS, IX: 159).

In the course of his engagement with these struggles, for which he mastered copious demographic, legal, and economic facts, Burke also theorised empire as a political form more deeply than anyone else of his time.[5] For

Burke, empires epitomised some of the central challenges and tasks of all political life: to reconcile diverse populations to a shared structure of governance; to cultivate mutual affection on the part of governors and governed; to ensure that those who exercise power do so with restraint and for the benefit of the governed as well as remaining accountable to them. In other respects, he understood the British empire to be a highly distinctive, indeed unprecedented, political entity (though he would sometimes look to Rome for instruction or admonition), one for which the British state and public were morally, politically, legally and institutionally ill-prepared.[6] Burke saw heterogeneity as the particular quality and challenge of empire: above all the diversity of forms of government among the various colonies and territories of Britain's 'great disjointed empire', and the religious pluralism within them, especially in India, Canada, and Ireland (WS, VI: 277). Burke's earliest experience of empire occurred in intimate view of the 'universal exclusion' and oppression of Irish Catholics, including his mother and the maternal relatives with whom he spent much of his childhood (WS, IX: 603). He was never tempted by the complacent view of the British empire as invariably a vehicle for liberty, or, as a dominant ideology of Burke's day held it, as 'Protestant, commercial, maritime, and free'.[7] On the contrary, he understood empire throughout his life as a political form beset by deep structural liabilities that engendered violence, instability and oppression, if also a form that might, if it were managed with sufficient far-sightedness and restraint, be capable of partly taming the violence endemic in an age of global movement and global commerce.

For many of Burke's contemporaries, the imperial crisis that stretched from the 1760s to the 1790s was above all one of control and stability: how was Britain to maintain the hard-won peace and unity that had, in 1689, followed decades of intermittent civil war and had then issued even more decisively from the final Jacobite defeat at Culloden in 1746? Many also took Rome to stand as a warning that overextended empire was unsustainable and that despotic power wielded abroad could undermine liberty at home. But Burke was perhaps unique in the degree to which he stressed that the crisis presented by Britain's global empire was a crisis of moral and political imagination. While others at this moment saw empire as a distinctly vulnerable political form primarily in a military or geopolitical sense, for Burke, empire's vulnerability lay in its particular susceptibility to the abuse of power and to the failure of sympathy and affection among its members.[8] Empires were, he held, structurally inclined to injustice in several ways. First, they were liable to the abuses almost inevitable when one party is judge in its own cause: 'When any community is subordinately connected with another, the great danger of the connexion is the extreme pride and self-complacency of the superior, which in all matters of controversy will probably decide in its own favour' (WS, III: 309).[9] This structural danger characterised all empires: it applied when the subordinated community was culturally familiar, as in the American case Burke referred to here, and even more exaggeratedly in the case of unfamiliar subject peoples for whom the dominant community could muster little sympathy, as in India. Empires were further given to abuse by imperial governors, unaccountable to their subjects and freed by distance from metropolitan oversight: 'Great Empire liable to abuse of Subordinate Authority – more [especially] if it is distant – most of all if the people have no distinct priviledges secured by constitutions of their own and able to check the abuse of the subordinate Authority' (WS, VI: 93). Burke's campaign against abuses in India involved the dual projects, legal-political and moral, of subjecting the East India Company to parliamentary control and attempting to instil in the British public some respect and sympathy for 'our distressed fellow-citizens in India' (WS, V: 552).

Given the fact of global commerce and exploration, in the context of European military superiority, Burke claimed that empire was, or could be, a desirable political form. He spoke of the 'communion and fellowship of a great empire', for which he maintained that Americans would be prepared 'to sacrifice some civil liberties', though not 'to pay for it all essential rights, and all the intrinsic dignity of human nature' (WS, III: 157). He invoked the glory of imperial power, as when he argued that 'what I think [parliament's] nobler capacity, is what I call her *imperial character*; in which, as from the throne of heaven, she superintends all the several inferior legislatures, and guides, and controls them all without annihilating any' (WS, II: 459–60). It has often been argued that Burke viewed the British empire as providential, as when he held that the British were 'placed [in India] by the Sovereign Disposer: and we must do the best we can in our situation. The situation of man is the preceptor of his duty' (WS, V: 404).[10] But that Burke did not presume to judge, much less approve, such divine dispositions is suggested by his use of a similar phrase when, lamenting the death of his much-loved son Richard, he deferred to 'a disposer whose power we are little able to resist, and whose wisdom it behoves us not at all to dispute' (WS, IX: 171). Burke arguably saw imperial governance as a painful if inevitable duty as much as a glorious or desirable vocation. He repeatedly stressed the possibility of counteracting imperial power's tendency to abuse, and the obligation on the British to try to do so – through structures of accountability, legal protections of subjects, restraint in the exercise of imperial power and prerogatives. But he also suggested that such reforms were hopeless without a transformation of British laws and morals, and he often stressed the dim prospects for such a sea change. Burke's commitment to extended empire, then, was highly qualified. He regarded the loss of Britain's imperial power, whether in America or Asia, with equanimity when compared with the abuse of that power, and the unifying thread of all his writings on empire is the project to contain and temper imperial power's abuse.

In speaking of all imperial subjects, including Indians, as fellow-citizens, Burke implied some united purpose or identity, or what he called 'a Unity of Spirit, though in a diversity of operations' (WS, III: 136).[11] He repeatedly identified with, or claimed to speak on behalf of, imperial subjects who lacked parliamentary representation, as when he wrote to his Bristol constituents, 'I am charged with being an American. If warm affection, towards those over whom I claim any share of authority, be a crime, I am guilty of this charge' (WS, III: 313), or to a family friend, about India, 'I have no party in this business, my dear Miss Palmer, but among a set of people, who have none of your Lilies and Roses in their faces, but who are the images of the great Pattern as well as you and I. I know what I am doing; whether the white people like it or not' (C, V: 255). But he emphatically distinguished empires from states or kingdoms for their diversity and structural complexity, calling an empire a 'great political union of communities' and 'the aggregate of many States, under one common head; whether this head be a monarch, or a presiding republick' (WS, III: 132–3). He saw institutional diversity as the essential feature of the British empire: as the *Account* put it in 1757, 'there is scarce any form of government known, that does not prevail in some of our plantations'.[12] In stressing the diversity constitutive of empire as a political form, Burke resisted the insistence, common in an era whose political imagination was still haunted by the English Civil War, that peace could be preserved only within an imperial 'unity'. 'It is said', he observed, 'that this power of granting vested in American assemblies, would dissolve the unity of the empire [...] Truly, Mr Speaker, I do not know what this unity means [...] The very idea of subordination of parts, excludes this notion of simple and undivided unity. England is the head; but she is not the head and the members too' (WS, III: 158). Burke was aware of the great obstacles to even virtual, much less direct, representation of colonial subjects in the imperial parliament, and of the dangers of authority exercised in the absence of the accountability that representation provided. He was undoubtedly less concerned than more democratic theorists would be about inconsistencies of representation within the empire, and he held parliamentary representation for distant colonies to be simply impracticable: '*Opposuit natura*' (WS, III: 145). But he also rejected the suggestion that the lack of representation for the colonies was no evil at all. Although he was later to argue strongly against the reform of England's uneven parliamentary representation – given what in another context he described as his 'insuperable reluctance in giving my hand to destroy any established institution of government, upon a theory' (WS, V: 387) – Burke also called that uneven representation one of the 'shameful parts of our constitution', 'our weakness' and 'our opprobrium', against those opponents who cited uneven representation at home as a reason to deny it to the American colonists (WS, II: 459).

One of Burke's most persistent themes was the inadequacy of conventional moral assumptions and legal procedures – what he called 'municipal maxims' – to the novel complexities of imperial politics, and the danger that unthinking reliance on parochial views would facilitate the abuse of power. 'I hope and trust there will be no rule, formed upon municipal maxims,' he declared, 'which will prevent the Imperial justice which you owe to the people that call to you from all parts of a great disjointed empire' (WS, VI: 277). The development of an adequate 'imperial constitution' demanded moral transformations of leadership and public at home, and the juridical status of the empire's various subjects, in his view, was inseparable from the moral relations between metropolitan and colonial citizens. Burke saw these connections between law and morals as running in both directions. First, and more obviously, failures of sympathy produced political oppression and legal exclusion. Attempting to secure legal rights was useless and even pernicious in the absence of appropriate sentiments and sympathies on the part of both governors and governed. The language of right, as he would famously argue in response to the French Revolution, invited an uncompromising absolutism, which defied the spirit of accommodation that he insisted was essential to politics. At the same time, he believed it impossible for the British to muster sympathy for those, especially in India, whom they saw as lacking recognisable laws and rights; governors could not govern with the necessary sympathy and restraint over subjects they believed to have 'no laws, no rights', whom they supposed to be 'in a degraded, servile state': for 'those whom you despise you will never treat well' (WS, VII: 264). This latter belief lies behind Burke's repeated insistence in the Hastings impeachment on India's legal complexity and sophistication. It lies too behind Burke's fierce rejection of Montesquieu's theory of Oriental despotism and the 'wild, loose, casual and silly observations on Government' by 'the whole rabble of Travellers' – in short, the belief that Asia was a scene of unrelieved lawlessness and arbitrary misrule – which he believed Hastings had relied on to justify his own corruption and despotism (WS, VII: 263).

Burke's distinctive view of imperial power, in which the imperial centre holds supreme dignity and authority but governs with extreme reserve, emerged in the American colonial crisis. He argued both for the 1766 Declaratory Act, which asserted parliament's right to legislate for the colonies 'in all cases whatsoever', and for the repeal of the Stamp Act, and more generally for allowing Americans to levy their own contributions to imperial defence through the colonial assemblies. This combination of measures, effected by the short-lived Rockingham administration of 1765–6, could preserve, he argued, both the 'authority' and the 'equity of Great Britain' (WS, II: 54, 443). Parliament could insist in principle on its supreme authority, and should reserve the right to impose on the colonies any legislation it deemed necessary to the well-being of the empire, but it should consider those powers a last resort of imperial policy, not an ordinary means of raising revenue. He called parliament's supreme authority 'very clear and very undeniable' in theory, but also 'little to the purpose' (WS, II: 47). This was a position that satisfied neither the leading colonists, who suspected that the Declaratory Act presaged further impositions on their right as Englishmen to tax themselves through their representatives, nor those, like Burke's adversary Josiah Tucker, who saw British opposition to the Stamp Act as rabble-rousing and as encouragement of American truculence.[13] Burke's policy of conciliation failed, of course, with the outbreak of war and the Declaration of Independence. He voted to repeal the Declaratory Act in April 1778, still hoping that perhaps 'thereby the minds of the Americans could be conciliated' (WS, III: 374), days before calling for parliament to recognise American independence rather than continue what he had called 'a fruitless, hopeless, unnatural civil war' (WS, III: 323).

Burke's analyses of the empire in Ireland, America and India share an insistence on the inefficacy of force as a tool of governance, or what Burke called the 'impotent violence of despotism' (WS, II: 461). Violence, that is, must not be confused with power; Burke sometimes suggested that power is instead found in the concerted actions of people united by some common project. He elaborated this theme most fully in his Conciliation speech, where he objected to force 'not as an odious, but a feeble instrument'. He argued that violence is, first, unpredictable in its effects: far from securing compliance, it cannot be relied on even to terrorise those subjected to it, for it may equally embolden them and harden resistance. Any success by violence is temporary, whereas when it fails, rulers who have resorted to it have depleted all the means at their disposal: 'Power and authority are sometimes bought by kindness; but they can never be begged as alms, by an impoverished and defeated violence' (WS, III: 118–19). Burke first made these arguments in debates over whether the American colonists should be compelled to comply with parliamentary taxation, that is, in the context of discussions about the use of force against colonial subjects widely regarded as members of a shared British moral and political community, as 'English' in spirit, and as sharing and even exceeding the English passion for liberty. In part, then, Burke was arguing in his American speeches against the use of violence toward people who would only participate in, or submit to, the British empire if they saw it as protecting rather than threatening their inherited British liberties. But he made, at the same time, a broader theoretical argument about the nature of power in any imperial polity. Like, but far more than, other states, empires must cajole their subjects, must solicit rather than compel their cooperation: 'In large bodies, the circulation of power must be less vigorous at the extremities [...] Despotism itself is obliged to truck and huckster [...] The Sultan gets such obedience as he can. He governs with a loose rein, that he may govern at all; and the whole of the force and vigour of his authority in his centre, is derived from a prudent relaxation in all his borders [...] This is the immutable condition; the eternal Law, of extensive and detached Empire' (WS, III: 125). This was as much a normative argument as it was a descriptive treatment of the facts of empire.

We have noted that Burke understood heterogeneity under structures of hierarchy to be the archetypal feature and challenge of empires. He suggested that the chief pathology of diverse, hierarchical societies is the oppression and exclusion of one people by another, or what he came to call 'oligarchical' domination. This was the great theme of his writings on Ireland from his early manuscript on the Popery Laws (c1762–1765) through his major statements of the 1790s, in public letters to his son Richard and to his friend Sir Hercules Langrishe, an Irish Protestant sympathetic to Catholic emancipation. As the English were claiming their own liberties at home, Burke noted, their countrymen in Ireland were depriving the local population of their property and of civil and political rights. Whereas in England the 1688 revolution had constituted a popular struggle for liberty, one rightly remembered as an emancipation from a minority of usurpers and oppressors, in Ireland the same revolution established the tyrannical power of a small faction, 'the establishment of the power of the smaller number, at the expence of the civil liberties and properties of the far greater part; and at the expence of the political liberties of the whole. It was, to say the truth, not a revolution, but a conquest, which is not to say a great deal in its favour' (WS, IX: 614).

Burke undoubtedly understood Ireland to be the starkest instance in the British empire of the evils of the oppression of one community by another, but he saw the danger as one inherent to empire, against which imperial policy would always have to struggle. In America, the problem was not, as in Ireland, that of dominant and subordinate populations sharing a colonial territory, with the subordinate people subjected to 'power unlimited, placed in the hands of *an adverse* description, *because it is an adverse description*' (WS, IX: 601–2). In America, the danger was rather that the politically superior metropolitan population would subject colonial subjects to invidious legal proscriptions they would never tolerate themselves. The partial suspension of *habeas corpus* protections in the American Treason Act of 1777 led Burke to note the danger of the legal exclusion of a whole class of subjects in a manner that recalls his chief critique of the regime in Ireland: 'Liberty, if I understand it at all, is a *general* principle, and the clear right of all the subjects within the realm, or of none. Partial freedom seems to me a most invidious mode of slavery'; 'Other laws may injure the community, this tends to dissolve it' (WS, III: 296–7). Burke's contemporaries tended simply to celebrate Britain's natural affinity for liberty and its empire as a vehicle for the spread of that liberty around the globe; as the Scottish Rockinghamite George Dempster told the House of Commons in October 1775, 'our wise ancestors have bound together the different and distant parts of this mighty empire' and 'diffused in a most unexampled manner the blessings of liberty and good government through our remotest provinces'.[14] Burke instead saw the project of combining empire and liberty as a Sisyphean struggle, and the unjust subordination of some subjects to others as empire's more habitual pattern: 'There is not a more difficult subject for the understanding of men than to govern a Large Empire upon a plan of Liberty' (WS, II: 47).

In India, imperial justice was threatened above all by the unprecedented power of the East India Company, which from its Elizabethan origins as a trading company, had 'by degrees' acquired 'those great, high prerogatives of Sovereignty, which never were known before to be parted with to any Subjects' (WS, VI: 282–3). As Adam Smith had done in the *Wealth of Nations*, Burke stressed the irregularity of the Company's combination of sovereign power and commercial activity, calling the Company 'a Republic, a Commonwealth without a people [...] The consequence of which is that there is no people to control, to watch, to balance against the power of office' (WS, VI: 285–6).[15] Burke spoke of Hastings as having 'disfranchized' Asia (WS, VII: 260), and he found the unavailability to Britain's Indian subjects of any means of complaint or redress one of the most egregious structural failings of Company rule (WS, V: 204, 436, 461). But he presumed that Indians' 'condition' was not yet 'capable' of more robust representation (WS, V: 386), and the British were the 'people' he envisioned as checking the Company's power, though he doubted their capacity to grasp the extent of its abuse of power (WS, V: 404). It is often and rightly emphasised that Burke's primary aim in the Hastings trial was moral suasion rather than legal conviction: that the British public, and posterity, were as much his audience as the Lords sitting in judgment.[16] At the same time, a central element of Burke's project of persuasion was his effort to prompt a reconception of law itself: more specifically, of the role of law in the British empire and its global commercial and political encounters.[17] By the end of the trial, Burke had come to characterise his dispute with Hastings as at bottom a controversy about law (WS, VII: 256), and he regarded the trial as a mobilisation of British law, through the rarely used mechanism of impeachment, to rein in and check the abuse of British power abroad. This meant soliciting from his British audience both a new respect for unfamiliar legal and normative systems and an unaccustomed sense of doubt about the adequacy of their own. As was typical of Burke, this was a project of both transformation and conservation, in the sense that he argued that British legal traditions were parochial and inadequate to a global politics, and that they contained the seeds of their own transformation.

Burke's political thought was undoubtedly shaped by his sense of the distinctively imperial space in which he acted. In the theory of representation for which he is famous, the representative is not an agent for the interests of his narrow constituency but a member of a deliberative body whose votes are guided by his judgment of the common good of the whole polity: 'Parliament is not a *Congress* of Ambassadors from different and hostile interests [...] but [...] a *deliberative* assembly of *one* Nation, with *one* Interest, that of the whole' (WS, III: 69). He later argued that this expansive understanding of the role of parliament had become imperative precisely under the conditions of imperial politics, when '[w]hat was first a single kingdom stretched into an empire; and an imperial superintendancy of some kind or other became necessary' (WS, III: 320). Burke's characteristic commitment to a politics of reverence, deference and affection on the part of subjects and reciprocal affection, magnanimity and benevolent superintendence on the part of rulers was suited to and perhaps shaped by the simultaneously hierarchical and vulnerable situation of empires. Finally, as we have seen, Burke's writings on empire offer some of the clearest evidence of his belief in the mutual dependence of legal, political and moral relations: the perniciousness of assertions of rights in the absence of shared sympathies, and the importance of respect for people's laws is a basis for sympathy and respect for the people themselves. Burke's belief that an uncompromising insistence on one's rights is dangerous politics is best known, of course, through his critique of the revolutionary rights of man. But he had made the case against truculent legal claims first in various imperial contexts where the claimants of rights were not the populace but the dominant. His horror of Jacobinism certainly drew from his sense of its affinities with the abuses of imperial power he had spent his career battling: 'I think I can hardly overrate the malignity of the principles of Protestant ascendency, as they affect Ireland; or of Indianism, as they affect these countries, and as they affect Asia; or of Jacobinism, as they affect all Europe, and the state of human society itself' (C, VIII: 254).

NOTES

1 For a superb argument for the centrality of conquest to Burke's political thought, including an analysis of the *Account*, see Richard Bourke, 'Edmund Burke and the Politics of Conquest', *Modern Intellectual History*, 4.3 (2007): 403–32. For an example of late concern with India, see Burke's letter to French Laurence calling the acquittal of Warren Hastings a 'barbarous and inhuman condemnation of whole Tribes and nations' (C, VIII: 63). On his 'spirited anxiety' for Ireland, see the letters of 1797 (C, IX: 277–359, passim).

2 See J. G. A. Pocock, 'Political Thought in the English-Speaking Atlantic, 1760–1790, Part 1: The Imperial Crisis', in J. G. A Pocock (ed.), *The Varieties of British Political Thought, 1500–1800* (Cambridge: Cambridge University Press, 1993), pp 246–82; H. V. Bowen, 'British Conceptions of Global Empire, 1756–1763', *Journal of Imperial and Commonwealth History*, 26.3 (1998): 1–27.

3 See Luke Gibbons, *Edmund Burke and Ireland* (Cambridge: Cambridge University Press, 2003), pp. 21–38, and Burke's own later account at (WS, IX: 602–3).

4 See, for example, William Gurthrie, *A New Geographical, Historical, and Commercial Grammar*, 10th edn. (London, 1787), p. 356.

5 For some others, less comprehensive and (except for Smith) less sophisticated, see Thomas Pownall, *The Administration of the Colonies*, 4th edn. (London, 1768) (Burke's own annotated copy is in the British Library, Shelfmark C.60.I.9); Arthur Young, *Political Essays Concerning the Present State of the British Empire* (London, 1772); Adam Smith, *An Inquiry into the Nature and Causes of the Wealth of Nations* [1776] (Indianapolis: Liberty Fund, 1981 [Glasgow edition]).

6 'We cannot resort to the example of Roman or Greek colonies. Nor must we seek for it in the older part of our constitution about the method of governing an Empire, the existence of which they could not even conceive' (WS, II: 50).

7 David Armitage, *The Ideological Origins of the British Empire* (Cambridge: Cambridge University Press, 2000), p. 8.

8 See, for example, Sir John Dalrymple on Grenville's concerns about imperial vulnerabilities: John Dalrymple, *Memoirs of Great Britain and Ireland* (Edinburgh, 1788), p 109. Also see P. J. Marshall, 'A Nation Defined by Empire, 1755–1776' in *'A Free though Conquering People': Eighteenth-Century Britain and Its Empire* (Aldershot: Ashgate, 2003).

9 See also (WS, III: 133), where Burke calls himself frightened and humbled by the imperial situation 'of being judge in my own cause'.

10 See, for example, Paul Langford, 'Introduction' (WS, V: 1–27).

11 Jane Burbank and Fredrick Cooper likewise characterise empires as above all both 'incorporative and differentiated': *Empires in World History: Power and the Politics of Difference* (Oxford: Princeton University Press, 2010), p. 10.

12 *An Account of the European Settlements in America*, 2. vols. (London, 1757), vol. II, p. 288.

13 Tucker, *Four tracts, on Political and Commercial Subjects* (Gloucester, 1774), p. 180.

14 George Dempster, speech, 27 October 1775; quoted by Jack P. Greene, 'Introduction: Empire and Liberty' in Jack P. Greene (ed.), *Exclusionary Empire: English Liberty Overseas, 1600–1900* (Cambridge: Cambridge University Press, 2010), p. 10.

15 Smith, *Wealth of Nations*, IV.vii.c.104–108.
16 See F. P. Lock, *Edmund Burke*, 2 vols. (Oxford: Clarendon, 1998–2006), vol. II, p. 468.
17 See, for instance, (WS, VII: 168), where Burke calls for 'the growing Melioration of the Law, by [...] conforming our Jurisprudence to the Growth of our Commerce and our Empire'.

12

HARRY T. DICKINSON

Burke and the American Crisis

During the American crisis of 1763–83, Edmund Burke was recognised, on both sides of the Atlantic, as 'a friend of America', primarily because of his determined efforts to seek a reconciliation between Britain and the American colonies on the question of taxation and his bitter criticisms of the efforts made by Lord North's ministry to subdue the American rebellion by oppressive legislation and military aggression. Modern scholars, however, are divided over Burke's response to the American crisis. Some maintain that Burke was well informed about American affairs, made vigorous and practical efforts to conciliate the American colonies, and played a leading role in attacking the war that Lord North's ministry waged against the American rebels.[1] Other scholars have argued that Burke never really fully appreciated the American position, wrongly believed that the root cause of the dispute was taxation, and used the war primarily to advance the interests of his own party.[2] This chapter will explore the evidence that can be used to sustain these contrasting viewpoints and will suggest that he was aware of the contradictions in his position and strove to reconcile them.

Burke's Knowledge of American Affairs

Among the many MPs who spoke or wrote on American affairs during twenty years of crisis, very few had any first-hand or deep knowledge of the situation in the American colonies. Only a tiny handful had been born in America or had spent substantial time in the colonies as merchants or landowners, civil administrators, or military officers. Burke himself never visited the American colonies, never corresponded regularly with any American Patriot during the crisis and never read widely in the American literature produced by the colonial critics of British policies. On the other hand, it is difficult to find many politicians of the period who made such an effort to educate themselves about American affairs as Burke did. Even before he entered parliament, Burke collaborated with his friend, William Burke, in producing a substantial *Account of the European Settlements in America* that was published in two volumes in 1757. Although a long-neglected source, it is now generally accepted that Burke played a significant part in producing these two volumes. He superintended the production of the *Account*, and the whole owed much to his ideas. More than 150 pages of the second volume deal with the English settlements that were to rebel against Britain in 1775. These pages make it clear that Edmund Burke fully appreciated the contribution that the American colonies made to Britain's prosperity and her strength. Although critical of the colonists' treatment of Native Americans, black slaves imported from Africa, and those of a different religious persuasion, Burke paid tribute to the efforts of the British migrants who had enriched and civilised the once barren lands of America.

What needs to be particularly noted in the *Account* are the frequent comments on the civil and religious liberty enjoyed by the American colonists and the extent to which they were already managing their own affairs, unencumbered by interference from the British government or parliament. In none of the colonies was there an hereditary aristocracy and in nearly all of them there were significant numbers of middling property owners, who enjoyed considerable personal liberty. In many colonies, there were elected legislative assemblies over which the governors exercised only limited control. The British parliament exercised too little control over these governors and imposed too many laws that were inappropriate for such infant settlements. Burke warned that great care needed to be exercised in the commercial regulation of the American colonies in order to avoid inappropriate restrictions on them (WS, II: 177). The American colonies had been permitted for many years to make their own laws, and Burke recognised, as early as 1757, that any dispute with them could not be easily resolved (WS, II: 142). He made much of the liberty enjoyed by the inhabitants of New England, and he was already conscious that these colonists in particular would resist any attempt by the British government or parliament to render them subordinate to their authority (WS, II: 161–62).

Burke's knowledge of America also owed much to the research he undertook in preparing the historical articles that he contributed to *The Annual Register* for almost a decade after its inception in 1758. From 1758 to 1763 Burke devoted a substantial and increasing space in his historical accounts to the war in North America, and hence he was well informed on the difficulties caused for the British troops in America by the size, climate and geography of the colonies. He had also studied the contribution made by the colonies to the war effort there, and he believed it was legitimate for the British government to expect the colonies to contribute to the costs of imperial defence after the end of the war. In *The Annual Register* for 1765, he praised the colonies for accepting Britain's post-war policies with patience and submission, but recognised that the colonies were justified in resenting the passing of the Stamp Act (AR, 1765: 23–26).

Burke's knowledge of American affairs expanded later, while he served as the colonial agent for the assembly of New York from December 1770 to August 1775. Through this connection he learned much about colonial resentment against the American policies pursued by Lord North's administration. He undoubtedly informed himself about the nature and extent of Britain's trade with the American colonies and how Britain's policies impacted on that trade. His duties also meant that he took a considerable interest in land grants made in the colony and in New York's claims to western lands, and he worked hard to protect the colony's boundary claims when these were threatened during the debates on the Quebec Act of 1774. It may be that Burke was more critical of the North ministry's policies towards the American colonies than he was sympathetic to the American position, but there are good grounds for maintaining that Burke was much better informed on American affairs than the vast majority of British politicians. In 1775, Burke informed the House of Commons, 'I was obliged to take more than common pains, to instruct myself in every thing which relates to our Colonies' (WS, III: 106). Two years, later he informed a wider public in his *Letter to the Sheriffs of Bristol* that 'I think I know America. If I do not, my ignorance is incurable, for I have spared no pains to understand it' (WS, III: 304).

The Stamp Act and the Declaratory Act

Burke became directly involved in political issues, rather than simply commenting upon them, as soon as he was elected to parliament in December 1765. His first task as an MP was to assist the new Rockingham ministry to deal with the American crisis created by the passing of the Stamp Act by the Grenville administration earlier in 1765. We can learn much of Burke's attitude to this crisis by examining the views he expressed on it in the historical essays in *The Annual Register* for 1765 and 1766 that T. O. McLoughlin has persuasively argued were written by Burke.[3] In these articles, Burke criticised the passing of the Stamp Act and explained at length how and why the American colonists opposed its implementation. He recognised the growing political maturity of the colonies and appreciated their claims that the British parliament had no constitutional right to impose an internal tax upon them when they had no representation in that legislature. Since colonial representation at Westminster was both impracticable and undesirable, Burke recognised that something else must be done to placate the colonies.

By early 1766, Burke was actively involved in trying to persuade the House of Commons to resolve this crisis. Burke was convinced of the expediency of repealing the Stamp Act, though he knew it would not be easy to persuade a majority of MPs to support repeal, because it would smack of retreating before American pressure. He therefore lobbied MPs and persuaded British merchants to send in petitions in favour of repeal and to appear before parliament to provide evidence of the serious damage that the American boycott was doing to British exports. These efforts undoubtedly had some positive effect on backbench opinion, but, in order to secure majority support, Burke agreed with his party that a bill should also be passed asserting parliament's right to pass laws or levy taxes on the colonies 'in all cases whatsoever'. Burke fully supported this strategy, although he was conscious of the danger of raising speculative discussions about abstract constitutional issues. While he was speaking in the Commons in early 1766 in favour of the Declaratory Act, he was writing in *The Annual Register* for 1765 that Grenville's ministry had unwisely maintained that the Stamp Act was a legitimate exercise of parliament's sovereign constitutional authority over the colonies: 'the bringing of which into question had been much better avoided [...] Decided in the affirmative, it must tend to alienate the affections of the colonies; in the negative, to increase their presumption; and left undecided, breed in them a complication of both these evils' (AR, 1765: 26).

In his historical essay for *The Annual Register* for 1766, Burke insisted that the Stamp Act could be implemented only with the backing of military force. He accepted, however, that this argument was not sufficient to persuade a majority of MPs to vote in favour of the act's repeal and hence the Rockingham ministry had no alternative but to pass the Declaratory Act. He did, however, genuinely believe that parliament possessed the constitutional right to exercise a superintending role over the American colonies. He wrote in *The Annual Register* for 1766 that there would be an entire dissolution of government if parliament gave up its authority over the colonies (AR, 1766: 41). In the notes he drafted for a speech he gave in the House of Commons early in 1766, Burke also acknowledged that the authority of parliament was unlimited in constitutional theory, but that the practical exertion of this authority in the form of taxation imposed on the American colonies could be unjust, inequitable and contrary to the spirit of the British constitution and the principles of liberty. A wise legislature should take cognisance of the particular circumstances of the American colonies since they were far distant from Britain and they had developed their own political institutions accountable to their own constituents (WS, II: 47–52).

Opposing Subsequent Ministerial Policies

The Rockingham ministry supported the Declaratory Act as an assertion of a constitutional position, but it had no intention of using the act to impose new taxes upon the American colonies. The ministry had no opportunity to demonstrate this since it lost power within months of passing the act, but, ever thereafter, Burke and his colleagues opposed all new efforts to tax the American colonies. The draft notes of a speech Burke delivered on 15 May 1767 proves that he thought the new Townshend duties were an unwise imposition that would alienate the American colonies (WS, II: 61–64). On several subsequent occasions he attacked the imposition of these duties for disturbing the good relations with the American colonies that he believed the Rockingham ministry had restored in 1766. On 8 November 1768, Burke condemned these duties as an attempt to strengthen Britain's authority in the colonies since the revenue was to pay the salaries of royal governors and other officials in the colonies in order to make them independent of their legislative assemblies (WS, II: 96). In his *Observations on a Late State of the Nation* in 1769, Burke insisted that it was impractical to grant the colonists representation in parliament and, hence, the principle of 'no taxation without representation' meant that all colonial taxation should be under the control of the local legislative assemblies (WS, II: 178–181). On 14 March 1769, he acknowledged that parliament had an undoubted right to tax the American colonies, but he denied that it was expedient to do so (PH, XVI: 605). A month later, he voiced concern over the colonial opposition to these duties and he wished to see them repealed rather than enforced (WS, II: 231–32). On 9 January 1770, he complained that these duties raised very little revenue, especially when most of them were in the process of being repealed, and that one of them, the tea duty was being retained simply to assert parliament's constitutional right to levy such a tax (PH, XVI: 725). Four months later, Burke again protested that there was no need to retain the tea duty simply to prove that parliament possessed this right (PH, XVII: 1003). By 13 November 1770, Burke was warning that the American colonists were firmly united in opposition to any British tax and that the British economy was suffering more from American opposition to British imports than parliament could possibly gain from any tax (PH, XVI: 1068).

When the Americans continued to resist parliament's authority in the colonies, Burke condemned successive governments for alternating between efforts to intimidate the American colonies and offering concessions to pacify the enraged colonists. Burke was critical of the extension of the power of the vice admiralty courts in the colonies, the decision to quarter British troops on the colonies, and the efforts to intimidate colonial assemblies into abandoning their resistance to British measures. When Americans attacked British tea ships in Boston harbour in December 1773, Burke could not condone such actions, but he was, nonetheless, deeply opposed to the Coercive Acts that Lord North's ministry brought before parliament in the spring of 1774 in order to punish Boston and the colony of Massachusetts for this attack on British property. On 25 March 1774, Burke attacked the Boston Port Bill because it would punish the innocent as well as the guilty. He regarded this bill as dangerously provocative because it would undoubtedly stiffen colonial resistance to Britain's authority across America (PH, XVII: 1182). In his speech against the Massachusetts Bay Regulating Bill, on 2 May 1774, Burke warned that the people of that colony would never accept this attack on their legislative assembly, and henceforward Britain would need an army to govern this colony (WS, II: 464–65). Burke opposed the Quebec Act of 1774, which many American colonists regarded as proof of the North ministry's authoritarian tendencies, because it did not offer the French inhabitants of that province an elected legislative assembly, and it imposed French civil law on that province. Burke's comments undoubtedly increased American suspicions of this measure: 'No free country can keep another in slavery [...] it is evident that this constitution is meant to be an instrument of tyranny to the Canadians, and an example to others of what they have to expect; at some time or other it will come home to England' (CD: 89).

Burke's Attempts at Conciliation

The coercive measures of 1774 convinced Burke that Lord North's ministry was threatening to drive the American colonies into armed resistance. He blamed British ministers for the growing crisis, though he recognised the colonists' excessive love of liberty. He believed that wise, moderate and consistent policies by Britain could conciliate the colonies and restore good relations. In 1774–5, he advanced his mature views on how to end the imperial crisis in his three great speeches delivered on 19 April 1774 and 22 March and 16 November 1775. These speeches have been praised as major efforts to improve relations between Britain and the American colonies, but they have also been criticised as inadequate responses to problems that Burke did not fully comprehend.

Ever since 1766 Burke had been struggling with the vexed problem of how to reconcile the resistance of the American colonies to parliamentary taxation and his belief that parliament was the sovereign authority in the British empire. He came to believe that Britain should abandon much of the legislation parliament had passed since 1763. He was convinced that the colonists would respond favourably to these concessions. He did not, however, advocate the repeal of the Declaratory Act of 1766, in part because his party had passed this measure and in part because he believed that the empire needed an acknowledged head and superintending power and this could only be the legislature of the king-in-parliament. On the other hand, he did try to avoid any open discussion on the question of sovereignty and on the relative constitutional rights of the British parliament and the American colonial assemblies. In his famous speech on American taxation on 19 April 1774, he refused to enter into a discussion of these issues since sophisticated and subtle discussions about them could only encourage the colonists to call parliament's sovereign authority into question. He warned his listeners, 'They will cast your sovereignty in your face. No body will be argued into slavery' (WS, II: 458).

Burke, however, did go on to explain what kind of superintending power parliament could legitimately exercise over the American colonies. He divided parliament's authority into two: an absolute legislative authority over Great Britain, but, in her 'imperial character', only a superintending power over all the inferior provincial legislatures, whose power she could guide and control, but not annihilate (WS, II: 459–60). By this, Burke appears to have meant that, in ordinary circumstances, each colonial legislature exercised the same authority over the people of these provinces as parliament did over the British people, and parliament had no authority over what these legislatures did. Only if they clearly acted in an unjust fashion and abused their power, could parliament act as the arbiter between the resulting conflict between the assemblies and the colonists. Furthermore, if the colonial assemblies absolutely refused to contribute to the costs of any war involving the British empire, then parliament retained the right to compel them to do so. This, however, should be an act of last resort.

By the time Burke delivered his Speech on Conciliation with America, on 22 March 1775, relations with the American colonies had deteriorated further. He condemned the recent policies of Lord North's ministry and advised parliament to recognise the colonists' love of liberty, the recent political developments that had occurred in America, and the difficulty of governing them from such a distance. Britain could not alter the temper and character of the colonists and should not try to govern them according to abstract constitutional rights. As before, he urged parliament to abandon its claim to possess the right to tax the American colonies, since it did not represent them, even virtually, and to repeal recent measures, especially the Coercive Acts of 1774. The colonial assemblies had granted financial subsidies to help the imperial war effort in the past, and parliament should count upon receiving these in future. Burke warned the House of Commons that the colonists would not accept Lord North's inadequate conciliatory proposals that the colonial assemblies could decide on the mode of taxation to meet the costs of imperial defence, but parliament must decide the amount to be collected and how this revenue was to be spent. This offered no solution to the American crisis and would simply perpetuate disputes between parliament and the colonial assemblies.

Once more, buried in this speech, Burke gave some indication of the constitutional authority of parliament over the colonial assemblies. He insisted that there could be no simple, undivided unity in the British empire and that the colonial assemblies legitimately possessed many privileges and immunities over the government of their provinces that parliament could not infringe or usurp. The colonists' defence of these should not be viewed by parliament as an attack on its own sovereign authority within the empire. When engaged in any dispute with the colonial assemblies parliament might be the final judge, but it should be very careful how it exercised its constitutional rights since some rights could be wrongly enforced. Parliament's sovereign authority should be used only to preserve liberty throughout the empire and not to impose burdens on distant colonies. The British empire should be held together by the spirit of the constitution and the principles of liberty, and parliament should therefore exercise its authority to those ends.

On 16 November 1775, after war had broken out, Burke delivered another great speech in the House of Commons, though one often neglected. He warned that France and Spain were likely to intervene in the conflict and hence a negotiated settlement was in Britain's best interests. To end the war, he proposed returning to the imperial system as it had been before 1763, advocated the repeal of the Coercive Acts, and proposed a general amnesty. While he advised parliament to put the control of colonial taxation into the hands of the colonial assemblies, he was still not ready to repeal the Declaratory Act because it might lead to unforeseen consequences. He wanted, instead, to repeal measures that had clearly provoked colonial resistance, to grant the colonies a considerable measure of self-government, and to restrict the exercise of parliament's sovereign authority (WS, III: 185–220).

Burke's great speeches on conciliation and his formal proposals to end the conflict with the American colonies failed to secure enough support in or out of parliament to halt the growing crisis. Many MPs undoubtedly believed that Burke was proposing to concede too much and was asking very little from the colonists in return. Outside parliament, Josiah Tucker observed: 'Why truly, if we will grant the Colonies all that they shall require, and stipulate for nothing in Return; they will be at Peace with us. I believe it; and on these simple Principles of simple Peace-making I will engage to terminate every Difference throughout the World'.[4]

These criticisms of Burke's efforts at conciliation have been endorsed by many modern scholars.[5] These modern critics have also insisted that Burke wrongly identified the levying of parliamentary taxation on the colonies, instead of parliament's claim to absolute sovereign authority over the colonies, as the root cause of the American crisis. By not supporting the repeal of the Declaratory Act, Burke proved himself to be wilfully blind to the greatest issue in dispute. Whereas Burke wanted to avoid any deep discussion of the respective constitutional rights of parliament and the colonial assemblies, a great many colonists wanted these to be clarified. Many colonists now fully recognised that, as long as parliament insisted on its sovereign authority over the colonies, they could never be sure that their rights and liberties would be secure. Burke seemed not to appreciate that, even if parliament did decide in 1775 to abandon its efforts to tax the American colonies and to repeal the many acts passed since 1763, the parliament of 1775 could not prevent a subsequent parliament from passing other taxes and acts that the colonists might regard as assaults on their rights and liberties. The colonists had come to believe that their rights and liberties could only be safeguarded if they became independent of parliament's authority altogether. There is much to be said for these criticisms of Burke's position in 1774–5, but some scholars, notably Richard Bourke and Peter J. Stanlis,[6] have argued that there are indications in Burke's three great speeches on American affairs that he was groping towards a sophisticated notion of a divided sovereignty rather than accepting the absolute sovereign power of parliament that had been asserted in the Declaratory Act. Although his language was obscure, Burke was not just asking parliament to repeal acts that had offended the American colonists or urging ministers to be wise and prudent. He was prepared to grant the colonists a very considerable measure of self-government and was advising parliament to impose real restrictions on the exercise of its sovereign authority. Parliament's role was to supervise the lawful and equitable operation of the colonial assemblies, not to usurp their authority or render them so subordinate that they could not defend the rights and liberties of their constituents. It is difficult to deny, however, that Burke still believed that a single power was needed to promote the commercial interests of all parts of the British empire and to settle disputes between these component parts, and that only parliament could fulfil this role.

Reactions to the American War

Burke came close to despair when war broke out and the conflict rapidly spread. He laid the blame for this on Lord North's ministry and, for years, his speeches and writings were full of criticisms of the management, expense and consequences of this war. He rarely advanced specific proposals for how the war should be conducted, though he did condemn the ministry for being undecided whether to prosecute the war with all the power at its disposal or to negotiate a settlement with the Americans. Lord North's attempts to make concessions to the Americans were attacked by Burke as being too little, too late (PH, XIX: 591). Almost every year he reminded the House of Commons how much more money was being wasted fighting this war than earlier parliamentary taxes had sought to raise from the American colonies. He condemned the ministers for so mismanaging the war that France, Spain and the Netherlands intervened in the conflict and expanded the war. He protested against the decision of the ministers to employ German mercenaries and savage Indians in the colonies and to encourage slave revolts in Georgia and South Carolina (PH, XIX: 699). Whereas ministers frequently claimed that many Americans were loyal to the British cause, Burke insisted on several occasions that most Americans were united in opposing the ministry's policies. By 6 December 1779, he was protesting that the American war had 'originated in injustice, was conducted with cruelty, and was likely to end in infamy, disgrace, and disappointment' (PH, XX: 1208).

As the war became wider, more expensive, and more threatening to Britain's interests, it became increasingly clear to Burke that America would settle for nothing less than complete independence. Even if Britain defeated America in the present conflict, Britain would need to station a large army in America to hold the colonies in subjection. He concluded that such a war was not worth fighting. In *A Letter to the Sheriffs of Bristol*, published in May 1777, Burke admitted that he would prefer to see the Americans independent than the continuation of a fruitless, hopeless and unnatural civil war. British interests would be better served by establishing good relations with an independent America than enforcing a submission that would produce mutual hatred and ruin both Britain and America (WS, III: 323). On 2 December 1777, Burke told the House of Commons that it would be foolish not to negotiate peace until the Americans had renounced their Declaration of Independence (WS, III: 344). On 6 April 1778, when Sir William Meredith moved for the repeal of the Declaratory Act, Burke insisted that the act had been wise when it was passed, that it had not been responsible for the disastrous policies adopted by subsequent ministers, and that repealing it would serve no purpose (PH, XIX: 1012). Four days later, however, he was ready to support a motion enabling peace commissioners to recognise America's independence (PH, XIX: 1088). By 14 December 1778, Burke was advocating an end to the war in America and a recognition of American independence so that Britain could concentrate on the war against France (PH, XIX: 81–5).

Burke became increasingly convinced that the American war was being continued to keep the present ministers in office and that it was being conducted in ways that were undermining Britain's reputation, liberties and free constitution. He complained about the way Henry Laurens was being treated as a prisoner in the Tower, and he protested against measures that would partially suspend *habeas corpus* and treat captured American seamen as pirates and others as traitors. British laws and legislative principles were being perverted by this war (WS, III: 300). When a British expedition captured the rich West Indian island of Eustatius, Burke lamented the way the private property of many innocent individuals was confiscated to reward those who had conquered the island. Burke's greatest concern, however, was the way the war was increasing the influence of the British executive over the legislature by the effective distribution of a vast amount of crown patronage. His views were shared by a growing number of MPs who supported John Dunning's famous motion of 6 April 1780 that 'the influence of the crown has increased, is increasing and ought to be diminished' (PH, XXI: 340–74). Burke himself set about diminishing the political influence that crown patronage could exert on parliament by putting forward resolutions in favour of measures of economical reform, in February 1780 and February 1781, that would reduce the number of offices, pensions and places that could be distributed by crown patronage to influence the behaviour of men sitting in parliament.

Britain's defeat at Yorktown in October 1781 was soon followed by the disintegration of Lord North's ministry. By February 1782, Lord North had resigned and was replaced by a ministry led by Lord Rockingham, with Burke serving in the minor office of paymaster-general of the forces. In this post, he was able to bring in a number of economical reforms to improve the running of the pay office and to abolish the Board of Trade, the American secretaryship of state and a number of sinecures and pensions in the royal household. When Rockingham died in July 1782, and his ministry fell, Burke went again into opposition. He soon expressed dissatisfaction with the economical reforms being proposed by the Shelburne ministry which he regarded as very different from his own proposals (PH, XXIII: 263). When he was back in office again during the short-lived Fox-North coalition in 1783, Burke was able to carry through further reforms of the paymaster's office. The American war had made Burke an advocate of economical reform (though not a supporter of parliamentary reform). His reforms did not achieve as much as Burke had hoped, but they did begin a long process of reducing crown patronage and the influence that the monarch could exercise over the composition of the House of Commons.

Burke had wanted peace with America long before it was finally negotiated in 1783 by Lord Shelburne's administration. Burke had no objection to the granting of American independence unconditionally, though he did fear that Britain made too many territorial concessions to her various enemies. He was critical of the ministry for not doing enough to achieve compensation for the American Loyalists, who had lost so much supporting Britain's cause during the war. Burke was even more critical of the ministers for not securing a commercial treaty with the independent United States of America. He had always stressed the contribution of the Atlantic trade to Britain's economic prosperity and he continued to believe that America's overwhelmingly agrarian economy and Britain's superior manufacturing base could restore a highly beneficial trade between the two countries. In order to restore this trade, he wished Britain would treat the Americans not as aliens, but, as far as possible, regard them, in his own words, as 'fellow subjects' (PH, XXIII: 611–14).

NOTES

1 See, for example, Peter J. Stanlis, 'Edmund Burke and British Views of the American Revolution: A Conflict over Rights of Sovereignty' in Ian Crowe (ed.), *Edmund Burke: His Life and Legacy* (Dublin: Four Courts Press, 1997), pp. 24–38.
2 See, for example, J. C. D Clark, 'Edmund Burke's Reflections on the Revolution in America (1777) Or, How Did the American Revolution Relate to the French?' in Ian Crowe (ed.), *An Imaginative Whig: Reassessing the Life and Thought of Edmund Burke* (Columbia and London: University of Missouri Press, 2005), pp. 71–92.
3 T. O. McLoughlin, *Edmund Burke and the First Ten Years of the 'Annual Register' 1758–1767* (Salisbury: University of Rhodesia, 1975), pp. 36–43.
4 Josiah Tucker, *A Letter to Edmund Burke* (Gloucester, 1775), pp. 44–5.
5 See the sources cited in this chapter in note 2.
6 Richard Bourke, 'Liberty, Authority, and Trust in Burke's Idea of Empire', *Journal of the History of Ideas*, 61 (200): 453–71; and Peter J. Stanlis, 'Edmund Burke and British Views of the American Revolution: A Conflict over Rights of Sovereignty' in Ian Crowe (ed.), *Edmund Burke: His Life and Legacy*, pp. 34–8.

13

FREDERICK G. WHELAN

Burke on India

India was one of the great causes of Burke's political career, one that he pursued from around 1780 until his retirement from parliament. Indeed, in his own retrospective judgement, it was the cause 'on which I value myself the most' (WS, IX: 159). By 'India' here is meant the incipient British empire in India or, more precisely, the regime of the English East India Company, to which parliament had ceded not only a commercial monopoly, but also authority over those parts of India that came under British control. 'India' also denotes the distant country and people as Burke tried to imagine them, and for whom he became a passionate advocate.

Burke became convinced that the East India Company (and by extension parliament) was abusing its trust by perpetrating (or permitting) severe forms of oppression and plunder of India and, more ominously, destroying the social foundations of a great, though alien, civilisation. Analysing and exposing the various abuses of imperial rule, Burke (together with his fellow Whigs under Fox) called for reforms. More dramatically, as a way of raising both parliamentary and public consciousness about the affairs of India, Burke pursued the prosecution and impeachment of Warren Hastings, the former governor-general of Bengal, whom Burke believed had directed and personified many of the abusive practices.

The study of Burke and India bears on the larger understanding of Burke in a number of ways. Since his Indian endeavours were pursued as a member of the House of Commons and its committees, they form an important chapter of his political career and provide material for judging whether Burke's political practice exemplified the ideal of statesmanship that he defended. The manifest intensity of Burke's hostility to Hastings, and his identification with Indian suffering, have led to speculations about the underlying motivations of some of Burke's stances, whether these are tied to his social or his Irish background. Burke's voluminous speeches on Indian affairs, which fill three volumes or nearly a third of his complete *Writings and Speeches*, offer material both for literary and rhetorical analysis as well as for scrutiny of his political and moral thought. They are indispensable for a full interpretation of Burke as a political theorist, the main focus of this chapter, despite their occasional and polemical character. Finally, Burke's engagement with India raises larger questions about his relation to the Enlightenment and its universalism, its treatment of cultural differences, and its assessments of non-Western societies. Aspects of these topics will be addressed here following an overview of Burke's Indian speeches and their background.

Overview

The English had been trading with India since Elizabethan times, when the (Muslim) Mogul empire was at its height. During the seventeenth century, the East India Company acquired from local rulers three enclaves with trading and fortification privileges at what became the thriving cities of Madras in the Carnatic, Bombay and Calcutta in Bengal. In the eighteenth century, the authority of the central Mogul government at Delhi declined, and power devolved to provincial rulers such as the Nawabs (Nabobs) of Bengal and of the Carnatic. Correspondingly, the economic rivalry between the English and other European trading companies, especially the French, developed political and military dimensions, as the Europeans sought to increase their privileges and spheres of influence by supporting factions in local power struggles and succession disputes. In the 1740s, Anglo-French hostilities in southern India (an echo of war in Europe) resulted in English victories and effective control over the Carnatic through a pliant nabob. Similarly, in 1757 (in events connected to the Seven Years' War), the English under Clive defeated – and soon replaced – the Nawab of Bengal at the momentous battle of Plassey, giving the East India Company an effective ruling position over that rich and populous province. In 1765, the year Burke entered parliament, the company's quasi-sovereign position there was formalised by a treaty between Clive and the Mogul emperor.

In a pattern that was to be repeated in the future, these events on the ground in India (then a six-months' voyage away) that created the British Indian empire reflected initiatives by local company officials in response to local threats and opportunities; they were not planned, and were sometimes disapproved of by governments in London, which nevertheless accepted them as *faits accomplis* and authorised the company to supplement its commercial activities with the military, administrative, judicial and taxing powers of a ruling agency. Adam Smith argued in *The Wealth of Nations* (1776) that the two roles of sovereign and merchant were incompatible, creating a conflict of interest in company officials that was bound to be oppressive to the Indian subjects. Burke grasped and came to agree with this general diagnosis, which underlay his unsuccessful attempt in 1783 to reform the empire by establishing more direct parliamentary oversight (Fox's India Bill). It was in the context of this argument that Burke's campaign against more specific abuses of power in India was waged.

From 1765 through the 1770s, misgivings about India increased in England with reports of abuses, a failure of expected profits, and a famine in Bengal, combined with conspicuously large private fortunes among return- ing company employees. During the earlier part of this period, Burke's brief statements (in WS II and V) reflected the Rockingham Whigs' support for the chartered rights of the company, a belief that it could reform itself, and a concern that its patronage not fall into the hands of the government – positions on which Burke was to change his mind as he learned more. Burke's first major intervention was his 1779 pamphlet, *Policy of Making Conquests for the Mahometans* (WS, V: 41–124), in which he opposed the annexation of the small state of Tanjore by the Nawab of the Carnatic with British assistance. The Nawab being Muslim and the Raja of Tanjore a Hindu, Burke embraced the cause (sometimes invoked by British officials as a justification for the empire) of defending peaceable Hindus against more warlike Muslim conquerors. This was a view of the peoples of India that Burke was to drop later when he became an advocate for the Muslim rulers and landowners of Bengal who were the main victims of Hastings's depredations. More importantly, Burke came to see the Tanjore episode as a corrupt manifestation of the financial interests of English speculators in Madras, whose control of the Nawab was the basis of their wealth. This line of criticism was continued in Burke's 1785 *Speech on [the] Nabob of Arcot's Debts* (WS, V: 478–617), in which he explains how the Nawab of the Carnatic's indebtedness to British creditors was guaranteed by the assignment of the public revenues of the country to the latter, and how the company's public authority was employed to protect this private inter- est. These investigations aroused Burke to an awareness of both financial exploitation and political corruption at the heart of the Indian empire that he found confirmed elsewhere. A further theme was that the 'Arcot' creditors had used their wealth to buy political influence in England, and even to procure seats in parliament, to protect their interests. Thus, as in the ancient Roman example, the ill-gotten gains of an Asian empire might return to corrupt the politics of the home country.

Burke began to acquire detailed knowledge of Indian affairs as a mem- ber of a parliamentary Select Committee in 1781–3, authoring its *Ninth* and *Eleventh Reports* as well as part of its *First Report* (WS, V: 144–89, 194–378), which detailed numerous abuses. These investigations turned Burke's attention to events in Bengal and adjacent territories and to the role of Hastings, and they unearthed evidence for charges that Burke was to pursue to the end of his career. They were soon followed by Burke's best-known and often-anthologised Indian text, the *Speech on Fox's India Bill* of 1 December 1783 (WS, V: 378–451), delivered in support of a reform measure when Burke's party was briefly in office as part of the Fox-North coalition. This speech touches on many of Burke's most important Indian themes and will be referred to later.

Fox's bill having been defeated in the House of Lords and his party defeated in the ensuing general election, Burke returned to his usual place in the opposition. His Indian campaign now took the form of a determination to prosecute the recently returned Hastings through impeachment, both as a matter of justice and as a way of keeping Indian abuses before the public. Procedural controversies relating to this somewhat archaic process are reflected in a number of short speeches. Substantively, Burke presented twenty-two 'articles of charge' against Hastings to the House of Commons in 1786. One that Burke considered especially important (but which the House rejected) was the Rohilla War charge (WS, VI: 79–113), which concerned the use of British troops by the company's ally, the ruler of Oudh, to expel and annex the lands of the small Rohilla nation – an unjust conquest tied to increasing British pressure on this province to the west of Bengal. With the surprising support of Pitt, the House of Commons approved eight charges against Hastings, and in 1787 Burke (appointed a manager of the impeachment) presented the 'Articles of Impeachment,' now drawn up in the form of legal indictments, to the House of Lords (WS, VI: 125–238).

The trial took place intermittently between 1788 and 1794, overlapping with Burke's engagement with the French Revolution and resulting formally in Hastings's acquittal. Burke presented one of the four major charges that were ultimately pursued: that concerning 'Presents' or bribes, in April–May 1789 (WS, VII: 31–64). In contrast to his practice elsewhere, the editor of this volume provides only what remains of Burke's manuscript version of this speech; a much longer version incorporating shorthand reports may be found in previous editions of Burke's works. More importantly, Burke delivered the four-day (February 1788) 'Speech on Opening of Impeachment' (WS, VI: 264–460) in which he laid out the entire case in the context of the history and society of India, to great public acclaim. Likewise, in May-June 1794 Burke delivered the even more massive, nine-day 'Speech in Reply' (WS, VII: 226–694), in which he reviewed and elaborated the case for the prosecution. These two speeches, which range from minute details to grand perspectives and principles, display Burke's oratory and provide, along with *Fox's India Bill*, the most important evidence regarding his thoughts on India and the empire. Notwithstanding the acquittal, Burke continued to insist that 'Indianism', along with Jacobinism, was the greatest threat facing his compatriots (C, VII: 553; VIII: 432).

India: Civilisation and Social Order

Burke's study of India convinced him that the company's misrule was being inflicted on, and disrupting, a stable social order that embodied an ancient and refined civilisation, a civilisation that was comparable to those of Europe and equally deserving of respect. This view may be compared to earlier eighteenth-century expressions of admiration for Chinese culture, especially in France, but it was not an attitude that normally accompanied imperial expansion.

Burke faced the difficulty of informing his audiences about this largely unknown world in conjunction with arousing their sympathy for Indian sufferings, as a condition (for Burke as for other sentimental moralists) of aligning their indignation and sense of justice with his own. This imperative led to a mixed rhetorical strategy of preserving some of India's exotic quality while at the same time trying to render its essential features familiar. Striking examples of the latter include Burke's extended comparison of the political geography of India to that of the contemporary German empire (WS, V: 389–90) and his portrayal of Indian aristocrats and gentry as equivalent to their English counterparts.

Burke's political thought is grounded in his conception of what may be termed the normal social order of a civilised country, one exhibiting the 'organic' elements of hierarchy, functional differentiation, evolved institutions and complexity of relations among the parts, all rooted in customary norms and prescription. These elements make traditional societies vulnerable to revolutionary assault, while making revolutionary programs self-defeating. Burke's description of India offers a good example of this conception:

> [There are] princes once of great dignity, authority, and opulence. There, are to be found the chiefs of tribes and nations. There is to be found an antient and venerable priesthood, the depository of their laws, learning, and history, the guides of the people whilst living, and their consolation in death; a nobility of great antiquity and renown; a multitude of cities, not exceeded in population and trade by those of the first class in Europe; merchants and bankers, [...] millions of ingenious manufacturers and mechanicks; millions of the most diligent, and not the least intelligent, tillers of the earth. Here are to be found almost all the religions professed by men, the Bramincal, the Mussulmen, the Eastern and the Western Christians. (WS, V: 389–90)

In such respects, Bengal resembled France (WS, V: 425) – the old-regime France whose destruction Burke would similarly deplore.

In their overseas explorations, eighteenth-century Europeans encountered both primitive tribal societies and, especially in Asia, agrarian states and empires that counted as civilised by any standard. Mogul and Hindu India, though in political decline, possessed monuments and literatures that impressed English observers and scholars. The foundations of Indian civilisation, moreover, were ancient, a feature that paralleled Europe's own classical culture and appealed to Burke's respect for tradition. Hence, Burke asserts that India 'does not consist of an abject and barbarous populace; much less of gangs of savages, [...] but a people for ages civilized and cultivated; cultivated by all the arts of polished life, whilst we were yet in the woods' (WS, V: 389), a view repeated in Burke's review of Indian customs in 'Opening' (WS, VI: 301–7). India thus provided an occasion for Burke to delineate a developed social order, with its culture and history, as well as its vulnerability to plunder by adventurers oblivious to its value.

Rejection of Oriental Despotism

In *The Spirit of the Laws* (1748), Montesquieu constructed a model of despotism in which a single ruler exercised arbitrary power over a large country through fear and without limitation by legal or social checks. Montesquieu sought to contrast despotism with European monarchies, but he also claimed that despotic rule was standard in most of Asia, thus reviving the older Western conception of oriental despotism. Montesquieu's view, in which Muslim countries (including Mogul India) figured prominently, was extremely influential. At his trial, Hastings asserted that his own forceful methods of rule were necessitated and thus justified by the incorrigibly despotic nature of the Asian environment.

Burke rejected this defense because it was not just shocking in an English governor (WS, VI: 346–9, 374–5) but also based on a false premise. Indeed, Burke stands out as one of the few major eighteenth-century European thinkers to repudiate Montesquieu's authority on this subject; according to Burke, Montesquieu had been misled by travelers' tales and self-serving European reports (WS, VII: 263–5). Hastings indeed governed in a despotic manner (WS, V: 406, 430, 434) but without the justification he claimed.

Despotism and the pervasive fear and passivity it created were incompatible with Burke's own view of Indian institutions as well as with the flourishing conditions that attracted Western merchants. In particular, Burke's studies convinced him that India (both Muslim and Hindu) possessed entrenched law, property and nobilities – three institutions excluded by despotism that went far, for Burke, to make Indian civilisation comparable in broad outline to European social structures.

The Analysis of Power and its Abuses

As a political thinker, Burke sometimes addressed the large themes and normative principles of political theory. On other occasions, he wrote as an analyst of concrete political institutions and dynamics with an astuteness that presumably reflected his experience as a practicing politician. At this level, Burke was usually in the position of a critic of injustices, of misguided policies, or of defective political arrangements, whether as a member of the parliamentary opposition (for example, opposing the government's American policy) or as an opponent of what he saw as sinister forces and interests (such as those embodied in Hastings and the Jacobins).

Much of what Burke wrote and said in his Indian campaigns, where the focus was on revealing abuses in the company's regime, falls in the latter category. His topics ranged from damning narratives of specific acts of injustice or corruption perpetrated by English officials in India to a critical analysis of the structural conditions that made such abuses likely. One guiding thread was concern with the uses and abuses of power, especially in the context of empire, where the dominance of armed and disciplined Westerners over disorganised subjects or inept native rulers invited oppression. Burke's sensitivity to power relations may have reflected his Irish background or his identification with the Whig tradition, in which the imperative to prevent tyranny by constitutional checks on executive power was deeply ingrained. One of Burke's basic insights was that young men who were removed from their English background and placed in positions of authority in an alien cultural environment tended to lose the moral inhibitions and character that (in Burke's view) usually require stable and supportive social surroundings.

The following list suggests the range of Burke's investigations of specific abuses: Hastings's techniques for soliciting large bribes through manipulation of the Indian custom of giving 'presents' to rulers; corrupt practices in the awarding of military contracts; various treaty violations, including the use of military force in unjust conquests, and the use of intimidation to pressure neighboring states; the use of renegade native agents to perform directly oppressive tasks, such as transmitting bribes and forcefully extracting taxes; the displacement and expropriation of insufficiently subservient native landowners; assaults on high-ranking women in violation of local custom; and the execution of one of Hastings's Indian enemies is what Burke interpreted as an act of judicial murder.

The institutional framework for these abuses was principally determined by parliament's grant of ruling authority to a commercial company without regular governmental oversight and control. This had been a long, cumulative, and unplanned process in which what at first made sense (for example, allowing the company to maintain its own armed forces to protect its trading stations) had grown into sovereignty over countries of European dimensions. This then was a case that rebutted Burke's usual view of the presumptive value of old, evolved institutions and the wisdom latent in them. That he recognised this and called for sweeping reform indicates that Burke's defense of traditional institutions was not uncritical. Other structural features of the imperial system that caught Burke's attention included the cynical use (and replacement when necessary) of compliant native rulers to disguise the company's actual ruling position; the company's personnel policy, in which teenage employees were sent to India, most with the intention of returning rich as soon as possible; and the formation of an Indian 'interest' in parliament to forestall political challenges to company practices.

Revolution in Bengal

It is well known that Burke fiercely opposed the French Revolution, and that this stance seemed to clash with both his defense of the Revolution of 1688 and his sympathy with the grievances that led to the American Revolution (see Chapters 11, 14 and 15 in this volume). It is less well known that Burke applied the term revolution(s) to describe the events by which the British acquired authority over Bengal (1756–65) and their consequences (WS, V: 427–9; VI: 317, 344). The first revolution, which Burke accepted, was Clive's defeat of the Nawab of Bengal in retaliation for the Nawab's previous attack on the English and his replacement, in exchange for lucrative presents, by a more dependent Nawab. Instead of restoring stability and good government, however, this event was followed by several more such political revolutions as subsequent officials sought to emulate Clive's example. The final stage, in the aftermath of these coups, consisted of ongoing upheavals in law, property, revenue and general administration that spread 'the miseries of a revolution' throughout Bengal (WS, V: 427). Burke rejected the French Revolution because, unlike the English and American Revolutions, it aimed at a repudiation of the past rather than a restoration of traditional principles, and because it was a social rather than a limited political revolution. The revolutions in Bengal began as a limited and justifiable turnover in the Bengal monarchy, but they grew into something more closely resembling the French Revolution, with similarly deplorable results.

It is noteworthy that Burke's references to the social and administrative 'revolution' in Bengal occurred prior to the French Revolution. When the latter began in the year following the opening of Hastings's trial, certain parallels emerged in his analyses of the two events; it is even possible to argue that Burke's conclusions about India predisposed him to discern dangerous elements in France as early as he did.

One parallel was in the social background and attitudes of the revolutionaries, who both in India and France were often provincial or parvenu adventurers whose aim was to enrich themselves (especially in India) or attain power (in France) quickly, without scruples, and oblivious to the destruction they were inflicting on the social fabric. Burke's later conjoining of Indianism and Jacobinism rested in part on his view of the similar qualities of these new ruling groups.

Another parallel involves what might be called the vicious-circle financing of a revolution, a topic that illustrates Burke's grasp of political realities. Both the original political and ensuing social revolutions in Bengal were motivated by company officials' quest for wealth (beyond the profits of legitimate commerce). A portion of these gains had to be diverted to pay for ever-larger military and administrative forces; some went back to the company directors and shareholders who approved these policies; and still more went to buy political influence in parliament. Thus, the revolution paid its own costs out of the plunder extracted from its victims. Similarly, Burke's *Reflections* analyses how the revolution's confiscation of Church property underlay the financial instruments that supported the revolution and enriched its backers.

Finally, both in Bengal and France the displacement and, to some extent, the revolutionary destruction of the landed gentry and nobility of the old regime was prominent among Burke's concerns (although his graphic descriptions of the sufferings of Indian peasants are also conspicuous). This focus reflected the fact that the wealth of the aristocratic class was a principal target of the revolutions, as well as Burke's respect for property and social hierarchy. It is noteworthy that he emphasises this theme especially in his 'Closing' speech at Hastings's trial, which was delivered to the House of Lords towards the end of the year of Terror in France.

Government (and Empire) as a Trust

The abuses Burke identified in the Indian empire stand out in contrast to his conception of the proper basis and duties of any ruling authority. A key idea, one that may derive from Locke's political philosophy, is that government is properly regarded as a trust from civil society and that magistrates and governors, like trustees, are accountable for ruling justly and in the best interests of the subjects as the beneficiaries of the trust (WS, V: 385–6). Hence Burke and his fellow members of parliament were trustees for the people of Great Britain; and when parliament conferred authority over India on the East

India Company, it established a derivative trusteeship structure on behalf of the people under its rule in India. The corrupt practices of the company therefore constituted derelictions of the obligations of a trust, and it fell to parliament (and to Burke) to call the company to account and remodel the system of imperial rule.

The legal instrument underlying the company's position was its periodically renewed and expanded charter, through which parliament had created the company as a legal corporation with its internal system of governance, granted it commercial privileges and ultimately delegated to it quasi-sovereign powers in its Indian dominions. To remodel the system of imperial rule therefore meant the revocation of the company's charter or its thorough revision to the detriment of the vested interests of its personnel and shareholders. Throughout the 1770s, Burke and his party (the Rockingham Whigs) hesitated to take up the cause of Indian reform in part because of their scruples about interfering with charters: Whig historical memories from the time of James II perceived political attacks on the privileges of chartered corporations as acts of tyranny, a view that corresponded to Burke's distinctive emphasis on prescriptive rights and venerable institutions.

Burke's detailed study of Indian affairs in his committee work in the early 1780s brought him to overcome these scruples and apply the moral logic of accountability inherent in the trusteeship conception of authority to the offending company. In his *Speech on Fox's India Bill*, he also famously distinguished different levels of charters, with different degrees of normative status and binding force: thus, the subordinate charter of a commercial company must give way before the more fundamental principles of justice – '*the chartered rights of men*', found in Magna Carta, 'a charter to restrain power, and to destroy monopoly' (WS, V: 384). Indeed, he proclaimed that the goal of Indian reform should be to provide a '*Magna Charta* of Hindostan' (WS, V: 386), in contrast to what had been perpetrated under cover of the company charter. In this manner Burke linked his trusteeship conception of government to the English constitutional tradition and suggested that the principles of that tradition were applicable to Britain's imperial possessions.

Moral Foundations: Natural Law and Alternatives

The nature and extent of Burke's adherence to natural law is considered in Chapter 9 of this volume. The topic must be mentioned here, however, since important textual evidence for this theme is found in Burke's Indian speeches, especially his speeches opening and closing the impeachment trial. Burke conspicuously invokes higher-law standards of political morality under such terms as the 'eternal law', the 'moral law', 'humanity and equity' and 'the law of nations and of nature' (e.g., WS, VI: 275, 350–1; VII: 256, 280, 291–2) – the last phrase referring to the eighteenth-century doctrine that international legal norms, for example on treaty obligations, were derived from natural law. These and similar phrases indicate commitment to objective and universal moral principles that properly guide and constrain the exercise of political authority, prohibiting in particular the use of arbitrary or willful power. These principles, moreover, were acknowledged in Asia as well as in Europe: 'their morality is equal to ours,' Burke asserted in reviewing Indian laws, 'as regards the morality of Governors, fathers, superiors' (WS, VI: 361). By appealing to these ideas with respect to India (and Ireland), Burke availed himself of the critical potentiality of the higher-law tradition vis-à-vis unjust practices.

When possible, for example on the charges of bribery and corrupt contracts, Burke sought to convict Hastings wholly by reference to company regulations and British laws. His appeal to natural law standards on the larger issues of arbitrary and oppressive rule suggests both the difficulty of grounding these offenses in positive law and Burke's sense of the importance of the matters at stake, both for India and for British public life. It should also be noted that Hastings presented powerful arguments in his own defense, appealing not only to local custom but also to state necessity: his forceful, if irregular, financial and military methods had after all 'saved the empire' in India, even as Britain was losing its North American colonies. In the dramatic confrontation between these two antagonists, only a compelling higher law could overcome such a claim.

Natural law is not the only or the most evident normative foundation for Burke's political judgements. Burke is famous for his frequent defence of traditional institutions, both because of the 'latent wisdom' contained in them and because of the prescriptive rights, generated by long usage, that are often attached to them. These concepts appear to provide a different basis for the justification of political and social arrangements, one that Burke also applied to India in his condemnation of the wanton company assaults on Indian tradition and customary rights. This standard may appear to be in tension with natural law insofar as it upholds diverse and particularistic practices in what might sometimes seem a relativistic spirit. In his confrontation with Hastings, however, it was the latter who embraced relativism, rejecting European standards of rule as irrelevant in Asia and justifying his actions as being in conformity with local (despotic) customs. Burke denounced this 'plan of Geographical morality,' asserting in response that 'the laws of morality are the same every where,' and that crimes are crimes in Europe, Asia and Africa alike (WS, VI: 346). Burke disputed

Hastings's interpretation of Indian custom, but the more general points are that Burke's traditionalism is not absolute, that 'latent wisdom' is presumptive and rebuttable, that bad customs may be distinguished from good ones by reference to moral principles, and that reform is sometimes called for.

Another approach appears when we inquire into the justification for British rule in India at all, rather than Burke's criteria for distinguishing just from unjust uses of imperial power. On the larger question Burke said:

> All these circumstances [e.g., its distance and unfamiliarity] are not, I confess, very favourable to the idea of our attempting to govern India at all. But there we are; there we are placed by the Sovereign Disposer: and we must do the best we can in our situation. The situation of man is the preceptor of his duty. (WS, V: 404)

This passage expresses Burke's view that the Indian empire had not been deliberately sought but had arisen incrementally through a series of unplanned events and circumstances. It also expresses a conception of what may be termed situational morality, in which individuals or entities like parliament may have valid obligations arising from a situation or role in which they find themselves, even if unchosen. Situational duties include the obligation of those in positions of authority to rule justly and as if exercising a trust for the benefit of the governed. Such duties may be dictated by the higher law, but their assignment to particular moral agents may be accidental – or providential.

Burke, the Enlightenment, and the Non-Western World

Finally, Burke's Indian texts provide a perspective on the interpretive question of his relation to the Enlightenment and the general character of his thought in this respect (see Chapter 2 in this volume). Burke explicitly attacked certain aspects of the theorising of the *philosophes*, and some have viewed his thought as having affinities to post-Enlightenment patterns of romantic, historicist and nationalist thinking. Burke's defence of Indian culture may be taken to imply a more general appreciation of cultural diversity and particularism, which might accord better with these emerging currents than with the typical abstraction and universalism of much Enlightenment thought. On the other hand, Burke's attempt to arouse sympathy for Indians and his demand for just rule in the Indian empire can be seen as expressions of alternative Enlightenment doctrines and of the humanism and universal values of his own century.

The context for this problem was the accumulation of knowledge available to eighteenth-century Europeans about the non-European world, which raised questions about the evaluation of non-Western institutions and the applicability of European standards to them. Burke stands out as one of the first major figures to incorporate these issues into his political thought. Unlike some of his contemporaries and successors, Burke accorded full respect to a major Asian civilisation (if not to the 'gangs of savages' with whom he contrasted the people of India). India was manifestly different from Europe, even exotic, at least on the surface; as we saw earlier, however, Burke compared Indian and European civilisations in a manner that suggested deeper similarities. More importantly, Burke underlined the common humanity (or human nature) of Indians and Europeans as the basis for his appeal on their behalf to his colleagues in parliament. Burke's impeachment of Hastings 'in the name of human nature itself', and 'by virtue of those eternal laws of justice which he has subverted' (WS, VI: 459), indicates a decisive orientation, in a distinctive voice, to the outlook of the Enlightenment.

14

IAN MCBRIDE

Burke and Ireland

One of the most notable developments in Burke scholarship during the last two or three decades has been the increasing attention paid to Irish experiences and contexts, and in particular to Burke's lifelong commitment to the abolition of the penal code. In 'Tracts on the Popery Laws', written at the very outset of his political career, Burke anatomised the inequalities that resulted from the incomplete conquest and colonisation of Ireland. The background was the agrarian unrest raging in the southern province of Munster, where oathbound gangs of Whiteboys were resisting the enclosure of common land. The vicious reaction of the local Protestant elite crystalised Burke's hostility to 'the unfeeling tyranny of a mungril Irish Landlord' (C, I: 147). Three decades later, in his *Letter to Sir Hercules Langrishe* (1792), Burke described the Protestant Ascendancy which ruled Ireland as a 'plebeian oligarchy', a monstrous contradiction in terms (WS, IX: 600). The natural relationship between property and authority, he contended, had been contorted by ethnic and religious antagonisms resulting from the Elizabethan, Jacobean and Cromwellian plantations, so that Protestant tradesmen and servants were raised above Catholic noblemen, whereas Catholic landowners, farmers, merchants and even 'titular' bishops were lumped together with a 'licentious populace' merely because of their religious beliefs (WS, IX: 602). In December 1796, shortly before the arrival of a French fleet in Bantry Bay, Burke continued to express his opposition to British policy in Ireland from his deathbed, writing sympathetically of 'the Jacobinism which arises from Penury and irritation' (C, IX: 162). In the periods between these well-known interventions, he frequently commented on Irish affairs, and he was an important influence on the Irish policy of Whig administrations. Moreover, this preoccupation with the social and psychological aftershocks of conquest would resonate throughout Burke's writings on England, North America, India and France.

It has long been recognised that Ireland constituted a major theme in Burke's writings. What is particularly striking about more recent interpretations is the conviction that Burke's Irishness provides the master-key to his broader political positions. For some, the frantic energy of Burke's conservatism is linked to the profound insecurities of the Anglo-Irish elite, committed to the maintenance of the very same British power structures which they themselves had experienced as a species of despotism.[1] Others situate Burke within a distinctively Irish tradition of counter-enlightenment thought which originated in the intellectual response of the Church of Ireland to the radical Deist John Toland.[2] The best-known of these 'Irish' interpreters, Conor Cruise O'Brien, presents a lengthy psychoanalysis of Burke (and, perhaps, of the author himself) as a closet Jacobite successfully making his way in a political landscape that had long been monopolised by varieties of Whigs. This chapter attempts to introduce and contextual-ise Burke's comments on Ireland. Without endorsing the more extreme claims that have been made for the priority of Burke's Irish commitments, it reasserts the importance of the link between Burke's denunciation of the Irish penal code and his response to both the Enlightenment and the French Revolution.

The Irishness of Burke

The image of Burke as a repressed Jacobite was first sketched by Conor Cruise O'Brien in his introduction to the 1968 Penguin edition of *Reflections on the Revolution in France*, and subsequently elaborated in *The Great Melody: A Thematic Biography and Commented Anthology of Edmund Burke* (1992). O'Brien's brilliantly sustained account turned on the hidden Catholic or Irish 'layer' he disclosed in Burke's psyche. The most impressive evidence for Burke's proximity to Catholic Ireland lies in the family's tradition of confessional ambivalence on the distaff side: his mother, Mary Nagle, con-formed shortly before marriage but remained a practicing Catholic; his sister Juliana was brought up as a Catholic; his wife Jane Nugent was the daugh-ter of a Catholic physician, and although she conformed to the Church of England she was described as 'a genteel, well-bred woman, of the Roman faith'.[3] These facts are more-or-less agreed. It is also well known that Burke spent much of his childhood staying with the Nagles in Munster where he would have acquired an unusual insight into the condition of the surviving Catholic gentry – families who had fought with the defeated Jacobite army in 1688–91. Much more contentious, however, are O'Brien's two central claims: first, that Edmund's father, Richard Burke, was a Catholic attorney who conformed to the established Church of Ireland in 1722; and, second, that his conversion followed his risky involvement in the case of Sir James Cotter, a flamboyant Jacobite gentleman and Catholic folk hero executed in

1720. The 'apostasy' of Richard Burke, O'Brien suggests, bequeathed to his son a profound guilt complex, which impelled him to defend his mother's people against the brutality of Protestant Ascendancy, to identify with other victims of colonial rule such as the suffering people of India, and ultimately to defend the Catholic inheritance of the French people against the revolutionary doctrine of Jacobinism.

As a public intellectual whose controversial career combined literary criticism, politics and journalism, Conor Cruise O'Brien had few serious rivals in post-war Ireland. His seminal writings still fizz with an energy that sets them beyond the reach of his many disciples and detractors. Like Burke, 'the Cruiser' was a brilliant polemicist; he was also histrionic, self-righteous, and unusually prone to conspiracy theories. His reputation as a principled critic of Western colonialism in Katanga and Vietnam left some admirers ill-prepared for his increasingly intemperate assaults on the 'sacral nationalism' that apparently fuelled the Provisional IRA and his sympathy with some of the more reactionary elements of Ulster Unionism.[4] To suggest that this idiosyncratic biographer identified strongly with his subject would be an understatement. While O'Brien regarded himself as a Burkean, it might be truer to say that Edmund Burke – as presented in *The Great Melody* – was an ardent O'Brienite. Although he accurately described *The Great Melody* as 'a rather weird combination of a sort of biography and a sort of anthology', O'Brien regarded the book as 'the principal achievement of my life'.[5] It is surely revealing that in his own unconventional memoirs he arranges the dilemmas of Irish history as a series of tensions between the discordant elements of his own mixed family background. As a Catholic educated in Protestant institutions, O'Brien felt that he had grown up as a kind of divided Irishman. His election to the Dáil for the constituency of Dublin North-East in 1969 thus closed 'a kind of schism in the soul', created by his defiance of the Catholic Church, 'which had long troubled me more than I had ever consciously acknowledged'.[6] If O'Brien analysed his own mental state in this way, then it becomes easier to understand his interpretation of Burke's *Reflections on the Revolution in France* as a spectacular return of the repressed.

Unfortunately, no hard evidence has been found for O'Brien's more speculative assertions concerning Richard Burke's conversion or his links with Jacobitism. Outside Ireland, consequently, many scholars have found it easy to dismiss a book whose enthusiasms and excesses they find rather embarrassing. Burke's most recent biographer deals with the Jacobite thesis only by politely avoiding it.[7] Neither of these positions entirely satisfies. Edmund Burke was one of the beneficiaries of British rule in Ireland who also possessed an unusually acute understanding of what it felt like to be one of its victims. As O'Brien put it, 'he came from an oppressed people but, as a privileged Protestant, he was part of an oppressive system'.[8] Burke consequently occupied an uneasy position among English Whigs, for whom tyranny was still inextricably linked with 'popery'. Ireland was not Burke's only obsession, or even his primary obsession, but it was certainly one of them. Numerous questions arise concerning Burke's enduring commitment to the repeal of the penal laws, the Irish friends and kinsmen whom he encountered in London, his willingness to jeopardise his parliamentary career by taking up unpopular Irish causes, and above all his highly distinctive attitudes to Catholicism: these are so striking that it is perverse not to consider their cumulative significance.

Although Edmund Burke was by birth and education a member of the established Church of Ireland it will already be obvious that he was not at all a typical product of the Protestant Ascendancy. Throughout the eighteenth century, Irish Protestants assembled to mark several important anniversaries that neatly encapsulated their own beleaguered history. They paraded through towns and cities, listened to sermons, held dinners, drank loyal toasts, illuminated windows, lit bonfires, and fired volleys of shots, all in commemoration of the great upheavals of the seventeenth century. Two of these annual holy days stand out. On 23 October, the date set aside by the Church of Ireland for the commemoration of the Irish uprising of 1641, Anglican clergymen solemnly recounted the barbarous massacre of 'many thousand British and Protestants' in the northern province of Ulster and the infliction on further thousands of 'the most exquisite tortures that malice could suggest' – all at the instigation of 'Romish' priests. Stories of these grisly atrocities, ultimately derived from Sir John Temple's *History of the Irish Rebellion* (1646), provided the standard justification for the penal code. Fear and hatred of Catholicism were recharged by formulaic 23 October sermons so that anxious Protestants felt 'locked into a cycle in which rebellion recurred every forty years' and concluded that the only means of protecting themselves was the exclusion of the Catholic population from political, social and economic influence.[9] Burke was a sincere Anglican, 'by choice and by Taste as well as by Education', but he did not belong to the righteous, embattled community that annually worshipped its own image during these fervid October rites (C, IV: 84). In the 1760s, when he compiled his unpublished 'Tracts on the Popery Laws', he accordingly censured Temple for his bigoted depiction of the Irish risings of the previous century. An examination of what he described as the 'interior' history of Ireland would one day reveal 'that these rebellions were not produced by toleration, but by persecution; that they arose not from just and mild government, but from the most unparalleled oppression' (WS, IX: 479).

The annual remembrance of 1641 was quickly followed by another key anniversary on 4 November (the birthday of William III), a day of celebration and thanksgiving for the blessings of the Glorious Revolution. Whereas the English remembered 1688 primarily as the triumph of parliamentary liberty over arbitrary monarchy, the Irish had experienced the Williamite revolution primarily as a war of religion. Three years of military campaigning, including the bloody battles of the Boyne and Aughrim, and the famous sieges of Derry and Limerick, had brought about the final, irreversible destruction of the old Catholic ruling class. In Irish history, Burke warned, the Glorious Revolution had actually been turned upside down:

> In England it was the struggle of the *great body* of the people for the establishment of their liberties, against the efforts of a very *small faction*, who would have oppressed them. In Ireland it was the establishment of the power of the smaller number, at the expence of the civil liberties and properties of the far greater part; and at the expence of the political liberties of the whole. It was, to say the truth, not a revolution, but a conquest [...]. (WS, IX: 614)

William III was celebrated as a parliamentary monarch in all three kingdoms. It was of course a 4 November sermon by the Rev. Richard Price, preached to the Revolution Society in London, that provoked Burke's *Reflections*. But Irish Protestants, especially those of the middling and lower sorts, also welcomed the anniversaries of Williamite victories as occasions for military triumphalism. Right from the 1690s, popular commemorations of 'the overthrow of the Irish at the Boyne' had been instituted.[10]

In 1779, the 4 November commemoration in Dublin took place against the background of the American War. The Irish volunteers had armed themselves when British troops were withdrawn from Ireland to fight across the Atlantic. By now numbering 40,000, these citizen militias quickly destabilised the predictable routines of Anglo-Irish politics. Before a massive crowd, ten volunteer companies staged a spectacular procession around the statue of King William, outside the Irish parliament, demanding an end to English regulation of Irish trade. When Lord North pushed concessions through the British House of Commons, Burke 'sat sullen and silent' (C, IV: 225). Dr William Drennan, the radical Dissenter from Belfast who later founded the Society of United Irishmen, began his literary career with a pamphlet entitled *A Letter to Edmund Burke Esq; by Birth an Irishman, by Adoption an Englishman* (1780), warning that a new '*amor patriae*' had energised the Irish (Protestant) nation. The experience of volunteering had levelled distinctions of rank among Ireland's citizen soldiers, inspiring the lower orders with a new 'independence and republicanism of spirit'.[11] Protestant resentment at the constitutional and commercial restrictions imposed on the kingdom of Ireland has often been viewed as a precursor of modern Irish nationalism. For the most part, however, Irish 'patriots' emphasised their similarities with the English rather than their cultural differences; like the enlightened Scots or the American colonists, theirs was a kind of 'emulative patriotism' concerned with reproducing English liberties in a provincial or 'colonial' setting.[12] In 1782, Lord North's government collapsed following defeat in America and the Volunteers went on to extort 'legislative independence' for the Dublin parliament.

The central claim of Irish patriots was that the legislative interference of Westminster in Irish affairs reduced the inhabitants of Ireland to the condition of slaves, since they were bound by laws to which they had not consented. This made little sense to an expatriate like Burke. Although tied to Ireland 'by [his] earliest instincts', he spent his adult life in England (C, IX: 277). Of course, Irish gentlemen in London, however much they emphasised their English ancestry and Protestant faith, were subject to the same repertoire of ethnic slurs hurled at lower-class Catholics. In 1759, the controversial playwright and novelist Henry Brooke lamented the humiliation of his countrymen in England, 'where, whoever is not smartly expert in the *English* Language, is immediately denominated a *Teague*, a *Paddy*, or I know not what'.[13] If Burke was stung by the critics who resorted to the stock anti-Irish images of bogs, whiskey and potatoes, he never showed it. His correspondence reveals none of the unease of the Irish immigrant, no 'identity crisis' or ambivalence about English culture. Financial rather than cultural insecurity was Burke's great anxiety. Moreover, the Burkes were part of an extensive Irish network in London, Bristol and Bath engaged in colonising the swollen apparatus of the British imperial state from the West Indies to Bengal. Among Edmund's close friends, Lauchlin Maclean was appointed vice-governor of St Vincent; Will Burke acted as receiver for Guadaloupe and deputy paymaster for forces in India; and his brother Richard was collector of customs for Grenada.[14] Burke's sincere belief that Ireland could not thrive without the British connection – a dependence he presented as a simple geopolitical fact – was also reinforced by the presence of Irish merchants of all denominations in and around the City of London and their investments in the business of empire.[15]

Burke's conviction that the Anglo-Irish relationship was based on a natural harmony of interests was no doubt related to his own upward mobility. In entering the Westminster parliament, 'the presiding council of the greatest empire existing, (and perhaps, all things considered, that ever did exist)', he found himself able to be 'somewhat useful to the place of my birth and education' (WS, IX: 561). But he also regarded the 'revolution' of 1782 as a triumph for the privileged minority rather than the nation as a whole. The constitutional status of Ireland was always regarded by Burke as secondary to the religious disabilities inflicted on the majority of its people. Protestant Ascendancy, he contended, was simply another name for arbitrary power: 'the resolution of one set of people in Ireland, to consider themselves as the sole citizens in the commonwealth; and to keep a dominion over the rest by reducing them to absolute slavery' (WS, IX: 644). Burke was by far the most important advocate of Catholic emancipation in the late eighteenth century.

Catholics and Converts

Those who framed the penal laws had envisaged them as a permanent barrier capable of providing Protestant Ireland with lasting protection from its implacable enemies. In fact, the cracks in the penal code were wide enough for enterprising Catholics to establish a foothold in public life. The legal profession was particularly important in enabling Catholic families to survive and even prosper in spite of penal legislation designed to dismantle their landed estates. As nominal converts to the established church, or as 'chamber counsellors' who advised clients outside the courtroom, Catholics were able to attract a substantial proportion of legal business in Dublin. From an early stage, for example, the sons of substantial Catholic/convert families from the west of Ireland were entering the legal profession: in 1709, the convert rolls recorded the conformities of Gerald Burke, Denis Daly, and Patrick French, all Galway lawyers.[16] These ex-Catholics devised the 'collusive discovery', the legal fiction whereby a 'discovery' action was brought by a friendly Protestant to pre-empt a genuine seizure of land. Such improvisations probably did more to determine the conditions under which propertied Catholics actually lived than the statute book. Although their main business was conveyancing, the convert lawyers and chamber counsellors also lobbied on behalf of their co-religionists in both Dublin and London. At Whitehall and Westminster, penal legislation was quietly opposed by a succession of Catholic/convert Irishmen who lived and worked around the Inns of Court: Dennis Molony (1650–1726), Peter Sexton (d. 1734), David Duane (d. 1736), Matthew Duane (1707–85), and Burke's friend Daniel Macnamara (1720–1800).

The conversion of barristers, solicitors, and attorneys occasioned alarm rather than relief among Protestants. Pragmatic conformists were not turncoats. Although they might occasionally attend an Anglican service, as one hostile observer explained, they retained 'their former Intimacy with the Papists, and are as well and as cordially received by them as ever'.[17] In the language of the period, converts were not treated as part of the 'Protestant interest', but rather as a distinct class of ex-Catholics who stood between the social worlds of the new Williamite elite and the old Jacobite gentry. As the Anglican primate noted in 1728, many converts 'have a popish wife who has mass said in the family, and the children are brought up papists'.[18] Even though it has not been possible to establish with certainty that Edmund's father, Richard Burke, was the Catholic attorney of that name who conformed in 1722, Burke's family was certainly typical of the so-called 'convert interest'. It is no coincidence that his sister Juliana married into the wealthy French family of Galway, one of the greatest convert dynasties, or that Burke's most intimate friend in Ireland was the independent country gentleman Charles O'Hara, the descendant of a Gaelic family that had been successfully integrated into the Protestant elite. It is not helpful to think of Burke as the product of a 'mixed marriage', with all the modern connotations of 'love across the barricades'. Nor should we imagine that sons of converts were ashamed of their fathers' actions. Converts, far from deserting their kin, had actually saved them from total ruin.

These speculations concerning Edmund Burke's origins among the families of the convert interest acquire a little more substance if we turn to a fresh source, so far neglected by Irish historians. All Irish law students were required to spend eight terms at one of the Inns of Court in London before being called to the Irish bar. At Middle Temple, the natural ties of kinship and patronage were reinforced by the system of manucapting, by which students were required to have bonds of up to £100 signed by two local guarantors.[19] Edmund's bond survives, complete with the signatures of his two sureties. One of these, Thomas Kelly, became a successful barrister in Dublin and eventually an MP. The son of a Catholic gentlemen from Galway, Kelly had married a daughter of James Hickey, a key figure in Burke's London circle. Even more interesting is the second bondsman: John Bourke of Serjeant's Inn, a Dubliner admitted to Middle Temple in 1722, was the father of Edmund's close friend, collaborator, and 'cousin', Will Bourke. Between 1730 and 1749 John Bourke signed bonds for at least thirteen students in addition to Edmund. A brief glance at his clients and his fellow-bondsmen reveals a predominance of Anglo-Norman and Gaelic names – Burke, Daly, Doyle, Macnamara, O'Malley, Sarsfield, and Staunton. Among other things, the identity of Edmund Burke's manucaptors strengthens the evidence for Galway connections in the family circle. The Galway region was one of two areas where a strong network of Catholic and ex-Catholic landowners survived (the other was the Blackwater valley in County Cork, home of the Nagles). Conversion in the history of eighteenth-century Ireland is best viewed not as the product of an individual spiritual decision but as a sociological phenomenon that allowed Gaelic and Anglo-Norman families to advance themselves and their kinfolk.

Enlightenment and Revolution

The Middle Temple bonds also reveal that the prominent writer and translator Thomas Nugent was linked to the same patronage network as the Burkes. If, as is generally supposed, the translator was the brother of Dr Christopher Nugent (Burke's father-in-law), he must have been a convert himself.[20] A number of Nugent's translations had a significant impact on Burke during the formative years of the 1750s: Dubos's *Critical Reflections on Poetry, Painting, and Music* (1748), Condillac's *Essay on the Origin of Human Knowledge* (1756), and above all Montesquieu's *The Spirit of the Laws* (1750). Burke's admiration for Montesquieu – 'the greatest genius, which has enlightened this age' (WS, I: 445) – was repeatedly acknowledged, from his *Abridgement of English History* (1757) to his *Appeal from the New to the Old Whigs* published in 1791 (WS, I: 445). Burke was indebted to Montesquieu for the key insight that, in reforming political institutions and legal structures, the legislator must work in harmony with the complex social and cultural factors that shaped his nation. *The Spirit of the Laws* was also cited *ad nauseam* by the Catholic pamphleteer Charles O'Conor to support two points in particular. First, on conquest, Montesquieu's masterpiece insisted that the rights of a conqueror leave intact the 'Liberty, Laws, Wealth and *always Religion*' of the defeated; and second that penal laws have only ever had a destructive effect.[21] In the 1774 parliamentary debate on the Quebec bill, Burke too would recommend 'Montesquieu's opinion' that a form of dominion founded upon conquest should leave the subject population secure in their 'Liberty – Property – always their Religion'.[22] Burke was no doubt comforted by Montesquieu's belief in the positive moral and cultural influence of Christianity on European civilisation.

Montesquieu's determination to locate the sociological underpinnings of constitutional forms appealed to those who wanted to bypass the sectarian frameworks within which the Irish conducted their politics. In general, however, the Enlightenment was difficult terrain for pro-Catholic writers. Daniel O'Conor was shocked when he met Helvétius in London in 1764 and found him indifferent to the sufferings of Irish Catholics. When he informed the *philosophe* that his brother Charles was an 'enlightened' man, Helvétius replied simply, 'And why does he not turn Protestant?'[23] Like the sermons preached on 23 October, the philosophical historians of the Enlightenment deplored the doctrines that allegedly freed Catholics from their obligations to Protestant neighbours and their obedience to non-Catholic sovereigns. First among these, of course, was the alleged power of the pope to depose secular rulers. Voltaire's battles with the French church meant that he always regarded the Catholic clergy as 'the perpetrators rather than the potential victims of persecution.'[24] Likewise Hume followed Sir John Temple's *Irish Rebellion* (1646) when he discussed the 1641 rising in his best-selling *History of England* (1754). The discreet lobbying of Charles O'Conor and Edmund Burke eventually persuaded Hume to moderate his account in later editions, with rather anti-climactic results: the Catholic insurgents were upgraded from 'barbarous savages' to 'enraged rebels', while 'insulting butchers' was softened to 'insulting foes'.[25]

In this unpromising climate, pleas for the modification of the penal code were usually presented as ways of strengthening rather than undermining the Protestant interest. The most prolific Catholic pamphleteer was Burke's friend Charles O'Conor, who often wrote in the guise of a moderate Protestant. Ireland's rulers, he believed, 'must properly be attended by their own physicians, not by a suspected and intruding prescriber'.[26] Where O'Conor gently suggested that the relaxation of controls on property would make Catholic capital available for investment in Irish land, Burke was strident and systematic in his denunciation of Protestant Ascendancy. Even in the early 1760s, as a secretary in the Dublin Castle administration, his core argument was that a law against the majority of the population was 'not particular injustice, but general oppression' (WS, IX: 454). Of course, Burke recognised that the established church possessed the allegiance of the landed elite; it was also the religion of the monarch and a vital institutional link between the two kingdoms. The problem was that the national church was rejected by 'the body of the people'. Two hundred years of plantation and persecution had not altered this power balance. After a century of legislation Ireland was 'full of penalties and full of Papists' (WS, IX: 464). Just as the people had been unable to overturn the Anglican regime, so the government was unable to eradicate the faith of the people. The *Letter to Sir Hercules Langrishe* therefore concentrated on the depravity of a state which could only maintain itself by the humiliation and subjection of the majority population. Whereas O'Conor sought to defuse Protestant fears, Burke simply ignored them. He found Protestant scaremongering so disgusting that he overlooked the actual or threatened invasions of 1708, 1715, 1719, and 1722, which had facilitated the passage of the 'popery laws'.

Anyone who reflected seriously on the history of Ireland had to confront the intractability of its ethnic and religious antagonisms. No other example could be found, as Archbishop King of Dublin once observed, 'of a country above 500 years in the possession of a people without settling it in a prospect of peace or bringing the conquered into the interest of the conquerors'.[27] Where the ruling classes traditionally posed the problem in terms of the violent intolerance of the Church of Rome, Burke naturally identified the obstacle as Protestant bigotry. 'Time has, by degrees, in all other places and periods, blended and coalited the conquerors with the conquered', he observed. Thus the Normans had been gradually 'softened' into the English; the Romans had 'blended' into the Gauls. Only the Protestant settlers in Ireland continued to see themselves as 'a sort of colonial garrison to keep the natives in subjection to the other state of Great Britain' (WS, IX: 614–5). Ultimately, he viewed the deficiencies in the government of Ireland in terms of moral failures rather than structural relationships. What we now call 'colonialism' did not have the automatic connotations of illegitimacy and exploitation that it has today; nor was modern colonialism sharply distinguished from older forms of territorial expansion or other processes of migration and settlement. The establishment of 'the first English races' in Ireland, moreover, was just one of several expansionary movements during the twelfth and thirteenth centuries, which saw the frontiers of Latin Christendom pushed into the peripheral regions of medieval Europe (WS, IX: 616). Burke had no quarrel with the English annexation of Ireland, which he regarded as an essential part of the progress of civilisation. His novelty was to insist upon the positive contribution of Catholicism to this history of progress, even those aspects of Catholicism that contemporaries found most abhorrent.

In an important article, Derek Beales has recently explored a completely neglected theme in Burke's rambling *Reflections*, his passionate defence of the French monasteries suppressed by the Revolution.[28] The seizure of ecclesiastical land by the National Assembly was of course a key theme in Burke's critique; but it is still puzzling to find the fate of the religious orders taking up ten pages of the whole book. No aspect of the *Reflections* was stranger than its rejection of contemporary attitudes towards Catholicism. Protestants in the British Isles and enlightened Europeans everywhere held that monasteries and nunneries were parasitic institutions characterised by sloth and superstition.

In 1783, Burke's *Letter from a Distinguished English Commoner to a Peer of Ireland, on the Penal Laws against Irish Catholics* was first published, apparently without the author's approval. Half of the pamphlet was taken up with the education of the Catholic priesthood. Astonishingly, the tract included a sympathetic discussion of such issues as clerical celibacy, conventual discipline, and the independence of the Catholic hierarchy, subjects which pro-Catholic writers wisely avoided like the plague. Burke recalled visiting the Collège des Lombards, the Irish seminary in Paris, in 1773, 'a very good place of Education, under excellent orders and regulations' (WS, IX: 571). He wrote approvingly of the custom whereby candidates for the priesthood were ordained *before* going abroad for their training, so that they could maintain themselves by 'performing now and then, certain offices of religion for small gratuities'. This irregular system, the target of much internal criticism, enabled priests to cheat the penal laws, just as the lawyers and land-owners had found their own complex methods of subverting the system. In Ireland, the monasteries had been destroyed, although the ruins were still regarded 'very holy ground' by Catholics who wanted to be buried there.[29] It was in fact the question of monasteries which prompted Burke's memorable pronouncement in favour of the cautious reform of established institutions in the *Reflections*. 'I cannot conceive how any man can have brought himself to that pitch of presumption, to consider his country as nothing but *carte blanche*, upon which he may scribble whatever he pleases.' This was of course what the Cromwellians had done, and what the Williamites in Ireland had attempted. A 'true politician', by contrast, must always consider 'how he shall make the most of the existing materials of his country' (WS, VIII: 206).

None of this is to argue that Burke 'was – as near as makes no difference – an Irish Catholic', or that he was in some way confused or 'conflicted' in his religious beliefs.[30] There is no reason to doubt Burke's attachment to the worship of the Church of England, even if he focused on its social util-ity rather than its theological rectitude. What was distinctive about Burke, however, was his determination to distinguish the Anglican creed from Protestantism, a word he came to dislike. Protestant belief was not defined by any positive doctrinal or liturgical content; it was not so much a reli-gion as the 'mere *negation*' of one (WS, IX: 604). This rhetorical move was original to Burke. What defined the eighteenth-century English, as recent historians have repeatedly emphasised, was their common Protestantism, or rather their common abhorrence of continental Catholicism. In the decades after 1707, one force above all shaped a broad British mentality capable of uniting England and Scotland: Protestantism.[31] And at the height of the Seven Years' War (1756–63) the vast assemblage of kingdoms, colonies, and possessions now known as the British empire was held together principally by a belief in a shared religious heritage; Irish patriots joined their fellow British and American subjects in the boast that their empire was free, com-mercial, maritime and, above all, Protestant.[32] In Burke's Irish writings, his strategy was to reduce Protestant Ascendancy to a 'spirit of domination' that England had outgrown. In place of Protestantism, he substituted pre-scription as the principle that underpinned the British constitution. It was prescription, the continuity of custom, that legitimised the Anglican commu-nion in England, the Presbyterian discipline in Scotland, the Catholic church in Quebec and perhaps in Ireland too. 'These things were governed', he explained, 'as all things of that nature are governed, not by general maxims, but by their own local and peculiar circumstances' (C, IV: 8).

NOTES

1 Seamus Deane, *A Short History of Irish Literature* (London: Hutchinson, 1986), pp. 49–57.

2 David Berman, 'The Irish Counter-Enlightenment' in Richard Kearney (ed.), *The Irish Mind* (Dublin: Wolfhound Press, 1985), pp. 119–40.

3 Conor Cruise O'Brien, *The Great Melody: A Thematic Biography and Commented Anthology of Edmund Burke* (London: Sinclair-Stevenson, 1992), pp. 10, 63–4.

4 Conor Cruise O'Brien, *Memoirs: My Life and Themes* (Dublin: Poolbeg, 1999), p. 122.

5 O'Brien to Valerie Jobling, 17 January 1991, 8 May 1991, mss in private possession.

6 O'Brien, *Memoirs*, p. 318.

7 See volume I of F. P. Lock's otherwise excellent *Edmund Burke*, 2 vols. (Oxford: Clarendon, 1998–2006).

8 O'Brien, *Great Melody*, p. 272.

9 T. C. Barnard, 'The Uses of 23 October and Irish Protestant Celebrations', *English Historical Review*, 106.421 (1991): 889–920, 897.

10 James Kelly, '"The Glorious and Immortal Memory": Commemoration and Protestant Identity in Ireland 1660–1800', *Proceedings of the Royal Irish Academy*, 94 (1994): 39–40.

11 [William Drennan], *A Letter to Edmund Burke Esq; by Birth an Irishman, by Adoption an Englishman* (Dublin, 1780), p. 16.

12 Colin Kidd, 'North Britishness and the Nature of Eighteenth-Century British Patriotisms', *Historical Journal*, 39.2 (1996), 361–82.

13 [Henry Brooke], *An Essay on the Antient and Modern State of Ireland* (Dublin, 1759), pp. 6–7, 35.

14 Craig Bailey, 'Metropole and Colony: Irish Networks and Patronage in the Eighteenth-Century Empire', *Immigrants & Minorities*, 23 (2005): 161–81.

15 David Dickson, Jan Parmentier, and Jane Ohlmeyer (eds.), *Irish and Scottish Mercantile Networks in Europe and Overseas in the Seventeenth and Eighteenth Centuries* (Gent: Academia Press, 2007).

16 T. P. Power, 'Conversions among the Legal Profession in Ireland in the Eighteenth Century' in Daire Hogan and W. N. Osborough (eds.), *Brehons, Serjeants and Attorneys: Studies in the Irish Legal Profession* (Dublin: Irish Academic Press, 1990), pp. 153–74, 156.

17 *The Conduct of the Purse of Ireland* (London, 1714), pp. 14–16.

18 *Letters Written by His Excellency Hugh Boulter*, 2 vols. (Oxford, 1769–70), I, pp. 229–30.

19 This paragraph is based on the bonds preserved in Middle Temple Archive (London), MT3/CBB/Boxes 12–14.

20 The translator left £50 to Christopher Nugent in his will to be given to charity: TNA, Prob 11/976.

21 [Charles O'Conor], *The Protestant Interest, Considered Relatively to the Operation of the Popery-Acts in Ireland* (Dublin, 1757), pp. 14, 15, 23, 26, 32, 34, 39 and 42.

22 Burke papers, Sheffield Archives, Wenthouse Woodhouse Muniments, 6.6. 'Canada Bill.' Quoted in Richard Bourke, 'Edmund Burke and the Politics of Conquest' *Modern Intellectual History*, 4.3 (2007): 403–432.

23 Daniel O'Conor to Charles O'Conor, 7 April 1764, Royal Irish Academy, BI1.

24 Graham Gargett, 'Voltaire's View of the Irish' in Graham Gargett & Geraldine Sheridan (eds.), *Ireland and the French Enlightenment, 1700–1800* (London: Macmillan, 1999), pp. 152–70, 161.

25 David Berman, 'David Hume on the 1641 Rebellion in Ireland', *Studies: An Irish Quarterly Review*, 65.258 (1976): 101–12.

26 Walter D. Love, 'Charles O'Conor of Belanagare and Thomas Leland's "Philosophical" History of Ireland', *Irish Historical Studies*, 13.49 (1962): 1–25, 10.

27 Toby Barnard, *A New Anatomy of Ireland: The Irish Protestants, 1649–1770* (New Haven and London: Yale University Press, 2003), p. 1.

28 Derek Beales, 'Edmund Burke and the Monasteries of France', *Historical Journal*, 48.2 (2005): 415–36.

29 James Kelly (ed.), *The Letters of Lord Chief Baron Edward Willes to the Earl of Warwick 1757–62* (Aberystwyth: Boethius Press, 1990), p. 88.

30 Siobhán Kilfeather, 'Edmund Burke's Gothic Imagination', *Irish Review*, 33 (2005): 118–24, 118.

31 Linda Colley, *Britons: Forging the Nation 1707–1837* (London: Pimlico, 1992).

32 See P. J. Marshall, *The Making and Unmaking of Empire: Britain, India, and America c. 1750–1783* (Oxford: Oxford University Press, 2005).

15

IAIN HAMPSHER-MONK

Reflections on the Revolution in France

Context, Origins, and Publication

Reflections on the Revolution in France was by far the most famous literary response to that liminal event of political modernity. It has often since been held to define and shape the conservative alternative to revolutionary principles. It purports to be a letter explaining, to a Frenchman, the author's views on the Revolution and distinguishing between what we would today call the political cultures of Britain and of revolutionary France. The epistolary device – widely used by Burke – had a basis in fact. Charles-Jean-Francois Depont, a young French acquaintance, had written asking Burke for assurance that the French were, 'worthy to be free, could distinguish between liberty and licence, and between legitimate government and despotic power' (C, VI: 32). Burke's initial reply, expressing grave misgivings about the Revolution, had been withheld, lest it compromise Depont, in favour of a brief noncommittal response, now lost. The opening of *Reflections* refers both to Depont's second letter pressing Burke for a reply and to the withheld letter, which had finally been sent. However, although Burke presents Depont's letter as the occasion for writing *Reflections*, it would be naïve to see it only in this way, or indeed, addressed only to the French.

Coincidently, on 4 November, the date of Depont's first letter, another event contributed decisively to the nature of *Reflections*, shaping its opening passages and rendering the English its real target audience (as Burke would put it in a letter: 'my Object was not France, in the first instance, but this Country' [C, VI: 141]). This was the address (Burke provocatively calls it a 'sermon') given by Rev. Richard Price to the dinner of the 'Revolution Society', an association of dissenting ministers meeting annually to celebrate the Revolution of 1688. Price's address, *A Discourse on the Love of Our Country*, deprecated a narrow patriotism and contrasted it with a wider concern for humanity. But it was Price's claim that the principles of England's Glorious Revolution of 1688 were one with those of the French Revolution to which Burke was to take such far-reaching exception. Price read 1688 as establishing a demotic basis for the regime that succeeded James II. The Glorious Revolution, he suggested, had established a popular right to 'cashier Kings for misconduct', an elective basis for royal succession (the right 'to choose our sovereigns'), and a democratic right 'to frame a government for ourselves'.[1] These principles, according to Price, were congruent with, albeit less explicit than, the claims the French were then making. It is this tactic of reading the France of 1789 back into the England of 1688 as a Trojan horse to insinuate its more explicit revolutionary principles into English political life that Burke would target as so dangerous and subversive of the constitution. Not only were the non-conformists (such as Price, who was legally excluded from political office) and other reformers enthused, but so were prominent parliamentarians. Amongst these was Burke's erstwhile political partner and leader of the parliamentary Whigs, Charles James Fox, who claimed he 'exulted' in the Revolution both 'from feelings and from principle'.[2]

Burke's repudiation of the Revolution was unexpected. He was a lifelong reformer and had sympathised with the American colonists in their struggle with the British. Tom Paine, an acquaintance of Burke's, wrote to him from France with news of events in a collusive tone, suggesting he expected Burke to agree with his optimism; and Paine was not the only friend of liberty to presume that Burke, like Fox, would greet that 'blissful dawn' (C, VI: 67).

However Burke drew a sharp distinction between gradualist reform (or even resistance to specific oppression) and any ideologically driven, totalising, revolutionary transformation. The opening of *Reflections* would be devoted to rebutting Price's reading of English constitutional history. Far from asserting the rights Price ascribed to them, the orchestrators of the Glorious Revolution of 1688 had, Burke claimed, sought to minimise any discontinuity in the hereditary character of the monarchy and the constitutional rights attached to it. Indeed, Burke insisted that so far from the Revolution having established, as Price claimed, the principle of elective magistracy; the fact was that if they had ever had such a right, 'the English nation did at that time most solemnly renounce and abdicate it, for themselves and for all their posterity for ever' (WS, VIII: 70). The English, moreover, claimed their rights as an historical inheritance grounded in national custom, not on the basis of abstract principles. Having sought to correct Price on a matter of historical fact, Burke strikingly concedes that even if the English were wrong in doing this, even if the reading of English history as a pedigree of rights was illusory, the fact of it being believed was enough to demonstrate and sustain the 'powerful prepossession to antiquity', which sustained English political liberty and stability (WS, VIII: 82).

Ultimately, for him it was historical belief, not historical fact that generated legitimacy.

Burke quickly decided that the Revolution was disastrous for France, but there are only hints that he saw any danger for England. In November, he wrote of France as 'a country undone', the Nobility and the Clergy, the chief supports of the Monarchy, 'extinguished' and of the 'pillage of their Church'. He continues, 'a public Bankruptcy seems the only remedy for the distempers of their Finances, and a civil war the only chance for producing order from their government'. Yet 'the interests of this country [England] requires, perhaps the interests of mankind require, that she [France] should not be in a condition to give the Law to Europe' (C, VI: 36). In December, criticising the plan for the new French Bank and currency, he still refers to the 'follies of France, by which we are not yet affected' (C, VI: 55).

It seems to have been his reading of Price's pamphlet in late January, following an account of it from a friend, that focused Burke's mind on the danger revolutionary ideas posed to English political life.[3] Burke's initial animus was as much affected by the aspersions Price cast on the character of his friend Fox (who had supported Dissenters politically), as it was on Price's attempt to recruit French principles for English politics (C, VII: 57). This must have deepened his feeling of betrayal when Fox too expressed extravagant support for the Revolution. In any event, from early in 1790, during the first phase of writing, which was directed at Price's pamphlet, Burke had already articulated the two main rhetorical features of *Reflections* – a deepening conviction of the illiberal character and violent potential of revolutionary politics and a determination to prevent their principles taking root in Britain.

Burke first publicly attacked the Revolution in the House of Commons on 9 February 1790, in a speech deprecating Fox's enthusiasm and expressing worries about the ideological danger revolutionary principles posed to England: 'some wicked persons', he warned, 'had shown a strong disposition to recommend an imitation of the French spirit of reform'. 'To prevent such innovations', he declared his readiness to 'abandon his best friends, and join with his worst enemies' (Works, III: 274). Although *Reflections* was already well under way, Burke had the speech published. His readiness to 'forsake his friends' proved prescient: a growing split within the ranks of the Whig party itself and an increasingly fractious relationship with Fox was to culminate in May 1791, in their very public and tearful break on the floor of the House of Commons. Over the summer parliamentary recess in 1790, Burke resumed work on *Reflections*, now with a much wider canvas, focussing on revolutionary France itself.[4] It was finally published in 1 November 1790.

The device of the 'letter to a gentleman in Paris' was brilliantly suited to his purpose of warning off those English who flirted with the Revolution. It positioned him rhetorically to appear to defend his version of English politics to foreigners ignorant of it, while, without condescension, playing tutor to his own countrymen, whom he clearly thought similarly in need of instruction. The work was hugely successful, the first impression of 4,000 copies selling so fast that four further impressions of 2,000 each were made within a fortnight, and an estimated 30,000 by Burke's death in 1797. As well as the London printings, editions were published in Dublin, Calcutta, New York and Philadelphia.[5] The work was translated, with Burke's assistance, into French and published in Paris the same month; pirated editions appeared in Lyons and Strasbourg.[6] Possession of it was later prohibited in France. Helen Maria Williams, then resident in Paris, records having first to bury, and then to burn her copy for fear of arrest.[7] An influential German translation by Gentz, was published in Berlin in 1793 and another in Vienna. Italian and Dutch translations and excerpts followed.

Philosophical Underpinnings

Burke's anti-revolutionary tirade was notoriously unsystematic, but it nevertheless invoked, alluded to, or otherwise hinted at a range of positions that were readily capable of being systematised by readers sympathetic to his political position. At the risk of over-schematising what was clearly intended as a rhetorical performance, what follows tries to provide a systematic account of those beliefs and Burke's deployment of them.

Burke's thinking was deeply grounded in early eighteenth-century issues. Central to the argument of *Reflections* lies a model of moral psychology, which is radically opposed to a rationalist and predominantly French strand of the Enlightenment. Broadly, both are heirs of Locke's epistemology, but each take Locke's strictures on the limits of human understanding in different ways – for the French, it implied both confidence in empirical knowledge and atheistic rejection of religious claims; for Burke it entailed scepticism about extra-sensory knowledge-claims (such as politics requires) and tolerance for a range of religious beliefs.

Burke's conception of human knowledge and his conception of the motivation needed to sustain the moral and political standards necessary for civilised life differed fundamentally from those espoused or presupposed by the revolutionaries.

Burke grew up in an Ireland where confessional divides and the insecurities of the minority Anglican establishment made rationalist critiques of religion – such as the radical Lockeanism of John Toland – threatening *causes célèbres* that structured philosophical debate.[8] Burke's first work (*A Vindication of Natural Society*, 1756) had been a satire on Bolingbroke's deistic and rationalist posthumous essays, which already presaged Burke's later reaction to the irreligion and confident rationalism of the Revolution. A year later, his one systematic work of theory – the *Philosophical Enquiry into the Origins of Our Ideas of the Sublime and the Beautiful* – had analysed our two principal aesthetic responses in terms that opposed epistemological clarity and emotional power. The beautiful was evoked by clear and small impressions – and hence they were susceptible to reasoned analysis, which to some degree robbed them of their affective power. The sublime, by contrast – found in impressions of the immense, the infinite, and the obscure – was incapable of forming clear and distinct ideas, and so overwhelmed the operation of (Lockean) reason. This suspension of reason rendered sublime impressions much more powerful than the beautiful. Although Burke does call attention in this work to the political and rhetorical importance of aesthetic considerations, they are not prominent either in it nor in his subsequent career – not, that is, until his response to the French Revolution, where the opposition between a would-be transparent (and so weak) revolutionary reason and the cognitively powerful, because sublime, resources of history, religion and eternity, becomes central.

Burke judges individual human beings for the most part to be incapable of adequately discerning the full meanings and modes of operation of social and political institutions and processes. This is not – as some reactionary romantics were to argue – because such social entities are mystical or divine creations (although, for Burke, ultimately they *are*), but because they are historical, the product of an iterated temporal process of trial and error that embodies accumulations of historical experience in an institutional reason that is simply inscrutable for individuals: 'We are afraid to put men to live and trade each on his own private stock of reason; because we suspect that this stock in each man is small, and that the individuals would be better to avail themselves of the general bank and capital of nations, and of ages' (WS, VIII: 138). The model for this is the operation of precedent within common law, which Burke had studied at Temple Inn, and with which most educated men of his generation in public life would have had some familiarity. Judgement according to the precedent of disparate cases thrown up by the diversity of life has the effect of refining rules to experience in a way that no rational *a priori* approach or codified law could do, because they could never possibly anticipate all the different circumstances that applications of the law would confront.[9] The revolutionaries' claim to be able to construct a constitution *ab initio* and on the basis of abstract first principles – those of the 'rights of man' – is diametrically opposed to this gradualist, incrementalist conception of political identity, knowledge, and change. Burke's opposition is thus not to reason, but to the arrogance of individual, *a priori*, deductive reason. His claim – a claim that has, until recently in Anglophone philosophy, been buried beneath a resolutely individual-centred cognitive tradition – is that political reason, and indeed knowledge itself, is socially constructed, collectively accumulated and held in suitably developed social institutions (establishments and corporations), practices (such as representation and consultation), and the dispositions they foster (most prominently, compromise). History, properly conducted, is the process by which such reason is accumulated, and a historically developed constitution is the repository of that reason.

The revolutionaries, in opposition to this, claim to be able to deduce institutional forms from an abstractly construed 'natural right'. Burke is often held to have simply rejected the whole concept of 'natural rights', but this misconceives his position, which is more subtle and explains why natural right is so threatening. Always mistrustful of appeals beyond positive law, Burke nevertheless acknowledged, most conspicuously in his Indian writings, that in the complete absence of positive juridical resources, recourse might be had to some trans-empirical juridical standards (more often natural law than natural right).[10] But in *Reflections*, and at length in the *Appeal*, he invokes a technically Hobbesian conception of natural right as pre-social and incompatible with society. 'Government,' he declared, 'is not made in virtue of natural rights, which may and do exist in total independence of it'. Within society, any appeal to such rights as a standard must be abjured: one of civil society's 'fundamental rules, is *that no man should be judge in his own cause*. By this each person has at once divested himself of the first fundamental right of uncovenanted man, that is, to judge for himself, and to assert his own cause' (WS, VIII: 110). Those invoking natural rights were thus to be understood as seeking, wittingly or not, to abandon the conventions (and accumulated historical experience) that had removed us from the state of violence and confusion, which is inseparable from their exercise and to plunge us back into Hobbes's brutish and uncivilised condition.

As well as its cognitive and moral indeterminacy, Burke has a second objection to revolutionary political thought: namely, its motivational inadequacy. This is not to say it does not have *energy* – indeed that is one of its most frightening properties: there is no guarantee that that energy will be focussed on the realisation of the doctrines professed. The spokespersons for the revolution seem to believe, Socratically, that a rationally adequate argument will *ipso facto* be motivationally compelling. Burke rejects this as naïve (or wicked). Even though a logically valid syllogism compels rational acceptance of the conclusion, this does not convert into a practical syllogism with an irresistible action as the conclusion. In this, as in other respects, arguments can be 'metaphysically true' but 'morally and politically false' (WS, VIII: 112). Not only is logical validity unrelated to motivational adequacy, the relationships between doctrines and outcomes is not a simple one, 'the real effects of moral causes are not always immediate [...] plausible schemes, with very pleasing commencements, have often shameful and lamentable conclusions' (WS, VIII: 111). It is absurd to suppose that natural rights principles, even if they were originally adequate in themselves, will, once they become policy 'continued in the simplicity of their original direction' (WS, VIII: 112).

The appropriate relationship between theory and political practice – in a properly conducted polity – is the *reverse* of that claimed by the revolutionaries. Theory is to be *derived from* established practice rather than imposed on it. In a speech against rationally inspired reformers (which rehearses the *Reflections'* defence of prescription) made as early as 1782, Burke argued that a 'prescriptive government, such as ours [...] never was made upon any foregone theory'. He adds that it is 'a preposterous way of reasoning [...] to take from the theories which learned and speculative men have made from that government, and then, supposing it made on those theories which were made from it, to accuse that government as not corresponding with them' (Works: VI: 148).

Why is prescription such a powerful source of legitimacy? Humans are predominantly creatures of habit. Settled societies *socialise* their members into predictable patterns of behaviour and allegiance. These may well not be underpinned by – or certainly held as – a readily available rational argument. Strikingly he asserts they may be held as 'prejudices' – indeed Burke seems to think they may be stronger for not being so underpinned (at least in the minds of those whose actions politicians are concerned to regularise). Prejudices are easier to deploy in moral practice than abstract principles:

> Prejudice is of ready application in the emergency; it previously engages the mind in a steady course of wisdom and virtue, and does not leave the man hesitating in the moment of decision, sceptical, puzzled, and unresolved. Prejudice renders a man's virtue his habit; and not a series of unconnected acts. Through just prejudice, his duty becomes a part of his nature. (WS, VIII: 138)

When we radically change institutions or principles, we disturb patterns of habitual behaviour; indeed, massive institutional change renders irrelevant habits, that have arisen from, constituted, or supported these former practices. Once this accumulated reason is broken, individuals are dislocated from the matrix of supportive, shared belief and become vulnerable to a range of motivational pathologies: naked self-interest, the pursuit of – or susceptibility to – unchecked power, irrational (and, more strikingly, rationalist) 'enthusiasms' of all kinds.

Burke agreed with the revolutionaries that creating a revolution was largely a matter of breaking long-held and widely shared patterns of socialised belief embodied in and re-enforced by institutional forms. Nevertheless, whilst they pursued this as a policy, Burke denounced it as destructive of the vulnerable fabric of society itself.

Embedded in the habitual picture of humans that informed Burke's rejection of these two core revolutionary beliefs – the cognitive and motivational inadequacy of reason – is a position on the relationship between art and nature, which highlights the role of aesthetics. The revolutionaries notoriously promoted nature as the standard against which morality, rights, and social institutions should be assessed – even the calendar was to be reconfigured, and months named according to their natural properties. Burke rejected this opposition between nature and convention as misconceived, for '[a]rt is man's nature' (Works, III: 86). Artifice, culture, refinement – all of them generated through history by human genius – is what separates us from the beasts. To reject this artifice, as the revolutionaries do, in pursuit of our aboriginal and pre-cultural 'nature' is itself *un*natural. However, this artifice, though natural, is not secure. Although it is our 'nature', civilised society is no easily recovered default position. It is not (as potentially in Hobbes) a product of instantaneous contract, rather it is the product of the long – and rather serendipitous – historical process referred to previously, and its loss is not easily remediable.

This claim that the constituent elements of a stable political culture could not be recreated through a process of deliberation or contract posed a very specific ideological problem for Burke's political identity as a Whig. Burke was heir to the troublesome, radical legacy of the idea of the social contract that had caused Whigs embarrassment as far back as the Sacheverell trial, but so closely was 'contract' identified with them, it could not be disowned. In this light, Burke's famous passage, claiming '[s]ociety is indeed a contract' but that it was a contract 'between those who are living, those who are dead, and those who are to be born' is a brilliant rhetorical move (WS, VIII: 146–7). His transfiguration of contract retains – indeed sublimates – its ideological power while draining it of its radical potential: a contract involving the dead and unborn could hardly be renegotiated. It is typical of Burke's rhetorical genius that this is not *merely* a rhetorical figure; it exemplifies Burke's deepest beliefs about the status of political establishments.

Our social institutions – and particularly those carrying political authority – cannot (like ordinary contracts) be the product of any individual's calculation or insight. 'Wisdom cannot create materials; they are the gifts of nature or of chance' (WS, VIII: 207); political authority must be created by '*a power out of*' [i.e., separate from] ourselves (WS, VIII: 111). In the absence of the intervention of the divine, the only source of that authority is history itself: 'Time is required to produce that union of minds which alone can produce all the good we aim at' (WS, VIII: 217). Institutions and dispositions cannot be created at will. If we are fortunate enough to have them (as the English were), we should cherish them. Since we do not quite know how they are formed, we cannot recreate them once lost. 'But that sort of reason which banishes the affections is incapable of filling their place,' and the compliance that flowed from customary allegiances has to be replaced by naked force (WS, VIII: 129). Hence, Burke predicts that the Revolution will descend into violence and coercion.

The French Revolution in Philosophical History

As well as appealing to an implicit epistemology, Burke's indictment of the Revolution also invoked a philosophy of history well canvassed in the later eighteenth century. Both Scots and French thinkers had schematised human history in terms of social stages characterised by their predominant economy each with its accompanying manners, laws and institutions. In some versions, dominant modes of subsistence – successively, hunting, pastoralism, agriculture and commerce – each generated their appropriate and supportive customs and morals.

But there was a less optimistic account according to which the *mores* on which modern commercial society relied – honour and trust, gentility, and aesthetic discrimination – were not themselves generated by that society but were inherited from a previous social form, namely feudalism.[11] This is Burke's view. The revolution's deepest threat was to the moral sensibilities and manners supplied to commercial society by an antecedent feudalism – which if lost could never be restored. His defence of chivalry – most extravagantly expressed in his 'purple passage' on Marie Antoinette, and famously lampooned by the cartoonists Byron and Cruikshank depicting him as a latter-day Don Quixote – is thus not mere conservative nostalgia or foolish gallantry, as his friend Francis chided him (C, VI: 86), for it is part of a proto-functional theory of the relationship between a society's mores and its institutions. A commercial society needs, but does not itself generate, a sense of honour and trust; *that* comes from feudal society. Moreover, it is not just a sense of honour and a softening of manners that feudalism has bequeathed us, it is a deeply religious sensibility, and this too is necessary to sustain social bonds:

> our manners, our civilization, and all the good things, which are connected with manners, and with civilization, have, in this European world of ours, depended for ages upon two principles; and were indeed the result of both combined; I mean the spirit of a gentleman, and the spirit of religion. (WS, VIII: 130)

The institutional vehicles of these two 'spirits' were the aristocracy and the clergy, and Burke increasingly comes to see the revolutionary process as one designed to destroy these institutions through destroying the belief system sustaining them. The elements of this revolutionary strategy emerge piecemeal as Burke deals with the failings and dangers of the Revolution.

The first in order of exposition is his sociological analysis of the composition of the National Assembly: this comprised those commoners and clergy who had withdrawn from the Estates General, swearing the famous 'Tennis Court Oath' not to disperse 'until the constitution of the kingdom is established and consolidated on firm foundations'.[12] Of these deputies, Burke points out, the majority are country lawyers, dispositionally quarrelsome and petty-minded, men not used to taking a large view of issues.[13] Among the clergy too, not educated Bishops, but small-town *curés* with limited administrative experience predominated. What really concerned Burke was the absence of any 'landed interest' or any concern with 'honour' and rank. The representation of land was a cornerstone of eighteenth-century political thinking. This was, of course, class interest, but it was not *mere* class interest. Wealth of any kind guaranteed independence, and independence was, at least *prima facie,* a political virtue. In addition, wealth based on possession of land – held and passed down in families – guaranteed a long-term interest in the flourishing of what was still a primarily agricultural economy. Having an interest in political stability, agricultural productivity, and the protection of property rights gave landowners a broad identity of interests, it was thought, with society as a whole. In thus recruiting self-interest for the collective good, the inheritance and the representation of landed property 'makes our weakness subservient to our virtue' and 'grafts benevolence even upon avarice' (WS, VIII: 102). This was political prudence, drawing on a realistic appraisal of how often base human motivations could be organised for the public good, rather than the French combination of foolish, idealistic, wishful thinking and *a priori* deductive reasoning.

But interest, for Burke, is always mediated by culture and manners. The country houses of the aristocracy were repositories of civilised values, of libraries and collections of artifacts, which engaged the cultivated aesthetic sensibilities of the educated mind with its society. Commitment to our inherited political culture and institutions required a deep susceptibility to the loyalties and emotional attachments that history, religion and art can evoke. Without these aids to attachment, humans would be at the mercy of either their passions, or – as Burke comes to realise – the destructive powers of un-anchored reason. Men would live rootless, chaotic lives, as ephemeral, as 'flies of a summer' (WS, VIII: 145).

Although understandably prominent in *Reflections*, stability was not the only political value. It needed balancing through an acceptance of the spirit of ability, enterprise and talent – a balance achieved in England through the ease with which rising families could eventually find a place in the aristocratic order. France had no such balance. By abolishing the distinctive political role of the aristocracy, the Revolution had shut out the propertied principle of stability and given free reign to social forces with no interest but innovation. An ideological offensive paralleled this – the claim that 'all occupations were honourable' was subversive of the deference that, in Burke's view, was needed to support the social structure (WS, VIII: 100). Such views fed the growing and misplaced confidence of politically unsophisticated deputies, freeing, indeed encouraging them to wilder and wilder political experiments – the geometrical division of France's ancient provinces into equalised electoral and administrative departments (something only a conqueror would have thought to do), the complex electoral balloting, the tortuous equivocation over property qualifications.

Burke's analysis thus exposes the way in which the course of the Revolution undermined the elements of the eighteenth century's 'modern monarchy'. But this is not merely an insight into a chaotic process, gained by reflection from a distance. Burke increasingly hints that, for at least some of the French, this was a 'fond election [choice] of evil', and his analysis of the causal aetiology of the revolution increasingly becomes an exposure of the strategy of a conspiracy (WS, VIII: 91). Burke identifies two groups, the 'men of letters' – philosophers and ideologues – and the 'monied men' – holders of the French national debt (WS, VIII: 159–60). The huge debt accumulated by the *ancien régime* was always vulnerable to the king cancelling it simply by declaring a bankruptcy, which, as an absolute monarch, he could do. Such a move had been actively discussed as one way of resolving the crisis. Creditors would be left with nothing. Parliamentary regimes, such as Britain and the Netherlands, had the edge here since their parliaments contained debt holders whose interest would never be served by a bankruptcy. This made them more creditworthy and so able to borrow money at lower interest rates. By recruiting the ideologues to take over the government, the financiers forestalled the bankruptcy. However, they still had to consolidate the debt. This they did by expropriating the property of the church, issuing paper money – *assignats* – backed by the value of church lands, which were then sold off to realise the value of the paper notes. Burke points out that the paper money backed, not by precious metal but by an auction of land (itself to be held in paper money the value of which is unpredictable) is like a share in a lottery. The revolutionaries have turned France into a great gambling den in which everyone who uses money must take part. The currency is like a share certificate in a volatile stock. No one who uses money can avoid the risk. The market in stocks and bonds was one of the most suspect aspects of the eighteenth-century economy. Burke's enthusiasm for the free market in agricultural produce did not extend to the stock market, about which he frequently expresses widely shared reservations.[14] Certainly the moral effects and vulnerabilities of a way of life, which was effectively based on gambling on future values inseparable from the adoption of the *assignat* as currency, ought not, he thought, to be widely dispersed among the population. In such a situation only the financiers would gain: the many who wished to use the currency as a means of exchange for their honest labour and produce would find themselves swindled by those skilled in manipulating the fluctuating value of the notes (WS, VIII: 240–41).

Stability of moral value and stability of economic value were implicated in each other – and 'speculation' was the antithesis of each. Respect for property and the institutions of civil government were an essential part of both forms of stability. The Church supported the moral deontology which protected us all from each other. The independence of the Church rested on its property from which it drew its income. Expropriating Church lands unravelled this virtuous circle turning the vicars into civil servants paid by the revolutionary state and, presumably, ultimately made the Church subservient to its atheistic will. Instead, a vicious circle was created where, by destroying the independence of the Church, the moral climate could be created in which property confiscations, the destruction of political institutions, and the moral emasculation and re-education of the public could all be conducted according to the will of the revolutionaries.

Burke deploys a striking range of ambivalent vocabulary to express the symmetry of effects in the moral and economic spheres – 'speculation' as both irresponsible moral philosophising and irresponsible economic investment. 'Creditworthiness' is a quality of both epistemological and economic enterprises. Revolutionary transformation in either sphere is stigmatised by a range of terms drawn from the tradition of pagan magic: the processes of the revolutionaries are 'arcane' and 'alchemical', their equipment includes the 'alembic', their knowledge is 'hermetic', and their economics is like the mythical philosopher's stone that could turn base metal into gold (WS, VIII: 172, 232, 142, 280). This transmutation of the moral certainty provided by a propertied religious establishment into a secular-atheistic regime supported only by the volatile value of a currency tied to the fluctuating bids of the auction house – or worse the gambling den – was not even an allegory of the difference between the eighteenth-century ideal of stable government and its nightmare opposite, it instantiated it. The melting down of Church bells for low-denomination coinage was a physical manifestation of the Revolution's secularisation of the Christian state.

The atheism of the revolutionaries' project – proclaimed by Burke before the regime itself – was to be a constant refrain in his other post-revolutionary writings. These, as well as pursuing and deepening the analysis offered in *Reflections*, would pursue new policies aimed not merely at the defence of the British constitution, but at the complete extirpation of the Revolution from the heart of France herself.

NOTES

1 Price, *A Discourse on the Love of our Country* ... in D. O. Thomas (ed.), *Political Writings* (Cambridge, 1991) pp. 176–196, 190.

2 Fox, 9 February, 1790, *Parliamentary Register, 1780–1796*, vol. XXVII, p. 75.

3 Indeed the original title had been *Reflections on certain Proceedings of the Revolution Society of the 4th November 1789*. See William B. Todd, *A Bibliography of Edmund Burke* (London: Rupert Hart-Davis, 1964), p. 143.

4 F. P. Lock, *Edmund Burke. Vol. II: 1784–1797* (Oxford: Oxford University Press, 2006), pp. 282ff.

5 Todd, lists four London editions of sixteen impressions, between 1790 and 1793, comprising sales of 30,000 by Burke's death in 1797. See, idem., *Bibliography*, pp.145, 150.

6 Edmund Burke, *Réflexions sur la Revolution de France et sur les Procédés de certaines Sociétés a Londres relatifs a cet Evénement* (Paris, 1790). The translation, by Pierre-Gaëton Dupont, had been begun, in London even before the English publication.

7 Helen Maria Williams, *A Residence in France*, ed. J. Gifford (London, 1797), p. 383, 386. Cited in Todd. *Bibliography*, p. 157.

8 John Toland, *Christianity not Mysterious* (London, 1696). See David Berman, 'The Irish Counter-Enlightenment' in Richard Kearney (ed.), *The Irish Mind: Exploring Intellectual Traditions* (Dublin: Wolfhound Press, 1985), pp. 119–40.

9 On Burke's debt to Coke and 'the Common Law mind', see J. G. A Pocock, 'Burke and the Ancient Constitution: A Problem in the History of Ideas', *Historical Journal*, 3.2 (1960): 125–43.

10 The approach taken here departs from interpretations of Burke as a neo-Thomist natural law thinker. See, for instance, Peter J. Stanlis, *Edmund Burke and the Natural Law* (Ann Arbor: University of Michigan Press, 1958); Francis Canavan, *The Political Reason of Edmund Burke* (Durham, N.C.: Duke University Press, 1960).

11 Philosophical historians who took this view include William Robertson, 'A View of the Progress of Society in Europe' in *History of the Reign of the Emperor Charles V*, 3 vols. (London, 1769), vol. I. and Adam Ferguson *An Essay on the History of Civil Society*, ed. Fania Oz-Salzberger (Cambridge: Cambridge University Press, 1995).

12 J. H. Stewart, *A Documentary Survey of the French Revolution* (London and New York: Macmillan, 1951), p. 88.

13 Fifty-three percent of the Third Estate were practising lawyers or members of the judiciary. See Harriet B. Applewhite, *Political Alignment in the French National Assembly, 1789–1791* (Baton Rouge: Louisiana State University Press, 1993) p. 42.

14 To be articulated in his *Thoughts and Details on Scarcity* (WS, IX: 119–145), a pamphlet written to advise Pitt in the famine winter of 1795, but unpublished until 1800.

16

IAIN HAMPSHER-MONK

Burke's Counter-Revolutionary Writings

Burke's *Reflections* generated a huge controversial literature directed at an increasingly wider and politicised public.[1] However, Burke neither responded directly nor addressed this emerging public. He claimed not to have read any of the responses – except Paine's – whose *Rights of Man* is quoted in the *Appeal*, without attribution, as the views of the Foxite Whigs (Works, III: 68–75). Burke's audience remained the traditional, and limited political 'public', a subset of the 400,000 or so voting individuals.

The first work to appear after *Reflections* was the *Letter to a Member of the National Assembly*. It remained – unlike *Reflections* – a true letter, to Francoise-Louis-Thibault de Menonville who had written to Burke praising *Reflections*. It contained Burke's first insistence on outside intervention to reverse the Revolution. *An Appeal from the New to the Old Whigs* defended his conservative interpretation of the Glorious Revolution of 1688, and his claim to be its true inheritor, exposing the 'new', Foxite Whigs' abandonment of the founding principles of their party. Following the split in the party, in *A Letter to a Noble Lord* (1796), he repudiated charges made by two 'new' Whigs, the Duke of Bedford and the Earl of Lauderdale, that it was he who was the turncoat and had reneged on his reformist past by accepting a pension from the (Tory) government. The *'Introduction'* to Brissot's *'Address'* (1794) was written for a translation – commissioned by Burke from his cousin Will – of Brissot's speech (May 1793), calling for revolution throughout Europe, so vindicating Burke's warnings about the revolution's expansionist character. Burke was seeking to influence a political public dismayingly unenthusiastic about counter-revolutionary war. His final published work, the *Two Letters on a Regicide Peace* (1796), urged continuation of an interventionist war and abandonment of the peace overtures begun that summer.

Strikingly, none of the other seven counter-revolutionary works was written for publication. They originated as private letters or briefing papers written to influence policy makers. Their publication was either later permitted by Burke or was undertaken posthumously by his executors.

In these works, Burke pursues two major counter-revolutionary political projects. First, he continued his vindication of the principles of English political life, identifying them with the Revolution Settlement (1689–1701), and distinguishing them from the wayward principles of revolutionary France. Second, he sought to justify a war to overthrow the revolutionary regime in France itself. We shall consider these in turn.

Burke's Defence of Himself and the Whig Tradition

Burke's theatrical break with Fox in the Commons on 11 May 1791 crystallised a new fault-line in English politics. It liberated Burke from a Whig–Tory party divide that he now thought irrelevant to the international situation. Although initially Burke's isolation seemed total – and was gloatingly so described in the press – he continued trying to win over those leading Whigs who had private reservations about Fox. And he continued to assert *his* view of the principles expressed in *Reflections*, insisting on the sharp and unbridgeable gulf between French revolutionary politics and the preoccupation with historical continuity and balance, and impatience with abstraction, that – for all the Whiggish commitments to 'liberty' – characterised English, 'Old Whig' views.

The *Appeal from the New to the Old Whigs* encapsulates these concerns. Burke defended the historical accuracy of his portrayal of the English constitution, but his own Whig credentials are deeply implicated in this. Burke was charged with reneging on his own past *and* Whig principles: he was, he said, 'reproached, as if, in condemning such [revolutionary] principles he had belied the conduct of his whole life, suggesting that his life had been governed by principles which he now reprobates' (Works, III: 94). His response was (i) that his position *was* consistent with that of the founding Whigs and *therefore* with the Revolution Settlement of 1689 and the constitutional foundation of the Hanoverian regime; (ii) that his political record, as a defender of that constitution, was also consistent with his opposition to French principles; (iii) that it was Fox and his followers who, in endorsing France, had subverted not only their party's founding principles but those of the English constitution. There were no gradations of position here; anyone who failed to denounce revolutionary principles was 'Paine at bottom' (C, VI: 312).

The *Appeal* opens by identifying the controversial circumstances of the work: the parliamentary rift between the author and Fox. There follow two documented proofs: a forensic demonstration of the principles of the 'Old' Whigs, as articulated by the Whig prosecution at the landmark trial of the Tory Dr Sacheverell in 1710, contrasted with quotations from Paine's *Rights of Man*, disingenuously presented as 'the sentiments of the modern whig'

(Works, III: 68). A final section offers one of the most sustained and systematic analyses of political concepts that Burke ever produced.

In the *Appeal*, Burke distinguished absolutely between the reformist politics of his previous career and those of the French Revolution (Works, III: 40). The Revolution had, as America and India had only threatened to, destroyed the stable ground of inherited institutions and prejudices against which a politics of judgement could conduct the pragmatic appraisal of benefit and possibilities of compromise, and entered the uncertain world of the political philosopher whose abstraction from practice, and 'stating of extreme cases', 'ever on the edge of crimes', 'may totally subvert those offices which it is their object to methodize and reconcile' (Works, III: 81).

The central, and for Burke irredeemably anarchic, political doctrine of the Revolution was popular sovereignty: 'that the *people*, in forming their commonwealth, have by no means parted with their power over it.' Burke recognised the Sieyesian foundation of this – that the people 'are masters of the commonwealth; because in substance they are themselves the commonwealth' (Works, III: 76).[2] Often explicit in this claim was that the people's 'will' constituted the standard of political legitimacy. Burke absolutely rejects claims about the legitimating powers of human will – individual or collective. Such voluntarist presumption would be inconsistent with any religiously grounded moral deontology – of the existence of which he was personally convinced. But he also invites a consequentialist consideration of its denial: without God's underpinning of morality, there would be no sanction for anything but force. A secular politics is neither credible nor practical.

Our personal experience of moral obligation confirms, he urges, the deontological hypothesis: our most fundamental obligations – to parents, to children – are not voluntarily incurred but given. Even in marriage 'the choice is voluntary, but the duties are not'. Likewise obligations to society and to 'mankind at large' do not derive from our will: 'Our country is [...] a social, civil relation' into which, 'every man [...] as much contracts by his being born into it, as he contracts an obligation to certain parents by his having been derived from their bodies' (Works, III: 79–80). Burke flirts with, without quite succumbing to, the venerable conservative *topos* of patriarchy.[3]

The statesman's duty is to maintain this background moral deontology. Unlike the philosopher, he must consider, not the intellectual defensibility or logical consistency of doctrines, but the practical consequences of their being believed (Works, III: 81, 92). Burke is helping to shape the emerging distinction between beliefs considered as philosophy and as ideology, and he attacks radical contractarianism on both levels. The former is strikingly Hobbesian in pointing to the destructively unbounded character of natural rights, and the necessity of their being abandoned on entering society. The revolutionary claim that individuals' natural rights trump conventional moral and political duties is both logically inconsistent with, and practically destructive of, the existence of a civil society – which comprises such duties. *Natural* rights 'admit no limit, no qualification whatsoever' (Works, III: 108). This is what makes their deployment within society so risky: to give such unlimited right to the multitude 'admits of no control, no regulation, no steady direction' (Works, III: 78). For rights to be exercised morally, or even practically, they must be conventionally limited and institutionally incorporated. The very concept of natural right logically presupposes the absence of all aspects of political society: 'to be a people, and to have these rights, are things incompatible. The one supposes the presence, the other the absence, of a state of civil society' (Works, III: 95). 'In a state of *rude* nature, there is no such thing as a people. A number of men in themselves have no collective capacity. The idea of a people is the idea of a corporation. It is wholly artificial'. Consequently, when people appeal beyond agreed positive conventions to natural rights, they are dissolving their social bonds: 'they are no longer a people; they have no longer a corporate existence; they have no longer a legal, coactive force to bind within, nor a claim to be recognised abroad. They are a number of vague, loose individuals, and nothing more. With them all is to begin again' (Works, III: 82).

Burke is insistent that 'nature' here possesses no immediately available moral or political resources. The revolutionaries' naïve presumption that even majoritarianism is some kind of natural, default decision-procedure is mistaken. In fact, it 'is one of the most violent fictions of positive law', and Burke is convinced that '[o]ut of civil society nature knows nothing of it'. Only persistent coercion resigns us to it. Moreover, in the natural (unincorporated) condition, what would a majority be a majority *of*? Burke insists that 'amongst men so disbanded, there can be no such thing as majority or minority' (Works, III: 82–3). It follows also that 'nature' supports no collective claim to land – either as a national territory or as an individual property. The current French government has no more right to France than Burke himself.

Burke's insistence on the thoroughly conventional character of political society was not intended to reveal its moral vulnerability, but to emphasise our good fortune in possessing one at all. Thus, Burke historicised Hobbes: political society is not the result of a single act of will (even a hypothetical one), but of the interaction of minds through time, the accumulation of habits of obedience and the acquisition of a culture of compromise and accommodation. In the British constitution there is 'a perpetual treaty and compromise going on' (Works, III: 110).

The utter contradiction between natural right and political society was not merely a logical proposition in political theory. It is, and must be assessed, Burke thought, as a claim about the sociology of political *belief*. Promulgating natural rights *teaches* individuals they may 'break the ties and engagements which bind [them]'. Believing in natural rights *leads* people to act as though they were true: they lose habits of obedience, social discipline, culturally acquired modes of interaction and end up *behaving* like men in a state of nature: 'all pious veneration and attachment to its laws and customs, are obliterated from our minds' (Works, III: 92–3).

The phenomenology of revolutionary belief, because it always couches propositions in universalist forms, licences extreme positions: 'these doctrines admit of no limit, no qualification whatsoever'. The sole restraint is 'the moral sentiments of some few amongst them to put some check on their savage theories' (Works, III: 108). But such 'commonsensical' restriction on universally framed propositions is no security against their more extreme implications – to believe so is naive or wicked – for individuals can be 'drawn to a connivance with sentiments and proceedings, often totally different from their serious and deliberate notions.' 'Doctrines limited in their present application, and wide in their general principles', he added, 'are never meant to be confined to what they at first pretend.' Consequently, reformers should take care that 'principles are not propagated for that purpose, which are too big for their object' (Works, III: 97–8).

There is, moreover, something in the quality of speculative belief that produces mental perturbations. Abstract ideas become detached from their real-world referents, gaining a power and volatility unrelated to their original properties. When a speculative principle supplants a practical aim as the object of political action, political demands cannot be met by addressing grievances – doing so may serve even 'further to irritate the adversary [...] as furnishing a plea for preserving the thing he wishes to destroy.' Then 'mere spectacles, mere names, will become sufficient causes to stimulate the people to war and tumult' (Works, III: 99). Abstractions render people susceptible to fanaticism or other mental derangements normally associated with religious enthusiasm: 'it must always have been discoverable by persons of reflection, but it is now obvious to the world, that a theory concerning government may become as much a cause of fanaticism as a *dogma* in religion' (Works, III: 98).

Although the logic of his natural right is Hobbesian, Burke's political sociology is decidedly not. Civil society requires an aristocracy whose wisdom, experience and moral discipline balances the power of the sovereign and evokes a 'state of habitual social discipline'. Against Sieyes (and Paine), Burke denies an aristocracy is an interest separate from the state; it is, rather, constitutive of it. Aristocracies enable populations 'to act with the weight and character of a people' (Works, III: 85). Burke surveys the range of experiences and features of a life that generate this respect:

> To be bred in a place of estimation; [...] to be taught to respect one's self; to be habituated to the censorial inspection of the public eye; [...] to be enabled to take a large view of the wide-spread and infinitely diversified combinations of men and affairs in a large society; to have leisure to read, to reflect, to converse; [...] to be habituated in armies to command and to obey; to be taught to despise danger in pursuit of honour and duty [...] these are the circumstances of men, that form what I should call a *natural* aristocracy, without which there is no nation. (Works, III: 86)

Such aristocracies are generated over time by well-conducted political societies – in *this* (not in the aboriginal sense) they are natural. Burke consciously plays on his century's equivocal conception of 'nature'. If '[a]rt is man's nature', he can denounce claims to deploy aboriginal right within society as *unnatural* (Works, III: 86).[4] Such claims undermine the natural aristocracy of a state, so destroying what may be called a 'people', and the resulting unstructured masses can have no claim to authority.

The revolution had substituted the Estates General (which, as originally assembled in separate estates, 'were the *people* of France') by 'voluntary clubs and associations of factious and unprincipled men'. It was made possible through the murder or exile of 'the weighty and respectable part of the people'; the debauch of the soldiery; and the loss of the 'weight and consideration' properly due to property (Works, III: 94–5).

The ideological properties of universalist principles exposed the more cautious, who drew only such limited conclusions as 'suits their premises' to become drawn into supporting the renegade leaders and, afraid of the mob, 'into schemes of politics, in the substance of which no two of them were ever fully agreed' (Works, III: 98).

Aristocracy was the natural safeguard against this: by setting the tone they might 'frown these wicked opinions out of the kingdom' (Works, III: 98). In the *Letter to a Noble Lord*, Burke would express outrage, at himself – a commoner – having to defend an aristocratic order from attacks by its own members who would be first to suffer if their views were to prevail. In some savage passages, he contrasts Bedford's inherited position with the difficulties of Burke's political career. No silver spoon had graced his infant mouth: 'I was not, like his Grace of Bedford, swaddled, and rocked, and dandled into a Legislator' (WS, IX: 160). When Burke writes how he has 'strained every nerve to keep the Duke of Bedford in that situation, which alone makes him [Burke's] superior', the 'alone' is pure vitriol (WS, IX: 162).

In closing his *Appeal*, Burke again underscores the difference in principle between France and England. Revolutionary principles, because of their universality and abstraction always tend to go to the extreme, the opposite was true for his – and English – political principles:

> The foundation of government is there laid, not in imaginary rights of men, (which at best is a confusion of judicial with civil principles,) but in political convenience, and in human nature; either as that nature is universal, or as it is modified by local habits and social aptitudes [...] in a provision for our wants, and in a conformity to our duties; it is to purvey for the one; it is to enforce the other. (Works, III: 109)

This difference he also characterises as a distinction between two conceptions of political theory – as prescriptive *for* or as abridgements *of* practice:

> The theory contained in his [Burke's] book is not to furnish principles for making a new constitution, but for illustrating the principles of a constitution already made. It is a theory drawn from the *fact* of our government. They who oppose it are bound to show, that his theory militates with that fact. Otherwise, their quarrel is not with his book but with the constitution of their country. (Works, III: 110)

Counter-Revolutionary War and International Community

A sequence of Burke's writings, beginning with *Thoughts on French Affairs* and culminating in the *Two Letters on a Regicide Peace*, urged the restoration of the French *ancien régime*. Almost all were letters or memoranda sent privately to policymakers. Only once negotiations with the French were being canvassed, did he publish these to a wider audience in a last desperate attempt to prevent a 'regicide peace'.

The danger of revolutionary ideology infecting Britain had worried Burke from his first public words on the matter (Works, III: 272–3), and he continued to regard the ideological threat as more formidable than the military one. The universal character of revolutionary claims, Burke pointed out, made them *intrinsically* expansionist. How could the rights of man be true *only in France*? How could the revolution co-exist with ancient regimes, the legitimacy of which it explicitly denied? Its very ambassadors were 'emissaries of sedition', revolutionary propagandists in the countries where they were sent (WS, VIII: 385). As a '*Revolution of doctrine and theoretick dogma*' it behaved more like a proselytising religion than a political revolt (WS, VIII: 341). Consequently, restoration was a condition of both domestic security and peace in Europe. Yet he recognised, and increasingly insisted on, the 'utter impossibility of a counter revolution from any internal Cause'

This section of the chapter draws on my more extensive discussion of this issue in 'Edmund Burke's changing justification for intervention', *Historical Journal*, 48.1 (2005): 65–100.

(C, VI: 241). The restoration of the French state 'must come from *without*' (WS, VIII: 305); as far as Burke was concerned, 'nothing else but a foreign force can or will do' (C, VI: 217). He was convinced that there must be a European military intervention for regime change, and he set himself to provide a justification for it consistent with international notions of legality.

The most authoritative treatise on international law in Burke's time was the Swiss jurist Emmerich de Vattel's *Le Droit des Gens, ou Principes de la Loi Naturelle, Appliqués à la Conduite et aux Affaires des Nations et des Souverains* (1758).[5] Vattel claimed that states were like individuals in a Grotian state of nature whose maximal duties were mutual respect for one another's autonomy: 'if a nation abuses its liberty 'others must put up with it [...] having no right to tell it what to do.'[6] Vattel thus provided a theoretical endorsement of the principle of non-interference in the internal affairs of states.

But there was one exception to this; that was 'the case of a divided kingdom.' In such cases, Burke claimed, 'the law of nations leaves our Court open to it's choice' as to which side to support (WS, VIII: 340). However, there were difficulties – both in Vattel's text and the political context – in exploiting this otherwise promising exception.

Burke evidently re-read Vattel at some point in 1792. His notes, headed 'Cases of Interference with Independent Powers', make clear what he is looking for.[7] The heading is not Vattel's, but Burke's. The exceptional grounds for intervention proved, in the end, to exclude the very case to which Burke sought to apply it. For even where injustice clearly existed, and subjects complained of it, Vattel denied the right to intervene while subjects were still actually obeying their government. Only where armed conflict already existed was intervention permitted and then not on the side of *their choice*: but only on the side of 'justice'. Where political bonds were irrevocably broken the parties become effectively new individual states in an international state of nature – each entitled to non-interference.[8]

Bluntly, for Vattel, if France really was irrevocably divided, the case for intervention *to reinstate the status quo ante* fell. If it was not irrevocably divided, intervention was not sanctioned. Burke increasingly acknowledged the nuances of Vattel's treatment, while still insisting international law did not support any blanket prohibition on intervention (C, VII: 176).

More troublesome, however, was the fundamental contradiction between Burke's conception of the state and the whole premise and tenor of Vattel's argument.

In the *Appeal*, Burke had insisted that the 'idea of a people is the idea of a corporation.' When that legal form is broken 'they are no longer a people' (Works: III, 82). This conception of the nation sounded almost transcendent at times: 'a nation is a moral essence' he declared in 1796. It remained so even though 'a tyrant or usurper should be accidentally at the head of it.' Such a fate may be lamented, 'but this notwithstanding, the body of the commonwealth may remain in all it's integrity' (WS, IX: 253). This exposed one of the most significant fault-lines between the politics of Burke and those of his adversaries: according to Sieyes, for instance, the nation as a people only emerged in the absence of corporate identities; for Burke, however, such corporate articulation was the very condition of statehood. He persistently repudiated the revolutionary principle that 'the majority told, by the head, of the taxable people [...] is perfectly master of the form, as well as the administration of the state, and that the magistrates, under whatever names they are called, are only functionaries to obey the orders [...] which that majority may make' (WS, VIII: 344). This corporate conception of the state made it virtually impossible to apply Vattel's criteria, which in any case seemed to presuppose geographical rather than social or corporate divisiveness. For Burke, the mere re-imposition of monarchy – 'absolute as over them, but whose sole support was to arise from foreign Potentates' – would have been a tyranny (WS, VIII: 393). The re-establishment of the 'state' required the re-establishment of its supporting 'orders'. He was thus committed to a restoration of 'the great judicial bodies [...] all the intermediate orders, the Nobility, Clergy, and to the body of the Law'.[9]

In *Heads for Consideration of the Present State of Affairs*, circulated in the winter of 1792 both to government ministers and sympathetic Whigs, Burke became more explicit about intervention. Brissot's infamous *Address* of 1793 had vindicated Burke's claims about the expansionist character of the revolution: 'We must', claimed Brissot, '*set fire to the four corners of Europe*; in that alone is our safety' (WS, VIII: 519). The outbreak of war raised Burke's hopes for an interventionist policy, and in 1793 he produced *Remarks on the Policy of the Allies* again for private circulation.

Burke now dropped Vattel as an authority; he was just another 'casuist[s] of public law' whose politics were 'rather of a Republican cast' and 'by no means as averse as [he] ought to be to a Right in the people [...] to make changes at their pleasure in the fundamental laws of their country' (WS, VIII: 474). Repudiating Vattel involved two important moves, which prepared the way for a quite distinctive argument for intervention. The first involved rejecting the entire post-Grotian jurisprudential construal of the international realm as a state of nature. Instead, he asserted the existence of a 'diplomatick Republick of Europe' with a collective right to decide whom to admit. The second move involved abandoning the casuistry of 'dividedness' on which, according to Vattel, the legitimacy of 'interference' supposedly hinged. On this question, Burke now claimed 'as on every political subject, no very definite or positive rule can well be laid down.' Instead, he characteristically insisted that circumstances 'directing a moral prudence and discretion [...] must alone prescribe a conduct fitting on such occasions' (WS, VIII, 474). Burke persistently asserted his view of the French people as an irreducibly corporate entity comprising 'the original individual proprietors of lands, [...] the states and the bodies politick, such as the colleges of justice called parliaments, the corporations noble and not noble of balliages, and towns, and cities, the bishops and the clergy, as [...] the legally organized parts of the people of France' (WS, VIII: 457). External powers, rather than considering how they might take sides in a divided state, must recognise that a state cannot be 'divided'. They could deal with 'France' only as its pre-existing moral whole, rather than seeking to take sides within it.

Finally, Burke pressed a theme that runs through all these later writings – the paradoxically zealous atheism of the revolutionaries. The counter-revolutionary war was not just regime-restoring, nor even a defence of the integrity of the European community of nations. It was a religious war – not a war *between* religions but a war between religion and atheism.

For Burke, the final nail in Vattel's coffin was his stress on the temporally limited obligations of other nations to oppose usurpers. Burke noted in his margin: 'not an eternal war'.[10] Vattel explicitly licensed the regicide peace that Burke would next have to oppose.

Abandoning Vattel had cleared the way for a new justification for intervention, but he finally assembled his thoughts to articulate that new case only in the *Two Letters on a Regicide Peace*. He based the new argument on a revised conception of the European international order, completely dissociated from Vattel's embarrassing, natural-rights-based principles.

The context and audience of the *Regicide Peace* series were quite different from the earlier papers on the war. By 1795 the government was pursuing peace overtures with the French. Lord Auckland's peace-kite pamphlet, *Some Remarks on the Apparent Circumstances of the War in the Fourth week of October 1795*, had been sent to Burke for comment. Convinced that private lobbying could no longer prolong the war, Burke decided to appeal to the public by publishing the *Two Letters on a Regicide Peace*.

Burke now abandoned *international* law as a basis for intervention. Instead, he invoked the growing literature on the importance of manners as constitutive of political ties. Europe, in view of its common manners, traditions, legal culture and – not least – religion, was, he claimed, a shared juridical space. Relations amongst its members could then be conceived of as domestic not international. This, he argued, made available positive, *domestic*, legal actions for redress, rather than the *a priori* deductions of Grotian international law. The Roman 'law of nations' – the legal customs found to be common to states engaged in relations – already formed part of the amalgam of practice, custom, shared inheritance and treaty that comprised international law. Burke now appropriated for himself the Grotian move of thinking of nations as individuals, asserting that nations, as well as individuals, might invoke actions from the Roman 'law of vicinage' and so override other states' claims to inviolability.

Burke had previously hinted that 'vicinage' (or laws organised around the concept of neighbourhood) were grounds for intervention, but had been challenged by Mackintosh, who pointed out that 'no case is in fact made'.[11] Burke now made that case.

Roman private law gave individuals rights of anticipatory defence against neighbours whose behaviour seriously threatened their interests. If individuals' rights held for states, then states too could act *in anticipation* against a danger to their polities from the conduct of their neighbours. These rights are articulated in the two remedial Roman law actions that Burke mentions. The *Praetorian Stipulation* allowed a proprietor to seek restraint on a potentially dangerous development in a neighbouring property, or seek indemnification from its owner. The *Missio in Possessionem Damni Infectum* involved seeking a declaration that the condition of a neighbour's property posed a threat of damage to one's own. Actions of this kind could even result in being granted possession of the delinquent's property.[12]

The rights of ancient regimes to intervene in France are analogous, Burke urges, to such Roman law remedies available to domestic proprietors. The analogy is relevant to European inter-state relations because all those states are inheritors of Roman legal culture.

The conception of the international arena not as a state of nature, but as a community sharing traditions, norms and even obligations, was an idea that was to have a long history, continuing into the present practice and theory of international relations.[13] It was in all sorts of ways more congenial to Burke's mind than his initial flirtation with Vattel: his new justification was historical and drew on positive law, rather than being an abstract deduction from metaphysical premises in the way that natural-rights-based thinking so often was. In invoking shared manners and dispositions, it provided a real and practical foundation for common expectations, which could also find a place for religion. It did not naively assume that deductions from first principles will invariably and unequivocally deliver the same prescriptions for practice to different people, or peoples. It provided him with a juridical justification for the restoration of France as a balanced, modern monarchy, supported by a nobility and restrained by representative and legal corporations, which was, after all, the only way eighteenth-century European states knew how to preserve liberty.

NOTES

1 For a bibliography, see Gayle Trusdel Pendleton, 'Towards a Bibliography of the *Reflections* and *Rights of Man* Controversy', *Bulletin of Research in the Humanities*, 85 (1982): 65–103.

2 Abbé Sieyes's famous pamphlet 'Qu'est-ce que le Tiers état?' (1789) derived his claim that the Third Estate *was* the nation from pointing out the privileged character of the other estates, who thereby departed from the common order and equal union that constituted the state. The Third Estate was the only one consistent with the constitutive features of the state. See Murray Forsyth, *Reason and Revolution. The Political thought of the Abbé Sieyes* (Leicester: Leicester University Press, 1987), ch. 3.

3 *Reflections* too, contrasted English filial political piety with the casual parricide of the French (WS, VIII: 146).

4 This may reflect Burke's debt to James Harris who had earlier declared: 'the only nature to which art belongs is human. See James Harris, *Three Treatises*, 8 vols. (London, 1744), vol. I, p. 12. Burke had this work in his library.

5 Emmerich de Vattel, *Le Droit des Gens, ou Principes de la Loi Naturelle, Appliqués à la Conduite et aux Affaires des Nations et des Souverains*, 2 vols. (London, 1758; repr. Washington: Carnegie, 1916).

6 Vattel, *Droit des Gens*, vol. I, p. 11.

7 Burke annotated notes in translation (in another hand) on Vattel's *Droit des Gens*. The originals are in the Sheffield Public Library Archive, Wentworth Woodhouse Muniments (hereafter WWM), Burke papers 10.27.

8 Vattel, *Droit des Gens*, I, pp. 297–8.

9 Burke papers, WWM, Sheffield Archives, 10.123, 'Sketch of a Declaration by the Emigrants.'

10 Burke papers, WWM, Sheffield Archives, 10.27: Burke's note from Vattel reads: 'Where king driven from his country allies are not obliged to support an eternal War … they must at length give peace to their people … and treat with him as with a lawful sovereign.'

11 'Reasons against the French War of 1793' *Monthly Review*, 40, p. 435. Reprinted in *Miscellaneous Works of the Rt Hon. Sir James Mackintosh* (London, 1851), p. 624–630.

12 Peter Stein, *A Textbook of Roman Law*, 3rd edn. (Cambridge: Cambridge University Press, 1963), pp. 724–8.

13 See Tim Dunne, *Inventing International Society: A History of the English School* (Basingstoke and New York: Palgrave, 1998).

17

SEAMUS DEANE

Burke in the United States

Leo Strauss's *Natural Right and History* (1953) marked an important stage in his evolution into America's Carl Schmitt. In its final chapter, he made the contentious claim that Burke, despite his readiness to invoke a universal natural law, was a historicist, in the sense that he regarded human rights, for instance, as the product of historical circumstances and not as deriving from abstract, universal principle. He was like Hegel in his preference for what is over what ought to be – a charge first made by Lord Acton that survives to the present day.[1] In Strauss's account, Burke unwittingly contributed to the erosion of the classical/Christian belief in a universal moral law and to the establishment in its place of the modern belief in the cultural relativity of values. This conclusion relocated Burke rather abruptly from what had seemed to be his increasingly secure position as an exemplary exponent of an anti-theoretical, pragmatic, even utilitarian approach to politics. His anti-revolutionary stance had regularly been praised as characteristically British or English, although his caution about circumstance and consequence was also often taken to be, at heart, utilitarian. These two elements formed a composite upon which his reputation rested easily for more than a century. Occasionally, tremors arising from his views on Ireland and India, or from allergic reactions to the florid complexion of his prose, or even, in Woodrow Wilson's case, to his 'brogue', or from an alleged incoherence in his political philosophy or even from the accusation that he didn't have one, shook the plinth on which he stood.[2] The Burke who had so successfully opposed 1789 to 1688, the Irishman who was more British than the English could ever be, the crypto-Catholic who had a deeper vision of Anglicanism than any Anglican since Hooker, the former supporter of rebellion who became the scourge and analyst of revolution, presented so great a paradox that for two hundred years its resolution or dissolution became a structuring feature of the commentary upon him. The fright of the French Revolution had brought out his deepest convictions in a suddenly articulated but long-implicit political theology. Even when the apocalyptic tone

faded, Burke's polemic against 'theory' retained its force as the most enduring and identifiable feature of his work, adopted and adapted in the service
of many causes. 'Burke's remarks on the problem of theory and practice are
the most important part of his work', says Strauss.[3] Yet he appeared to yield
at a critical moment to the idea that since the French Revolution was itself
part of the Providential order, it should be accepted; he showed himself
to be 'oblivious of the nobility of last-ditch resistance'.[4] This sudden shift
in the tenor of Strauss's argument presents a Burke who promoted both a
fatal resignation to what is, and who denied a presiding law of what ought
to be, thereby giving to relativism an unwitting but decisively important
impetus.

Founding Father

Strauss's intervention was especially controversial in the United States where
Burke had always retained a special position as the defender of a specifically Christian society against a desolating modernity. Rousseau, so identified by Burke himself, was his scandalous and dangerous rival; from Irving
Babbitt's *Democracy and Leadership* (1924) to J. L. Talmon's *The Origins
of Totalitarian Democracy* (1952), the battle between these avatars of the
contemporary world was regularly and histrionically restaged in academic
publications and in journalism as the primal scene in American political
philosophy. In Talmon's work, Rousseau was the prophet whose Messianic
fantasy of revolutionary redemption was brought to life in the Terror and the
Robespierrian dictatorship which were harbingers of the twentieth-century
phenomenon of the totalitarian state. Talmon's was an incomparably coarser
work than Hannah Arendt's *Origins of Totalitarianism* (1951) in which,
by the author's own admission, Burke's thinking on human rights played
an important role. However, his promotion of the rights of Englishmen, as
opposed to those of humankind in general, seemed to anticipate, she suggested, the state-based racism of the British imperial system. Obviously, the
question of a conflict between the universal and the national dimension of
Burke's notion of rights arose out of readings of his interpretation of the
French Revolution and of the accompanying ideas of national and popular
sovereignty.[5] Michael Halberstam's analysis of Arendt's theory of totalitarianism discovered within it crucial features of Burke's theory of the sublime,
such as terror and a psychic dislocation leading to a dissolution of subjectivity.[6] This was a more glamorous version of Walter Lippmann's earlier
explanation for the atrocities of Lenin, Hitler and Stalin, with their common
root in Jacobinism – for all such figures, 'inhuman means are justified by the
superhuman end: they are the agents of history or nature'.[7]

Francois Furet's *Penser la Revolution francaise* (1978), a hostile interpretation of the presiding liberal and Marxist interpretations of the Revolution, intensified the Anglophone applause for Burke. It helped to renew the double claim that he was a founding figure for a specifically Anglo-American tradition of political philosophy and that he had so effectively annihilated the intellectual claims of radical revolution (both Russian or French), that they could no longer be entertained in respectable company, although their dire consequences would have to be forever resisted. In opposing the French and supporting the American Revolution, Burke had become the great prophetic voice of the Christian West against a revolutionary, alternative, secular gospel. The Cold War struggle between capitalism and communism was presented as a re-run of that ideological battle. This analogy, pursued relentlessly until the fall of the Soviet system in 1989, then adjusted for the new war with Islam, drew much of its energy from a supposedly archetypal opposition between aggressive, doctrinal beliefs and more politically passive, but deeply-seated convictions. In the United States of the fifties and sixties, there was a receptive audience for Burke's transposed call to Britain to awake from its non-dogmatic slumber to counter the missionary appeal of Jacobinism and to find a political language for the inarticulate mass of convention that was menaced by a revolutionary rhetoric in favour of all that was new and violently hostile to all that was old. Here again, Strauss's version of Burke seemed to be at odds with the views of a whole generation of commentators who had made Burke a hero of his and of their own times.

A concerted campaign to rehabilitate Burke's reputation began. Russell Kirk devoted a chapter of his influential book, *The Conservative Mind* (1953), to a polemical endorsement of Burke that was very far removed from Strauss's infinitely more educated and piercing critique. But it was Kirk's apocalyptic populism that set the tone for a discussion of Burke that was driven by hostility to the 'modern world' and by the ambition to counter modernity's presiding political heir, liberalism. In Kirk's account, the United States had to be awakened to its world role and duty as an aggressive defender of the integrity of an ancient, Christian inheritance so derided that it had almost been lost. To win the Cold War against the Soviet Union, it was necessary to win the internal battle against the liberal and communist view of the world political order. All radicals, whatever their disagreements among themselves, 'unite', according to Kirk, 'in detesting Burke's description of the state as ordained by God…[as] the community of souls'. Burke had survived Liberalism's 'hundred years of ascendancy', he 'knew history to be the unfolding of a Design' and 'never would concede that a consumption society, so near to suicide, is the end for which Providence has prepared man'.[8] This doomsday evangelism, as kitsch as can be, is yet a founding tract for the politics and aesthetics of American conservatism of the next sixty years. To effect Burke's transition from the central figure of British to that of American conservatism, the conceptual architecture of his political thought had to be altered.

As part of Kirk's continued crusade on behalf of his version of Burke, the Jesuit priests Peter J. Stanlis and Francis Canavan published respectively *Edmund Burke and the Natural Law* (1958; new ed. 2003) and *The Political Reason of Edmund Burke* (1960). All three writers were continuing rather than initiating an attempt to reanimate American conservatism. Conservatism had begun a rebuilding programme in the aftermath of the Wall Street Crash and at the beginning of the Great Depression, with the collection of essays *Twelve Southerners: I'll Take my Stand: the South and the Agrarian Tradition* (1930). The Agrarian and the Fugitives movements took the industrialisation of the South as an example of the destructive force of 'Northern' capitalism and of the peril faced by all traditional ways of community life caught up in its marauding energies. This agrestian politics reached an epitome in the work of Wendell Berry, whose opposition to the United States' recurrent wars from World War II to Iraq, highlights the isolationist and anti-imperial streak, once notable in American conservatism.[9] Burke was often, if rather casually, invoked in this literature in defence of the organic community and its 'traditional' class distinctions. Additionally, hostility to the secular state and a corresponding fetish of individualism had been central to conservative thinking in the thirties, as in the writings of an admirer of Burke such as Albert Jay Nock.[10] But Kirk and the Jesuit scholars opened up an unexpected new space for the reception of Burke as a defender of anything that could be claimed as traditional, organic, historic, communal, and, most of all, religious. This was the Irish-American Catholic space.

It was not a region, like the American South, but a virtual space, a new Catholic medieval Europe for political philosophy. It had already flashed up in Agrarianism, as an after-image of G. K. Chesterton's and Hilaire Belloc's economic theory of 'Distributism' and their medievalist ideal. In this less literary version, intellectual dominion was exercised by St. Thomas Aquinas whose exposition of the natural law had long been the basis for political thought and action in the Christian world before the Enlightenment and the Revolution. Two elements had to be repositioned. One was the estimate of the presence and influence of natural law, the other was the meaning and role of prudence in his work. In this new account, Burke, being at once Irish and Catholic, Protestant and British, retained a living relationship with that old European world and with the British tradition of liberty. By drawing on these resources, he had been enabled to outface the Revolution and expose its demonic energies and potential. Yet the Revolution's gains were already so great that Burke's attack was totally darkened to a lament for a world suddenly awakened to the recognition of its imminent dissolution. The violent destruction of traditional societies in India and Ireland by the British was akin to the destruction of traditional France by the revolutionaries, although the latter were pursuing the logic of a new secular theory, while the colonising groups were betraying the principles of an ancient, Christian polity and thereby unwittingly colluding in a universal devastation.

This is the Romantic reading of modernity as catastrophe transposed to Cold War conditions. Burke is its sovereign authority in whom the tradition of a natural law, in its Christian, Thomist formulation – although bearing the impress of its classical precedents, as represented by Cicero – is revived at a critical moment in history. However, it was claimed, Burke's thought had been stealthily disengaged from its Christian sources by a strategy that had allowed him to remain a champion against revolution but had defamed him as a utilitarian who advocated cautious, incremental reform, thus entirely disavowing the moral nature of his political thought. It was the aim of the Irish Catholic appropriation of him in the United States to demonstrate that he was not a utilitarian (and therefore open to the charge of 'relativism' in its many guises), but a Christian thinker in the natural law tradition for whom prudence was the virtue that enabled the principles of that law to be realised in widely different sets of circumstance. In the terms of this debate, the exercise of prudence was in itself a moral action, far removed from any Benthamite calculus, but easily mistaken for it, because both reckonings acknowledged the complex variety of the actual and both derided uniform, abstract, or 'theoretic' systems. Utilitarianism was the appropriate ethical system for the materialist secular view of the world; it was, indeed, a product of this outlook. Burke's prudential view (or vision) of the world, subtler and more nuanced than the 'mechanical' estimates of utility, was founded in a metaphysical belief. Thus, practical judgement in politics was an exercise in moral thinking which Burke exemplified by his tacit or explicit allegiance to the natural law. To retrieve this dimension of Burke's thought was part of a much more general restoration.[11]

In 1993, Joseph L. Pappin III published *The Metaphysics of Edmund Burke*, a full-length argument in favour of the natural law and against utilitarianism. The second edition and third printing of Stanlis's *Edmund Burke: the Enlightenment and Revolution* (1991), which appeared in 2003, had a chapter 'Burke and the Moral Law', subtitled 'Burke's supposed utilitarianism'; it emphasised Burke's account of Ireland as ruined by the Penal Laws, an instance of a morally and politically criminal system that he had condemned on natural law, not utilitarian, principles. The 2003 edition of

Stanlis's *Edmund Burke and the Natural Law* bore an Introduction by V. Bradley Lewis, who claimed that when the book was first published in 1958, 'it was with a sense that natural law thinking about ethics and politics was under siege'. But, 'by now the revival in Natural Law has happened'.[12]

Such unforgivingly eristic discourse needs a certain stylistic glamour to leaven the monotony of its address. Only William F. Buckley Jr., among American conservatives, achieved this at times – more effectively on television than in print. His journal, *National Review*, for which Russell Kirk wrote 500 articles in 20 years, helped to establish Burke's name as the password for entrance to the newly reified 'Conservative Mind' with its 'Tradition' and 'Beliefs'. Kirk's grim, hectoring tone in his 'From the Academy' column in the *National Review*, which paraded the absurdities of American higher education, needed Buckley's smiling company and his journal's circulation to make 'Burkean' a stock, laudatory epithet.[13] Willmoore Kendall, a mentor to Buckley and no admirer of Kirk, who was said to have harboured the ambition to become 'the American Burke', wrote in 1963 that modern conservatives are 'simply those who resist the revolutionary program Burke identified and opposed in the *Reflections*'.[14] In his attempt to distinguish a conservatism that would be less literary, and less intellectually arthritic than Kirk's, Kendall was one of many who took as an example, not Strauss, but another influential German émigré, the Catholic Eric Voegelin, who, like Babbitt before him, regarded modernism as a Gnostic heresy.[15]

Culture Wars

The events of 1968 at Berkeley and Columbia accelerated the tempo of defection from liberalism as intellectual conviction or public practice, most prominently among those Jewish academics and writers who had come to be known, not affectionately, as the New York intellectuals. Perhaps the most revered among them Lionel Trilling, intimated in his book *Beyond Culture* (1972) how troubling, as a teacher, he found the antinomianism of a modernist literature (which had elective affinities with radical modernist political thought) that exhilarated a generation of students wholly ignorant of the dangers it posed for a liberal democracy. The culture of a (largely European) modernism menaced the politics of (a predominantly American) modernity. Trilling's rehearsal of anxious scruple seemed to many to exemplify liberalism's deadly failure to confront the Schmittian-Straussian enemy; he was altogether too fascinated by and fascinating on the subtleties of betrayal in relation to his own Jewishness, to Israel, to the United States and to a lingering sentiment for a socialism that retained a dangerous cultural appeal when politically it had mutated into the Soviet menace. Teachers on American campuses were still praising the doctrines of the God that Failed; merely to be anxious about that was farcical. Was the enemy the Soviet Union or was it possible to be so removed from the real world as to think it was the New Criticism? Apparently so; Trilling 'stood against the New Criticism as Edmund Burke had once stood against the ideologues of the French Revolution'.[16]

The counter-parade of toughness, which presented worried distinctions in cultural matters as the sign of a fatal liberal dalliance with irrelevancy that ultimately subverted the decisiveness, even the idea, of authority, was led by Norman Podhoretz, best-known as a former editor of the *Partisan Review*, a coarse and effective propagandist for whom someone like Trilling was an indulgence America could ill afford. Curiously, the assault on liberalism often took the form of an attack on the prestige it assigned to the idea of complexity; this was reconstrued as, in effect, an idiotic or sinister readiness to dissolve all certainties in the bonfires of an intellectual vanity that opposed the principles of that parental humanism, which had allowed it to flourish in the first place. The reception of Jacques Derrida in the United States is perhaps the most spectacular example of this reaction to the liberalism, allegedly now transmogrified into an ideology, that had corroded the assumptions of democratic civilisation and exchanged its former suavity for an apocalyptic vacuity by which higher education had been swallowed.[17] These culture wars, as they came to be called, revived the commercial-cultural idea of the Great Books of Western Culture, through a knowledge of which Tradition could be revived and the security of the state and society assured. New editions of many of these canonical authorities, financed by foundations and institutes, appeared. Burke could not but be a beneficiary. No Great Books listing would exclude him, and no opportunity was lost to affirm that in him an Anglo-American, economically liberal, free society had an anchor. Reading for America was a serious and sustained project, even if the choice of recommended readings might be in the insecure hands of a Straussian epigon like Allan Bloom or if the ponderous, educated hero of the bewildering hour might take the comic form of one of Saul Bellow's heroes, such as Moses Herzog.[18] The point was to get back to the basics (Basic Books, Anchor Books) and renew the Western Tradition in the United States. The basics were, in that light, simple by definition.

But in another light they were not. Burke's hostility to the French intellectuals of his day was that they shoehorned complex matters to make them fit with an ideology which could never apprehend the infinite variety of human, historical circumstance and experience. Theory simplified; history, which Burke had made its antithesis, restored a sense of complexity. Stark theoretical radicalism, Irving Kristol argued, in *Reflections of a Neoconservative* (1983), belonged to the French, not the British Enlightenment which, in men like Adam Smith or Burke, had provided a secure basis for a libertarian or neo-conservative politics.

Another identifying feature of radical politics was said to be a homelessness that expressed itself as or in abstraction. Burke's attack on theory was always reinforced by his complementary support for attachment, especially in the endlessly repeated citation from *Reflections* about loving 'the little platoon we belong to in society' (WS, VIII: 97). For Jewish intellectuals in the United States, after the Second World War, this phrase had a particular attraction, since the claim to belong to such a group would counter the stereotype of the intellectual and of the Jew as someone who, precisely in not belonging to one country, thereby belongs to the world. Burke's attack on the intellectuals and on the Revolution as *une cause théoretique*, had almost criminalised rootlessness; the 'justifiable' exclusion of the intellectual from a national consciousness or consensus became a reactionary commonplace as much as the neighbouring accusation that intellectual exclusiveness is the condition for the abstraction of radical thought.

Once again, it was in Hannah Arendt's writings that the issue received a decisive political articulation. In the most Burkean of her books, *On Revolution* (1963), she contrasted the partial success of the American with the total failure of the French Revolution in producing a democratic polity. In an important modification of what she had previously said about the limitations of Burke's notion of human rights, she now claims that it is a human right to have civil rights. The tension between these two orders of right is peculiar to the political realm and the assertion that this needs to be addressed and resolved as far as possible, is made on behalf of all those who are stateless, homeless or in a minority and yet who have a claim on the specific civil rights available in any given society to the presiding majority. This claim was developed in relation to Burke by Michael Walzer in an essay of 1984, and later in *Thick and Thin: Moral Argument at Home and Abroad* (1994) – both echoed by Jennifer Welsh in 2004.[19] The reconciliation of the local, historically grounded values and their universal and abstract dimensions is foundational to liberal communitarianism. But much of its impetus originated in the specifically Jewish attempts to solve the apparent antinomies of assimilation and disassimilation, diaspora universalism and an at-homeness in the chosen double homes, 'the little platoon' of the United States and of Israel.

Liberals and Communitarians

The Burke of 'the little platoon' proved to be a creature of almost infinite adaptability. In 1976 (and again in 1986), Robert Nisbet called for a renewal of this Burkean spirit, a Tocquevillian citizenship rooted in localities as against the 'bankrupt [Jacobin] idea of *patrie*'.[20] This gave a stimulus to the communitarianism associated with Michael Sandel, Michael Walzer, and others.[21] In 1984, in another example, Richard John Neuhaus had called for the 'Christian community', which he distinguished from 'the religious new right', to enter upon 'the public square' and challenge the languages of liberalism with 'the very new-old language of Christian America'.[22] Neuhaus is one of those – Peter Viereck, Edward Banfield, Gary Wills among them – who recognises and demonstrates that what Sharon Crowley calls the 'discursive climate' in the United States is 'dominated by two powerful discourses: liberalism and Christian fundamentalism'.[23] Communitarian political philosophy supported the declaration that, in the grievous circumstances of the present, the local is the only arena for a possible politics. It was at pains to distinguish itself from a rights-based liberalism, and from the grip of the polemical opposition between 'reason' and 'tradition' that was widely taken to be Burkean. Philip Selznick announced that 'Burke's reason was an *anchored* rationality'.[24] In him, sociology and the natural law tradition were finally introduced to one another, although the accounts of Burke's political philosophy in the ensuing debates became alarmingly perfunctory. But his reputation was such that he could then and still can be used as a brand name, little more than an organic ingredient in an advertisement for a new political health food. Selznick's real interest is organisation theory, which has a considerable overlap with communitarianism.

The corporation or organisation has now become the most recent version of 'the little platoon'. This new formula, according to Sheldon Wolin, 'is not pure Leninism, but Leninism clothed in the language of Burke.'[25] However, the further perfection of organisation is sought in Systems Management Theory. Here again, Burke survives in a grotesque after-life in which his name and a pseudo-Burkean language are flourished in an attempt to allow budget accounting, public administration, and 'the new science of organization' to affect a status comparable to political philosophy.[26] It's a long way from Leo Strauss.

The increasing feebleness of the name 'Burkean conservative', was forecast by David Bromwich in 1996.[27] It is appropriate that the warning came from someone who has himself at times made even Burke seem not Burkean enough and is one of the most caustic critics of the right's detention, even rendition, of Burke for its own purposes. He pleads that we learn from Burke 'the possibility of holding politics and imagination together in a single thought'.[28] The echo of Yeats in that phrase would be both appreciated and suspected by Alasdair MacIntyre, who sees in the Burkean myth of continuity in English history, both in itself and in its adaptation by Yeats, 'a prototype in and for the modern world' in that it provided for the modern state 'a much-needed mask'.[29] In MacIntyre's Catholic conservatism, there is a lingering aroma of the anarchism that had been much earlier attributed to Burke by Murray Rothbard.[30] Burke's linkages of the ethical and the political, so heavily eroded by political polemics and in part redeemed as a philosophical issue in itself by MacIntyre's work, has been further restored by the work of Bromwich and James Chandler, especially through an understanding of his impact on Wordsworth.[31] Similarly, the tacit affinities between Burke and de Tocqueville, explored with such mastery by Sheldon Wolin, have enriched our understanding of their analyses of the French Revolution and of the emergent democratic polities of the modern era.[32] Such work is especially consolatory and politically important in the face of the Disney versions of Burke that have become the soft modern equivalent in the United States of the vicious cartoons that so successfully misrepresented him in eighteenth-century Britain. We read, for instance, that the American 'Old Right' had a 'Burkean veneration of antiquity, history and tradition, a sense of the mystical charm of things that gave to otherwise mundane and quotidian commonalities of experience a special place in the imagination'.[33] The vocabulary is there, but in such examples, Burke himself has faded to a melancholy spectre of the giant figure he once had been in American political philosophy. Even now some conservative writers strive to rescue his version of 'civil society' from the radical right to restore to politics some sense of public virtue.[34]

NOTES

1 Leo Strauss, *Natural Right and History* (Chicago: University of Chicago Press, 1953), p. 319. Acton MSS at Cambridge University Library, Add. 4967.74.

2 Woodrow Wilson, 'The Interpreter of English Liberty' in *Mere Literature and Other Essays* (Boston: Houghton Mifflin Co., 1896), pp. 104–60, 104.

3 Strauss, *Natural Right and History*, p. 303.

4 Ibid., p. 318. See Steven J. Lenzer, 'Strauss's Three Burkes: The Problem of Edmund Burke in *Natural Right and History*', *Political Theory*, 19.3 (1991): 364–90; for a hostile account of Strauss on Burke, meant to be scathing, see Claes G. Ryn, *A Common Human Ground: Universality and Particularity in a Multicultural World* (Columbia: University of Missouri Press, 2003), pp. 58–59, p 70.

5 Hannah Arendt, *Origins of Totalitarian Democracy* (New York: Harcourt Brace, 1951), pp. 290–302; Cornelius Castoriades, *Fragments: Writings on Politics, Society, Psychoanalysis, and the Imagination* ed. and trans. D. A. Curtis (Stanford: Stanford University Press, 1997), p. 96; Peg Birmingham, *Hannah Arendt and Human Rights: The Predicament of Common Responsibility* (Bloomington: Indiana University Press, 2006), p. 45; Michael Hardt and Antonio Negri, *Empire* (Cambridge, MA: Harvard University Press, 2000), pp. 104–5.

6 Michael Halberstam, *Totalitarianism and the Modern Conception of Politics* (New Haven: Yale University Press, 1999), 113–16; Stephen K. White, *Edmund*

Burke: Modernity, Politics and Aesthetics, (Thousand Oaks, CA: Sage, 1994), pp. 32, 47.

7 *Essays in The Public Philosophy* (New York: Mentor, 1955), p. 68.

8 Russell Kirk, *The Conservative Mind from Burke to Santayana* (Washington: Regency Gateway, 2001) reprint of the 7th edn. (1985), pp. 10, 13, 11. From 1960, the title became *The Conservative Mind from Burke to Eliot*.

9 See Wendell Berry, *Citizenship Papers* (Washington, DC: Shoemaker and Hoard, 2003).

10 Albert Jay Nock, *Our Enemy, the State* (New York: W. Morrow & Co., 1935).

11 For a recent discussion of prudence, with some specific relation to Burke, see Richard Bourke, 'Theory and Practice: The Revolution in Political Judgement' in Richard Bourke and Raymond Geuss (eds.), *Political Judgement: Essays for John Dunn* (Cambridge: Cambridge University Press, 2009), pp. 73–109.

12 V. Bradley Lewis, Introduction to Peter J. Stanlis, *Edmund Burke and the Natural Law* (New Brunswick: Transaction Publishers, 2003), pp. ix-x.

13 See Jeffrey Hart, *The Making of the American Conservative Mind: National Review and Its Times* (Wilmington, DE: ISI Books, 2006).

14 Willmoore Kendall, *The Conservative Affirmation* (Chicago: Henry Regnery Company, 1963), p. 142; see George H. Nash, 'The Place of Willmoore Kendall in American Conservatism' in John A. Murley and John E. Alvis (eds.), *Willmoore Kendall: Maverick of American Conservatives* (Lanham, MD: Lexington Books, 2002), pp. 3–16.

15 See, for example, Eric Voegelin, *The New Science of Politics: An Introduction* (Chicago: Chicago University Press, 1952).

16 William M. Chace, *Lionel Trilling, Criticism and Politics* (Stanford: Stanford University Press, 1980), 64.

17 See Christopher Norris, *Derrida* (London: Fontana, 1987), pp. 142–61.

18 Allan Bloom, *The Closing of the American Mind: How Higher Education Has Failed Democracy and Impoverished the Souls of Today's Students* (New York: Simon & Schuster, 1987); Bellow wrote a Foreword to Bloom's book; *Herzog* was published in 1964.

19 See Albrecht Wellmer, 'Arendt on Revolution' in Dana Richard Villa (ed.), *The Cambridge Companion to Hannah Arendt* (Cambridge: Cambridge University Press, 2000), pp. 220–41; Pierre Birnbaum, *Geography of Hope; Exile, the Enlightenment, Disassimilation* (Stanford: Stanford University Press, 2008), pp. 203–41, 374–80; Michael Walzer, 'Edmund Burke and the Theory of International Relations', *Review of International Studies*, 10 (1984): 205–18; Jennifer Welsh, 'Burke's Theory of International Order' in David Clinton (ed.), *The Realist Tradition and Contemporary International Relations* (Baton Rouge: Louisiana State University Press, 2007), pp. 137–60.

20 Robert A. Nisbet, *Twilight of Authority* (New York: Oxford University Press,1975), pp. 286–7; See also *The Sociological Tradition* (New York: Basic Books, 1966) and *Conservatism: Dream and Reality* (Minneapolis: University of Minnesota Press, 1986).

21 Michael J. Sandel, *Liberalism and the Limits of Justice* (Cambridge: Cambridge University Press, 1982); see Daniel Bell, *Communitarianism and Its Critics* (Oxford: Clarendon Press, 1993).

22 Richard John Neuhaus, *The Naked Public Square; Religion and Democracy in America* (Grand Rapids, MI: Eerdmans Publishing Company, 1984), pp. 7, 19, 93.

23 Sharon Crowley, *Toward a Civil Discourse: Rhetoric and Fundamentalism* (Pittsburgh: University of Pittsburgh Press, 2006), p. 2. For Peter Viereck, see *Conservatism Revisited: The Revolt Against Ideology* (New York: Scribners, 1949); Edward Banfield, *The Unheavenly City Revisited* (Prospect Heights, IL: Waveland Press, 1990); Gary Wills, *Under God: Religion and American Politics* (New York: Simon and Schuster, 2007).

24 Philip Selznick, *The Moral Commonwealth: Social Theory and the Promise of Community* (Berkeley, Los Angeles: University of California Press, 1992), p. 40.

25 Sheldon S. Wolin, *Politics and Vision: Continuity and Innovation in Western Political Thought*, new ed. (Princeton: Princeton University Press, 2004), p. 383.

26 Akhlaque U. Haque and Anwar-ul-Haque, *Edmund Burke: Limits of Reason in Public Administration Theory* (Cleveland: Cleveland State University, 1994); Akhlaque U. Haque, 'Edmund Burke, The Role of Public Adminstration in a Constitutional Order' in Thomas D. Lynch and Todd Dickers (eds.), *Handbook of Organization Theory and Management: The Philosophical Approach* (New York: Marcel Decker, 1998), pp. 181–202; 'Moral Conscience in Burkean Thought: Implication of Diversity and Tolerance in Public Administration' in Thomas D. Lynch and Peter L. Cruise (eds.), *Handbook of Organization Theory and Management*, 2nd edn. (Boca Raton, FL: Taylor and Francis Group, 2006), pp. 283–300; Thomas D Lynch and Cynthia F Lynch, 'Philosophy, Public Budgeting, and the Information Age' in Aman Khan and W. Bartley Hildreth (eds.), *Budget Theory in the Public Sector* (Westport, CT: Quorum Books, 2002), pp. 259–305 (especially pp. 266–7 on Burke); Michael C Tuggle, 'Snowstorms and Saigon: Knowledge and Control' in *Confederates in the Boardroom: the New Science of Organizations* (College Station, TX: Traveller Press, 2004), 33–60.

27 David Bromwich, 'Review of James Conniff, *The Useful Cobbler: Edmund Burke and the Politics of Progress; Stephen K. White, Edmund Burke: Modernity, Politics, and Aesthetics*', *Political Theory*, 24.4 (1996): 739–46, 739.

28 David Bromwich, 'Review of Paul Langford et al (eds.), *Writings and Speeches of Edmund Burke*, Vols. II, V, VIII', *Political Theory*, 19.4 (1991): 662–667, 667. See also David Bromwich, *A Choice of Inheritance: Self and Community from Edmund Burke to Robert Frost* (Cambridge, MA: Harvard University Press, 1989).

29 Alasdair MacIntyre, 'Poetry as Political Philosophy: Notes on Burke and Yeats' in *Ethics and Politics: Selected Essays*, 2 vols. (Cambridge: Cambridge University Press, 2006), vol. II, pp. 159–71, 163.

30 Murray Rothbard, 'A Note on Burke's *Vindication of Natural Society*', *Journal of the History of Ideas*, 19 (1958): 113–18.

31 James K. Chandler, 'Wordsworth and Burke', *English Literary History*, 47 (1980): 741–71; David Bromwich, *Disowned by Memory: Wordsworth's Poetry of the 1790s* (Chicago: University of Chicago Press, 1998). Bromwich's *Edmund Burke: An Intellectual Biography* is due for publication in 2011.

32 Sheldon S. Wolin, *Tocqueville Between Two Worlds: the Making of a Political and Theoretical Life* (Princeton: Princeton University Press, 2001).

33 J. David Hoeveler, Jr., *Watch on the Right: Conservative Intellectuals in the Reagan Era* (Madison: University of Wisconsin Press, 1991), p. 178.

34 See, for example, Sam Tanenhaus, *The Death of Conservatism* (New York: Random House, 2009).

FURTHER READING

Burke's Life and Reputation

Biographies and Memoirs

Bisset, R. *The Life of Edmund Burke*, London,1798.

Cone, C. B. *Burke and the Nature of Politics*, 2 vols., Lexington, University of Kentucky Press, 1957–64.

Kramnick, I. *The Rage of Edmund Burke: Portrait of an Ambivalent Conservative*, New York, Basic Books, 1979.

Lock, F. P. *Edmund Burke*, 2 vols., Oxford, Clarendon Press, 1998–2006.

Macpherson, C. B. *Burke*, Oxford, Oxford University Press, 1980.

M'Cormick, C. *Memoirs of the Right Honourable Edmund Burke*, London, 1797.

O'Brien, C. C. *The Great Melody: a Thematic Biography and a Commented Anthology of Edmund Burke*, Chicago, University of Chicago Press, 1992.

Prior, J. *Memoir of the Life and Character of the Right Hon. Edmund Burke*, London, 1824.

Life of the Right Honourable Edmund Burke, 5th ed., London, 1854.

Stanley, A. *Edmund Burke*: His Life and Ideas, London, Murray, 1988.

Burke's Legacy

Bell, D. *The Radical Right,* 3rd edition, New Brunswick, New Jersey, Transaction Publishers, 2001.

Buckley Jr., W. F. and Kesler, C. R. (eds.), *Keeping the Tablets: Modern American Conservative Thought*, New York, Harper & Row, 1988.

Crowe, I. (ed.), *Edmund Burke: His Life and Legacy,* Dublin, Four Courts Press, 1997.

Dwan, D. *The Great Community: Culture and Nationalism in Ireland,* Dublin, Field Day, 2008.

Dunn, C. and Woodward, D. *American Conservatism from Burke to Bush: An Introduction,* Lanham, MD, Madison, 1991.

Friedman, M. *The Neoconservative Revolution: Jewish Intellectuals and the Shaping of Public Policy,* Cambridge, Cambridge University Press, 2005.

Muller, J. Z. *The Mind and the Market: Capitalism in Modern European Thought,* New York, Knopf, 2002.

Nash, G. H. *The Conservative Intellectual Tradition in America since 1945*, New York, Basic Books, 1976.

Musselwhite, D. 'Reflections on Burke's Reflections, 1790–1990' in Hulme, P. and Jordanova, L. (eds.), *The Enlightenment and Its Shadows*, London, Routledge, 1990.

Pitkin, H. F. *The Concept of Representation*, Berkeley and Los Angeles, University of California Press, 1972.

Scruton, R. *'Man's Second Disobedience: a Vindication of Burke'* in Crossley, C. and Small, I. (eds.), *The French Revolution and British Culture*, Oxford, Oxford University Press,1989.

Wolin, S. *Democracy Incorporated*: *Managed Democracy and the Specter of Inverted Totalitarianism*, Princeton, Princeton University Press, 2008.

Intellectual Contexts

Enlightenment and Romanticism

Berlin, I. *The Roots of Romanticism*, Princeton, Princeton University Press, 1999.

Beiser, F. C. *Enlightenment, Revolution, and Romanticism: The Genesis of Modern German Political Thought, 1790–1800*, Cambridge, MA, Harvard University Press, 1992.

Bourke, R. 'Edmund Burke and Enlightenment Sociability: Justice, Honour and the Principles of Government', *History of Political Thought*, 21:4 (2000), 632–55.

Brunschwig, H. *Enlightenment and Romanticism in Eighteenth-Century Prussia*, Chicago, University of Chicago Press, 1974.

Cobban, A. *Edmund Burke and the Revolt Against the Eighteenth Century: A Study of the Political and Social Thinking of Burke, Wordsworth, Coleridge, and Southey.* London, George Allen and Unwin, 1960.

Hampsher-Monk, I. 'Burke and the Religious Sources of Sceptical Conservatism' in van der Zande, J. and Popkin, R. H. (eds.), *The Skeptical Tradition around 1800*, Dordrecht, Kluwer, 1998.

Pocock, J. G. A. 'Clergy and Commerce: The Conservative Enlightenment in England' in Ajello, R. et al. (eds.), *L'età dei lumi: studi storici sul settecento europeo in onore di Franco Venturi*, 2 vols., Naples, Jovene, 1985.

Young, B. *Religion and Enlightenment in Eighteenth-Century England: Theological Debate from Locke to Burke*, Oxford, Oxford University Press, 1998.

Aesthetics and the Sentiments

Bromwich, D. 'The Sublime before Aesthetics and Politics', *Raritan: A Quarterly Review*, 16 (1997), 30–51.

Bullard, P. 'The Epicurean Aesthetics of the *Philosophical Enquiry*', in *Edmund Burke and the Art of Rhetoric*, Cambridge, Cambridge University Press, 2011, pp. 79–108.

Dwan, D. 'Edmund Burke and the Emotions', *Journal of the History of Ideas*, 72:4 (2011), 571–93.

Ferguson, F. 'The Sublime of Edmund Burke, or The Bathos of Experience', in *Solitude and the Sublime: Romanticism and the Aesthetics of Individuation*, New York and London, Routledge, 1992, pp. 37–54.

Gibbons, L. 'The Sympathetic Sublime: Edmund Burke, Adam Smith, and the Politics of Pain', in *Edmund Burke and Ireland*, Cambridge, Cambridge University Press, 2003, pp. 83–120.

Hinnant, C. 'Shaftesbury, Burke, and Wollstonecraft: Permutations on the Sublime and the Beautiful', *Eighteenth Century: Theory and Interpretation*, 46 (2005), 17–35.

Huhn, T. 'Burke's Sympathy for Taste', *Eighteenth-Century Studies*, 35 (2002), 379–93.

Nicholson, M. J. *Mountain Gloom, Mountain Glory: The Development of the Aesthetics of the Infinite*, Ithaca, Cornell University Press, 1959.

Sarafianos, A. 'Pain, Labor, and the Sublime: Medical Gymnastics and Burke's Aesthetics', *Representations*, 91 (2005), 58–83.

Turner, J. 'Burke, Paine, and the Nature of Language', *Yearbook of English Studies*, 19 (1989), 36–53.

Wood, 'The Aesthetic Dimension of Burke's Political Thought', *Journal of British Studies*, 4 (1964), 41–64.

Rhetoric and Oratory

Browne, S. H. *Edmund Burke and the Discourse of Virtue*, Tuscaloosa, University of Alabama Press, 1993.

Bryant, D. C. '*The Contemporary Reception of Edmund Burke's Speaking*' in Howes, R. F. (ed.), *Historical Studies of Rhetoric and Rhetoricians*, Ithaca, Cornell University Press, 1961, pp. 271–93.

Bullard, P. *Edmund Burke: Rhetoric and Ethics,* Cambridge: Cambridge University Press, forthcoming.

De Bruyn, F. 'Burke and the Uses of Eloquence: Political Prose in the 1770s and 1780s' in Richetti, J. (ed.), *The Cambridge History of English Literature: 1660–1780*, Cambridge, Cambridge University Press, 2005, pp. 768–94.

Hampsher-Monk, I. 'Rhetoric and Opinion in the Politics of Edmund Burke', *History of Political Thought*, 9 (1988), 455–84.

Harris, I. 'Publishing Parliamentary Oratory: The Case of Edmund Burke', *Parliamentary History*, 26 (2008), 112–30.

Law and Jurisprudence

Donlan, S. P. 'Beneficence Acting by a Rule: Edmund Burke on Law, History, and Manners', *Irish Jurist*, 36 (2001), 227–64.

'Little Better than Cannibals: Property and Progress in Sir John Davies and Edmund Burke', *Northern Ireland Legal Quarterly*, 54 (2003), 1–24.

'"A Very Mixed and Heterogeneous Mass": Edmund Burke and English Jurisprudence, 1757–62', *University of Limerick Law Review*, 4 (2003), 79–88.

'Law and Lawyers in Edmund Burke's Scottish Enlightenment', *Studies in Burke and His Time*, 20 (2005), 38–59.

McDowell, R. B. 'Edmund Burke and the Law' in Greer, D. S. and Dawson, N. M. (eds.), *Mysteries and Solutions in Irish Legal History: Irish Legal History Society and Other Papers, 1996–1999*, Dublin, Four Courts Press, 2001.

Pocock, J. G. A. 'Burke and the Ancient Constitution – A Problem in the History of Ideas', *Historical Journal*, 3 (1960), 125–143; reprinted in Pocock, J. G. A. *Politics, Language, and Time: Essays on Political Thought and History*, Chicago, University of Chicago Press, 1973.

Schwartz, B. 'Edmund Burke and the Law', *Law Quarterly Review*, 95 (1979), 355–75.

Sunstein, C. R. 'Burkean Minimalism', *Michigan Law Review*, 105 (2006), 353–408.

Political Economy

Armitage, D. 'Edmund Burke and Reason of State', *Journal of the History of Ideas*, 61:4 (2000), 617–34.
Bourke, R. 'Liberty, Authority and Trust in Burke's Idea of Empire', *Journal of the History of Ideas*, 61:3 (2000), 453–71.
'Edmund Burke and the Politics of Conquest', *Modern Intellectual History*, 4:3 (2007), 403–32.
Hampsher-Monk, I. 'Edmund Burke's Changing Justification for Intervention', *Historical Journal*, 48:1 (2005), 65–100.
'Edmund Burke and Empire', in Kelly, D. (ed), *Lineages of Empire*, London, British Academy, 2009, pp. 117–36.
Pocock, J. G. A. 'The Political Economy of Burke's Analysis of the French Revolution', in *Virtue, Commerce and History: Essays on Political Thought and History, Chiefly in the Eighteenth Century*, Cambridge, Cambridge University Press, 1985, pp. 193–212.
'Edmund Burke and the Redefinition of Enthusiasm : the Context as Counter-Revolution', in Furet, F. and Ozouf, M. (eds.), *The French Revolution and the Creation of Modern Political Culture*, 3 vols., Oxford, Pergamon, 1990, Vol. III. 'The Transformation of Political Culture 1789–1848', pp. 19–43.
Winch, D. *Riches and Poverty. An Intellectual History of Political Economy in Britain, 1750–1834*, Cambridge, Cambridge University Press, 1996.

Religion

Aston, N. 'A "lay divine": Burke, Christianity and the Preservation of the British State, 1790–1797', in Aston, N. (ed.), *Religious Change in Europe 1650–1914. Essays for John McManners*, Oxford, Clarendon Press, 1997, pp. 185–211.
Beales, D. 'Edmund Burke and the Monasteries of France', *Historical Journal*, 48:2 (2005), 415–36.
Clark, J. C. D. 'Religious Affiliation and Dynastic Allegiance in Eighteenth-Century Britain: Edmund Burke, Thomas Paine, and Samuel Johnson', *English Literary History*, 64: 4 (1997), 1029–67.
Cowling, M. *Religion and Public Doctrine in Modern England*, 3 vols., Cambridge, Cambridge University Press, 1980–2001, vol. III, pp. 25–35.
Dreyer, F. A. 'Burke's Religion', *Studies in Burke and His Time*, 17 (1976), 199–212.
Harris, I. 'Paine and Burke: God, Nature and Politics' in Bentley, M. (ed.), *Public and Private Doctrine. Essays in British History Presented to Maurice Cowling*, Cambridge, Cambridge University Press, 1993, pp. 34–62.
Hart, J. 'Burke and Pope on Christianity', *Burke Newsletter*, 8 (1967), 702–13.
'Burke and Christianity. A Response to Harvey Mansfield', *Studies on Burke and His Time*, 9 (1968–9), 866–7.
Lambert, E. 'Edmund Burke's Religion', *English Language Notes*, 32 (1994), 19–28.
Lock, F. P. 'Burke and Religion', in Crowe, I. (ed.), *An Imaginative Whig: Reassessing the Life and Thought of Edmund Burke*, Colombia, University of Missouri Press, 2005, pp. 19–36.
Mahony, T. H. D. 'Edmund Burke and Rome', *Catholic Historical Review*, 43:4 (1958), 401–27.

Edmund Burke and Ireland, Cambridge, MA, Harvard University Press, 1960.
Mansfield Jr., H. C. 'Burke on Christianity', *Studies on Burke and His Time*, 9 (1968–9), 864–5.
O'Flaherty, E. 'Burke and the Catholic Question', *Eighteenth-Century Ireland*, 12 (1997), 15–27.
Rothbard, M. 'A Note on Burke's Vindication of Natural Society', *Journal of the History of Ideas*, 19 (1958), 114–18.
Weston Jr., J. C. 'The Ironic Purpose of Burke's Vindication Vindicated', *Journal of the History of Ideas*, 19 (1958), 435–41.

Natural Law and Utility

Bourke, R. 'Edmund Burke and Enlightenment Sociability: Justice, Honour and the Principles of Government', *History of Political Thought*, 21:4 (2000), 632–56.
Canavan, F. *The Political Reason of Edmund Burke*, Durham, Duke University Press, 1960.
Dinwiddy, J. R. 'Utility and Natural Law in Burke's Thought: A Reconsideration', *Studies in Burke and His Time*, 6 (1979), 105–28.
Freeman, M. *Edmund Burke and the Critique of Political Radicalism*, Chicago, University of Chicago Press, 1980.
Morley, J. *Edmund Burke: A Historical Study*, London, 1869.
Burke, London, 1879.
Nelson, D. *The Priority of Prudence: Virtue and Natural Law in Thomas Aquinas and the Implications for Modern Ethics*, University Park, Pennsylvania State University Press, 1992.
Insole, C. J. 'Two Conceptions of Liberalism: Theology, Creation and Politics in the Thought of Immanuel Kant and Edmund Burke', *Journal of Religious Ethics*, 36:3 (2008), 447–90.
The Politics of Human Frailty: A Theological Defence of Political Liberalism, Notre Dame, University of Notre Dame Press, 2005, ch. 1.
Irwin, T. *The Development of Ethics: A Historical and Critical Study*, 3 vols., Oxford, Oxford University Press, 2008, Vol. II, 'From Suarez to Rousseau'.
Pappin III, J. *The Metaphysics of Edmund Burke*, New York, Fordham University Press, 1993.
Porter, J. *Nature as Reason: A Thomistic Theory of the Natural Law*, Grand Rapids, MI and Cambridge, William B. Eerdmans Publishing Company, 2005.
Schneewind, J. B. *The Invention of Autonomy: A History of Modern Moral Philosophy*, Cambridge, Cambridge University Press, 2005.
Stanlis, P. *Edmund Burke and the Natural Law*, Ann Arbor, Michigan, University of Michigan Press, 1958.

Political Contexts

Empire and India

Bayly, C. A. *Imperial Meridian: The British Empire and the World, 1780–1830*, London, Longman, 1989.
Bourke, R. 'Edmund Burke and the Politics of Conquest', *Modern Intellectual History*, 4:3 (2007), 403–32.

'Liberty, Authority, and Trust in Burke's Idea of Empire', *Journal of the History of Ideas*, 61 (2000), 453–71.

Bowen, H. V. 'British Conceptions of Global Empire, 1756–1763', *Journal of Imperial and Commonwealth History*, 26:3 (1998), 1–27.

Carnall, G. and Nicholson, C. (eds.) *The Impeachment of Warren Hastings: Papers from a Bicentenary Commemoration*, Edinburgh, Edinburgh University Press, 1989.

Conniff, J. 'Burke and India: The Failure of the Theory of Trusteeship', *Political Research Quarterly*, 46 (1993), 291–309.

Deane, S. *Foreign Affections: Essays on Edmund Burke*, Notre Dame, University of Notre Dame Press, 2005.

Dirks, N. *The Scandal of Empire: India and the Creation of Imperial Britain*, Cambridge, MA, Harvard University Press, 2006.

Greene, J. P. (ed.), *Exclusionary Empire: English Liberty Overseas, 1600–1900*, Cambridge, Cambridge University Press, 2010.

Hampsher-Monk, I. 'Edmund Burke and Empire', in Kelly, D. (ed), *Lineages of Empire*, London, British Academy, 2009, pp. 117–36.

Janes, R. 'At Home Abroad: Edmund Burke in India', *Bulletin of Research in the Humanities*, 82 (1979), 160–74.

'Edmund Burke's Flying Leap from India to France', *History of European Ideas*, 7 (1986) 509–27.

'Edmund Burke's Indian Idyll', in Ruate, R. (ed.) *Studies in Eighteenth-Century Culture*, vol. IX, Madison, University of Wisconsin Press, 1979.

Koebner, R. *Empire*, Cambridge, Cambridge University Press, 1961.

Marshall, P. J. '*A Free though Conquering People': Eighteenth-Century Britain and Its Empire*, Aldershot, Ashgate, 2003.

Mehta, U. S. *Liberalism and Empire*, Chicago, University of Chicago Press, 1999.

Pitts, J. *A Turn to Empire: The Rise of Imperial Liberalism in Britain and France*, Princeton, Princeton University Press, 2005.

Pocock, J. G. A. 'The Political Economy of Burke's Analysis of the French Revolution,' in *Virtue, Commerce and History, Cambridge*, Cambridge University Press, 1985.

'Political Thought in the English-Speaking Atlantic, 1760–1790, Part 1: The Imperial Crisis', in Pocock, J. G. A. (ed.) *The Varieties of British Political Thought, 1500–1800*, Cambridge, Cambridge University Press, 1993, pp. 246–82.

Travers, R. *Ideology and Empire in Eighteenth-Century India: The British in Bengal*, Cambridge, Cambridge University Press, 2007.

Whelan, F. G. *Edmund Burke and India: Political Morality and Empire*, Pittsburgh, University of Pittsburgh Press, 1996.

Enlightenment Political Thought and Non-Western Societies: Sultans and Savages, New York, Routledge, 2009.

'J. C. D. Clark's Reflections and the Place of Contract in Burke's Political Theory', *Studies in Burke and His Time*, 20 (2005), 95–126.

Britain and the Constitution

Brewer, J. *Party Ideology and Popular Politics at the Accession of George III*, Cambridge, Cambridge University Press, 1976.

Bourke, R. 'Edmund Burke and Enlightenment Sociability: Justice, Honour and the Principles of Government', *History of Political Thought*, 21 (2000), 632–56.

Coniff, J. 'Burke, Bristol and the Concept of Representation', *Western Political Quarterly*, 30 (1977), 329–41.

Hill, B. W. 'Fox and Burke: the Whig Party and the Question of Principles, 1784–1789', *English Historical Review*, 89 (1974), 1–24.

Kriegel, A. D. 'Edmund Burke and the Quality of Honor', *Albion*, 12 (1980), 337–49.

Phillips, N. C. 'Edmund Burke and the County Movement, 1779–80', *English Historical Review*, 76 (1961), 254–78.

Pocock, J. G. A. 'Burke and the Ancient Constitution: A Problem in the History of Ideas', *Historical Journal*, 3 (1960), 125–43.

Ireland

Cullen, L. M. 'Burke, Ireland, and Revolution', *Eighteenth-Century Life*, 16 (1992), 21–42.

Deane, S. *Foreign Affections: Essays on Edmund Burke*, Notre Dame, University of Notre Dame Press, 2005.

A Short History of Irish Literature, London, Hutchinson, 1986.

Gibbons, L. *Edmund Burke and Ireland*, Cambridge, Cambridge University Press, 2003.

McBride, I. *Eighteenth-Century Ireland: The Isle of Slaves*, Dublin, Gill and Macmillan, 2009.

Mahoney, T. H. D. *Edmund Burke and Ireland*, Cambridge, MA, Harvard University Press, 1960.

O'Brien, C. C. *The Great Melody: A Thematic Biography and Commented Anthology of Edmund Burke*, Chicago, University of Chicago Press, 1992.

Power, T. P. and Whelan, K. (eds.), *Endurance and Emergence: Catholics in Ireland in the Eighteenth Century*, Dublin, Irish Academic Press, 1990.

America

Clark, J. C. D. 'Edmund Burke's Reflections on the Revolution in America (1777) Or, How Did the American Revolution Relate to the French?' in Crowe I, (ed.), *An Imaginative Whig: Reassessing the Life and Thought of Edmund Burke*, Columbia and London, University of Missouri Press, 2005, pp. 71–92.

Hoffman, Ross J. S. (ed.). *Edmund Burke: New York Agent*, Philadelphia, The American Philosophical Society, 1956.

Langford, P. 'The Rockingham Whigs and America, 1767–1773' in Whiteman, A., Bromley, J. S., Dickson, and P. G. M. (eds.), *Statesmen, Scholars and Merchants*, Oxford, Clarendon Press, 1973, pp. 135–52.

Mahoney, T. H. D. 'Edmund Burke and the American Revolution' in Browning, J. and Morton, R. (eds.), *1776, Toronto and Sarasota: Samuel Stevens* Hakkert & Company, 1976, pp. 53–71.

McLoughlin, T. O. *Edmund Burke and the First Ten Years of the 'Annual Register' 1758–1767*, Salisbury, University of Rhodesia, 1975.

O'Brien, C. C. 'Edmund Burke and the American Revolution' in Doyle, D. N. and Dudley Edwards, O. (eds.), *America and Ireland, 1776–1976*, Westport, CT and London, Greenwood Press, 1976, pp. 3–13.

O'Gorman, F. *Edmund Burke: His Political Philosophy*, London, George Allen & Unwin, 1973.

Reitan, E. A. 'Edmund Burke and Economical Reform, 1779–83', in Brack Jr., O. M. (ed.), *Studies in Eighteenth-Century Culture*, vol. XIV, Madison, University of Wisconsin Press, 1985, pp. 129–58.

Ritcheson, C. R. *Edmund Burke and the American Revolution*, Leicester, Leicester University Press, 1976.

Stanlis, P. J. 'Edmund Burke and British Views of the American Revolution: A Conflict over Rights of Sovereignty' in Crowe I. (ed.), *Edmund Burke: His Life and Legacy*, Dublin, Four Courts Press, 1997, pp. 24–38.

France

Clark, J. C. D. *'Introduction'* in Clark, J. C. D. (ed.), *Edmund Burke Reflections on the Revolution in France*, Stanford, Stanford University Press, 2001, pp. 23–111.

Lock, F. P. *Burke's Reflections on the Revolution in France*, London, Allen and Unwin, 1985.

Goodwin, H. 'The Political Genesis of Edmund Burke's Reflections on the Revolution in France', *Bulletin of the John Rylands Library*, 50 (1967–68), 336–64.

Hampsher-Monk, I. 'Rhetoric and Opinion in the Politics of Edmund Burke', *History of Political Thought*, 9 (1989), 455–84.

'Edmund Burke's Changing Justification for Intervention', *Historical Journal*, 48:1 (2005), 65–100.

Mosher, M. 'The Skeptic's Burke', *Political Theory*, 19 (1991), 391–418.

Pocock, J. G. A., 'Burke and the Ancient Constitution: a Problem in the History of Ideas', *Historical Journal*, 3 (1960), 125–43.

'The Political Economy of Burke's Analysis of the French Revolution', *Historical Journal*, 25 (1982), 3311–49.

INDEX

Banfield, Edward, 228–29
Baumgarten, Alexander, 53
Beaconsfield house and estate, Burke's
    purchase of, 19, 25–26
Beales, Derek, 191
the beautiful, 60–64
Bedford, Duke of, 26, 209
Beiser, Frederick, 37
Belloc, Hilaire, 224
Bellow, Saul, 227
benevolence, 33, 34–36, 69, 136
Bentham, Jeremy, 5, 7, 131–33, 225–26
    'greatest happiness principle' and, 135–36
    on natural law, 138–39
    utilitarianism and, 131–33, 137
Bergersdicius, Franciscus, 27
Berry, Wendell, 224
Beyond Culture (Trilling), 226–28
Blair, Hugh, 44–45
Bloom, Allan, 227
Boileau, Nicholas, 54–55
Bolingbroke, Henry St. John Viscount, 28,
    29–30, 107, 198–99
    Burke's satire of, 30–31
Boston Port Bill, 160–61
Boswell, James, 44, 45–46, 72
Bourke, John, 188
Bourke, Richard, 5–6, 8, 27–37, 164
Brady, Robert, 69
Brissot, Jean-Pierre, 209, 217–18
Bromwich, David, 229–30
Brooke, Henry, 186
Brown, John, 53–54, 87–88
Buck, Andrew, 42
Buckley, William F. Jr., 226
Bullard, Paddy, 5–6, 53–64
Burke, Edmund
    aesthetic psychology of, 53–64
    American crisis discussed by, 156–67
    ancient influences on, 44–49
    on Christianity *vs.* deism, 94–97
    chronology of, xx
    Cobban's evaluation of, 28–29
    on the constitution, 104–15
    context and principle in political life of, 3
    counter-revolutionary writings of, 209–19
    early life and education, 15–17, 92–94
    Enlightenment and Romanticism, 27–37
    on India, 168–80
    on Ireland, 181–92
    Irish background of, 182–87
    law and legal theory in work of, 27, 67–77
    life of, 15–26

on natural law, 1–2, 6–7, 117–29
political economy and, 7, 25–26, 80–90
reception in America, 222–30
political philosophy of, 1, 198–203
on reason and imagination, 28–31
religion in writings of, 92–103
as rhetorician and orator, 5–6, 41–50
utility and in writings of, 7, 33–34,
    131–42
Burke, Gerald, 187–88
Burke, Juliana, 182, 188
Burke, Richard, 182–83
Burke, Richard Jr., 25–26, 147, 151
Burke, William
    on Burke's oratorical skills, 47
    colonial positions held by, 186
    financial difficulties of, 19
    friendship with Burke, 16, 17, 188
    political economy and, 7
    writing collaboration with Burke, 27,
        85, 145
Burney, Frances, 46
Butler, Joseph, 95

Canavan, Francis, 224
Cassirer, Ernst, 8
casuistry, Burke's interpretation of natural
    law and, 123–24
Cavendish, John (Lord), 17–22
Chandler, James, 229–30
*Characteristiks of Men, Manners, Opinions,
    Times* (Shaftesbury), 33–34, 61–63
Charles I (King of England), 33
Chesterton, G. K., 224
chivalry, Burkes defense of, 203–04
Choiseul, Étienne François, duc de, 86
Christenheit oder Europa (Novalis), 35–36
Christianity
    Burke's early views on, 92–94
    communitarianism and, 228–30
    deism *vs.*, 94–97
    French Revolution and, 100–03
    natural law and, 122–29
    politics and society and, 97–100
Christianity not Founded on Argument
    (Dodwell), 31
Christianity not Mysterious (Toland), 30–31
Church of Ireland, 92–94, 181–82, 184–85,
    187–88
Cicero
    casuistry discussed by, 123–24
    De Finibus treatise of, 62
    De Oratore treatise of, 48

Dickinson, Harry, 10
*Discourse on the Origin and Foundations
of Inequality amongst Men* (Rousseau),
96–97
Discourse on the study of the law, A
(Blackstone), 67–68
Dissenters, 73
French Revolution and, 195–98
'Distributism' (economic theory), 224
divine power, Burke's discussion of, 60
Dodwell, Henry, 31
Donlan, Seán Patrick, 6, 67–77, 105–06
"double cabinet," Burke's theory of, 108
Drennan, William, 185–87
Duane, David, 187–88
Duane, Matthew, 187–88
Dwan, David, 7, 131–44

East India Company
abuse of power by, 174–75
Burke's criticism of, 32
Burke's speech on, 22
Hastings impeachment and, 119–20,
152–53
history in India of, 169–72
Lord North and, 48
William Burke's financial crisis and, 19
'Economic Reformation,' Burke's support
for, 21
economics. *See* political economy.
Edmund Burke and the Natural Law
(Stanlis), 224, 225–26
*Edmund Burke: the Enlightenment and
Revolution* (Stanlis), 225–26
Edward the Confessor, 105, 106
electoral politics
Burke's discussion of, 108–10, 111–12
representation and reform of, 110–13
Elliot, Gilbert, 46
Emile (Rousseau), 35
emotion, Burke on reason and, 50
empire. *See also* colonialism
Burke's discussion of, 9–11, 145–53
just and unjust uses of, 177–79
role of government and, 145–46, 176–77
Enlightenment
Burke and, 8, 27–37
and Catholicism,
French Revolution and, 32–34
Irish politics and, 189–92
non-Western world and, 179–80
in *Reflections on the Revolution in France*,
198–203

religion and, Burke's discussion of, 8–9
revolution and, 31–34
Epicureanism and Burke's aesthetic theory,
55–57
Essay Concerning Human Understanding
(Locke), 55–57
Essay on the Origin of Human Knowledge
(Condillac), 189
'Essay towards an History of the Laws of
England' (Burke), 27
Estates General (France), 33, 204, 213–15
*Estimate of the Manners and Principles of
the Times* (Brown), 87–88
Europe
Burke's fears concerning, 7–8, 80–82
Burke's legal interpretations of, 218–19
Christianity in, 100–03
France seen as threat to, 88–90
Eustatius, Island of, 166

Fate of Eloquence in the Age of Hume, The
(Potkay), 44
feudalism, 81, 203–04
Fitzwilliam, William Wentworth (Earl),
25–26
Forbes, Duncan, 105
Fox, Charles James, 21–22
Burke's break with, 210
Dissenters and, 197–98
French Revolution and, 195–96
impeachment of Hastings and, 23–24,
168–69
India Bill of, 169–70, 171–72
parliamentary career of, 45–46, 115
Whig party and, 104
France
British war with, 25, 89–90
Burke's view of, 85–88
the Clergy in, 101
economic strength of, 88–90
political economy of, 82–85
presence in India of, 169–72
reception on Burke's *Reflections* in, 198
restoration of aristocracy in, 215–19
Francis, Philip, 22–25, 88–89, 203–04
Frederick William II of Prussia, 89
French, Patrick, 187–88
French Revolution
American views of, 222–26
Arendt's discussion of, 228
British political economy and, 88–90
in Burke's counter-revolutionary writings,
209–19

Reflections of a Neoconservative (Kristol),
227–28
Reflections on the Revolution in France
(Burke), 1
conservative interpretations of, 226
constitution discussed in, 105–06
context, origins and publication of,
195–98
enlightenment in, 32–34
French monasteries defended in, 191
legacy of, 24–25, 37
legal theory in, 71, 74–76
manners in, 141
O'Brien's interpretation of, 183
political economy discussed in, 88–89
politics of the beautiful in, 64
religion in, 100–03, 175–76, 191, 198–203
translations of, 198
Reformer, 15–16
Regency Crisis
Burke's oratory during, 50
Burke's views on, 5, 24–25
constitutional theory and, 73–74
Reid, Christopher, 5
religion. *See also* Protestantism; Roman
Catholicism
aesthetics and, 33–34
Burke's writing on, 8–9, 92–103
enlightenment and, 27
French Revolution and role of, 100–03,
203–04
natural law and, 119, 122–29
in *Reflections,* 175–76, 191, 198–203
sectarianism and, 27–28
society and politics and, 97–100
religious toleration, Burke's advocacy of,
8–9, 99, 102–03, 170–71
empire and role of, 145–46
Remarks on the Policy of the Allies (Brissot),
217–18
representation in government
constitutional reform and, 110–13
empire and, 148–49, 153
resistance, natural law and rights of,
126–28
revealed theology
Burke's discussion of, 94–97
politics and society and, 97–100
revolution. *See also* American Revolution;
French Revolution
in Bengal, Burke's discussion of, 175–76
in Britain, Burke's concern about, 215–19
enlightenment and, 31–34

Revolution Settlement, 210
Reynolds, Joshua, 16–17
rhetoric
Burke's use of, 5–6, 41–50
Rights of Man (Paine), 209, 210–11
Rockingham, Lord. *See* Wentworth, Charles
Watson (Lord Rockingham)
Roman Catholicism. *See also* religion
Burke's defense of, 16–17, 70, 75–76,
98–99, 145, 181
Burke's family ties to, 182
Enlightenment and, 189–92
Roman law, Burke on law of nations and,
218–19
Romanticism
Burke and, 27–37
in England, 36–37
in Germany, 36–37
political aspects of, 37
Rousseau and, 34–37
Romantic Revolt, The (Vaughan), 28–29
Romilly, Samuel, 45–46
Rothbard, Murray, 229–30
Rousseau, Jean-Jacques, 34–37, 83–84,
96–97
American view of, 223
Romanticism and
Royal Marriage Bill, Burke's oratory in
debates on, 46–47

Sacheverell, Henry, 210–11
Sandel, Michael, 228–29
Savigny, Frederick von, 71
scepticism, influence on Burke, 8–9, 198
Schlegel, Friedrich, 35–36
Schmitt, Carl, 221–22
Scholastic philosophy, 27–28
science
Bolingbroke's discussion of, 30
Burke on religion and, 8–9
Scottish Enlightenment, 75–76
Scottish law, Burke's knowledge of, 69–70
sectarianism, Burke's criticism of, 27–28
self-preservation, 132, 140–41
Selman, John, 69
Selznick, Philip, 228–29
Sermon on the Mount, Burke's discussion
of, 93–94
Seven Years' War, 32, 85, 86, 87, 145, 192
Sexton, Peter, 187–88
Shackleton, Abraham, 15–16, 41
Shackleton, Richard, 27–28, 61
Shaftesbury. *See* Cooper, Anthony Ashley

Cambridge Companions to...

Thomas Mann edited by Ritchie Robertson

Christopher Marlowe edited by Patrick Cheney

Andrew Marvell edited by Derek Hirst and Steven N. Zwicker

Herman Melville edited by Robert S. Levine

Arthur Miller edited by Christopher Bigsby (second edition)

Milton edited by Dennis Danielson (second edition)

Molière edited by David Bradby and Andrew Calder

Toni Morrison edited by Justine Tally

Nabokov edited by Julian W. Connolly

Eugene O'Neill edited by Michael Manheim

George Orwell edited by John Rodden

Ovid edited by Philip Hardie

Harold Pinter edited by Peter Raby (second edition)

Sylvia Plath edited by Jo Gill

Edgar Allan Poe edited by Kevin J. Hayes

Alexander Pope edited by Pat Rogers

Ezra Pound edited by Ira B. Nadel

Proust edited by Richard Bales

Pushkin edited by Andrew Kahn

Rabelais edited by John O'Brien

Rilke edited by Karen Leeder and Robert Vilain

Philip Roth edited by Timothy Parrish

Salman Rushdie edited by Abdulrazak Gurnah

Shakespeare edited by Margareta de Grazia and Stanley Wells (second edition)

Shakespearean Comedy edited by Alexander Leggatt

Shakespeare and Contemporary Dramatists edited by Ton Hoenselaars

Shakespeare on Film edited by Russell Jackson (second edition)

Shakespeare's History Plays edited by Michael Hattaway

Shakespeare's Last Plays edited by Catherine M. S. Alexander

Shakespeare's Poetry edited by Patrick Cheney

Shakespeare and Popular Culture edited by Robert Shaughnessy

Shakespeare on Stage edited by Stanley Wells and Sarah Stanton

Shakespearean Tragedy edited by Claire McEachern

George Bernard Shaw edited by Christopher Innes

Shelley edited by Timothy Morton

Mary Shelley edited by Esther Schor

Sam Shepard edited by Matthew C. Roudané

Spenser edited by Andrew Hadfield

Laurence Sterne edited by Thomas Keymer

Wallace Stevens edited by John N. Serio

Tom Stoppard edited by Katherine E. Kelly

Harriet Beecher Stowe edited by Cindy Weinstein

August Strindberg edited by Michael Robinson

Jonathan Swift edited by Christopher Fox

J. M. Synge edited by P. J. Mathews

Tacitus edited by A. J. Woodman

Henry David Thoreau edited by Joel Myerson

Tolstoy edited by Donna Tussing Orwin

Anthony Trollope edited by Carolyn Dever and Lisa Niles

Mark Twain edited by Forrest G. Robinson

John Updike edited by Stacey Olster

Mario Vargas Llosa edited by Efrain Kristal and John King

Virgil edited by Charles Martindale

Voltaire edited by Nicholas Cronk

Edith Wharton edited by Millicent Bell

Walt Whitman edited by Ezra Greenspan

Oscar Wilde edited by Peter Raby

Tennessee Williams edited by Matthew C. Roudané

August Wilson edited by Christopher Bigsby

Mary Wollstonecraft edited by Claudia L. Johnson

Virginia Woolf edited by Susan Sellers (second edition)

Wordsworth edited by Stephen Gill

W. B. Yeats edited by Marjorie Howes and John Kelly

Zola edited by Brian Nelson

TOPICS

The Actress edited by Maggie B. Gale and John Stokes

The African American Novel edited by Maryemma Graham

The African American Slave Narrative edited by Audrey A. Fisch

Allegory edited by Rita Copeland and Peter Struck

For EU product safety concerns, contact us at Calle de José Abascal, 56–1°, 28003 Madrid, Spain or eugpsr@cambridge.org.

www.ingramcontent.com/pod-product-compliance
Ingram Content Group UK Ltd.
Pitfield, Milton Keynes, MK11 3LW, UK
UKHW020336140625
459647UK00018B/2165